Praise for *Inglorious*

A po ... grouse shooting industry, ... its
illegal s... propaganda war against the Hen Harrier.

Guardian

No other book this year put the cat amongst the pigeons (or
rather, the game birds) like Avery's impassioned investigation into
driven grouse shooting and its impact on moorland ecology.

The Times

This book pulls no punches... This is a book you must read
whether or not you support such shooting.

Highland Press

Avery is not afraid to ruffle feathers, but his unapologetically
polemical book also happens to be utterly fascinating... Pacy
and passionate, this is nature writing that insists you sit up and
take note.

The Lady

Mr Avery writes with a light touch and endearing self-
deprecation. He's passionate (obsessed?) about the Hen Harrier.

Country Life

Mark Avery makes a persuasive case for abolishing driven grouse
hunts. Expansive in scope yet forensic in detail ... This clearly
reasoned and well-written book is inspired by the author's
exasperation ... It's a powerful message.

BBC Wildlife

It is well-documented and impeccably logical; I find it convincing.

The Independent

Inglorious is fuelled by hard and difficult facts, which the author
has presented without getting them too caught up in his own
emotional bias, but we, as the readers, can allow ourselves to be
affected by this awful tale and can pass on the message of this
book. I am angry about what I have learnt in reading this and I
will suppo... ...hideous pastime.

River

A NOTE ON THE AUTHOR

Mark Avery was the Conservation Director of the RSPB for thirteen years. A scientist by training and a conservationist for most of his life, Mark is now a well-known and highly respected blogger, public speaker and writer on UK nature conservation and environmental issues. His previous book for Bloomsbury was *A Message from Martha,* the story of the extinction of the Passenger Pigeon.

@MarkAvery

Inglorious

CONFLICT IN THE UPLANDS

Mark Avery

BLOOMSBURY

LONDON · OXFORD · NEW YORK · NEW DELHI · SYDNEY

Bloomsbury Natural History
An imprint of Bloomsbury Publishing Plc

50 Bedford Square   1385 Broadway
London   New York
WC1B 3DP   NY 10018
UK   USA

www.bloomsbury.com

First published 2015. Paperback edition 2016.

British Library Cataloguing-in-Publication Data
A catalogue record for this book is available from the British Library.

Library of Congress Cataloguing-in-Publication data has been
applied for.

ISBN (hardback) 978-1-4729-1741-6
ISBN (paperback) 978-1-4729-1743-0
ISBN (ebook) 978-1-4729-1742-3

2 4 6 8 10 9 7 5 3 1

Typeset in Bembo Std by Deanta Global Publishing Services,
Chennai, India
Printed and bound in Great Britain by CPI Group (UK) Ltd,
Croydon CR0 4YY

Contents

Foreword

Lack of parity in justice is something that aggrieves us all. From the time when our little sister or big brother gets a cuddle and an ice cream and we get told off and sent to our room when 'they did it', to Maradona's 'Hand of God', from *Dances with Wolves* beating *Goodfellas* to the Best Picture Oscar in 1991 to the Sex Pistols being denied the number one spot with 'God Save the Queen' in 1977, the rancour, the rage, the anger when things just aren't fair seizes us all, fuelling our fury probably more than anything else. It is primal; it has led to words, wars, revolutions, divorces and lifelong disagreements, and it's fundamentally what this book is all about. That, and grotesque acts of vicious vandalism that rob us of our natural heritage. And lies, lots and lots of lies. Mostly fusty old lies, but damned lies all the same. So this book is going to get your goat, enflame your ire and make you cross, but if it achieves its purpose it will motivate you to help put an end to an insidious, hugely destructive and outdated practice that isn't ethically or morally fit for the twenty-first century – driven grouse shooting.

I like Mark Avery's outlook and attitude. He's fairly unique among contemporary conservationists for two important reasons – he doesn't sit on the fence, and he doesn't pull his punches. Thus he isn't afraid to say it like it is and doesn't shy away from a fight. If only significant others were of the same ilk – but they're not. In these risk-averse, politically correct and cowardly times they are responsible for putting the 'con' in conservation, which is shameful given the dire straits our wildlife is in. Here, on the other hand, is a frank and uncompromised missive about a very hot topic. Mark has laid out the facts for us to digest, and most of those facts are ugly, so while you will probably not enjoy this book in the true sense of the word, it is undeniably essential reading if you have any interest in wildlife and conservation in the UK. It is an important book – in fact, it's a must-read.

Despite centring predominantly on two bird species, the Red Grouse and the Hen Harrier, *Inglorious* is mainly about people: those who shoot and those who would rather enjoy life than take it. At certain points I sat back, sighed and couldn't believe I was reading about events that were happening *now*. It is as if all the science, all the ecology, the knowledge, the respect and the understanding that we have so diligently and passionately evolved simply didn't exist. Aspects of this 'industry' seem to persist in a vile vacuum rooted in an ignorant, intolerant and inglorious past. And to try and justify its stance, it trots out a shabby litany of idiotic lies that may somehow have been believable to previous generations but are frankly embarrassing to this one, given the sophistication our public now has in ecological matters. For instance, in recent years a number of grouse moors have eradicated all the mountain hares on their land – they've enacted lagomorphicide – because the hares can transmit a parasite to the grouse. There cannot be a single viewer of wildlife television who doesn't realise that such lunacy will have a profound effect on the ecology of that community, a community equally devoid of predators of all kinds; it will damage it irreparably. So when we are told by the shooting fraternity that they are 'looking after the uplands' the joke simply isn't funny any more. They burn it, drain it, poison it, denude it of any life that may possibly harm a grouse, and then kill the grouse themselves. How absurd.

So why does it continue? Why has Mark had to sit down and detail the anatomy of this atrocity? Basically, money and psychosis. A tiny, selfish, destructive minority who measure their pleasure in the number of things they can kill. Well, I say 'bollocks' to money and psychosis, and when you've read this I'm sure you will too. Because this minority doesn't 'own' the things they kill – *we* do. They're *our* Hen Harriers, our Peregrines, our Golden Eagles, Goshawks, Buzzards and Kites that rot on the moors to sustain this insanity. These birds are our national natural treasures, which we are being unjustly and illegally robbed of, and the 'getting away with it' has gone too far. If I walked into an art gallery and slashed and smashed a Constable or a Gainsborough or a Landseer beyond repair I'd be pilloried across the globe as a vandal, as a monster who had stolen the world's right to enjoy a great masterpiece. And I'd hopefully be jailed. But when a gamekeeper shoots a raptor, even if they are caught, and even if they are prosecuted (which is a rarity), nothing effectively happens. The punishment never fits the crime.

Okay, so let's imagine you've read the book, you are now as furious about this evil fiasco as Mark is, and as I am; what are you going to do to actually make a difference? Because I'm afraid caring is not enough – action is required to effect change. Well, you have to make your voice heard, so use Twitter, Facebook, YouTube … any social medium to communicate your opinions to others. Write letters to the press, to the NGOs, to MPs, or blog to the world, and support the newly inaugurated Hen Harrier Day, which will run annually in August until we can rid our countryside of illegal raptor persecution. Refute apathy, empower yourself and make a difference.

One day this horror will end, of course, but with your help it will end a lot sooner, and your grandchildren and those of the rotten criminals will thank you for it.

Chris Packham
New Forest 2015

Preface

This book has a point of view – it sets out the case for ending driven grouse shooting in our uplands. In some ways that is quite a 'big ask', as grouse shooting is a favoured sport of the rich and powerful in the UK, and so the vested interests are immense. Nevertheless, its demise is inevitable, because it is a practice pursued by the few to the detriment of the many. I am sure that driven grouse shooting will be consigned to history within the next few years and, if you agree with the case made in this book, you can help to hasten that end.

The whole business of shooting grouse is a rather parochial and peculiarly British affair, of little interest to most of the world. Indeed, it is of equally little concern to most of us in Britain, but when people learn about what grouse shooting entails then most become far less inclined to tolerate it. Shooting Red Grouse in huge numbers for fun is such a ridiculous pastime that only those closest to it will seek to support it – those who find the shooting of a hundred or more birds in a day an attractive way to spend their time, those who are employed by the industry, and a few hangers-on. The rest of us, who suffer the harmful side effects of this industry on our enjoyment of the countryside, on our water bills and on the climate that we all experience, and who are subsidising grouse shooting to an enormous extent, will eventually wake up and decide that a couple of centuries of intensive upland management to produce artificially high densities of one species of gamebird is quite enough.

In conservation terms, too, grouse shooting is an oddity. Nowhere else in the world do the same issues arise, and nowhere else are the same arguments made in quite the same way, or with the same venom. This is a peculiarly British conservation issue, deeply rooted in Britain's class system and played out according to class lines. As such, it is not only an interesting case study in nature conservation, but an enlightening object lesson in what really makes Britain tick – even in the early years of the twenty-first century.

The book starts with some biology, as it's always good to start with something that seems reassuringly eternal. But we start not with the biology of the grouse themselves but with that of a bird that eats grouse, namely the Hen Harrier. Hen Harriers have been on Earth since long before men in tweed started shooting Red Grouse for pleasure. They are completely protected by the law, on paper, although not in practice in the hills where grouse shooting takes place. And so this book starts with an appreciation of a victim of the grouse-shooting industry. As we move through its pages we will find that the conflict between Hen Harriers and grouse shooting has been an important one, but also that there are other victims of grouse shooting – other animals, some plants, and quite a lot of people too.

The second chapter takes us through a short history of grouse shooting and explains where it came from, how the method of killing grouse has changed over time, who does it and where it is done. Chapter 3 looks at the conflict between the Hen Harrier (the subject of Chapter 1) and grouse shooting (the subject of Chapter 2) through a study carried out on the Scottish estate of the Duke of Buccleuch in the mid-1990s. Everything was different after that study, and Chapter 4 describes the events between the end of the study on the Buccleuch land and the end of the year 2013. It also describes how I weighed up the evidence both for and against driven grouse shooting, and eventually came down in favour of radical change. Chapter 5 describes the events of 2014, which might justifiably be called the 'Year of the Hen Harrier' from the point of view of someone (myself) intimately involved in many of those events. Chapter 6 looks 25 years into the future, to a time when driven grouse shooting is banned, and comments on the position then from the point of view of an ex-gamekeeper whose life has changed dramatically. Chapter 7 briefly describes how the demise of driven grouse shooting is inevitable, and how you can help bring it about.

I wrote this book because I wanted to, and because I felt I ought to. I also wrote it with the aim of getting the subject out of my system. Writing these last few words now, in early March

2015, I am glad I wrote *Inglorious* and I hope you like reading it (or hate reading it, depending on who you are) – but I am not entirely sure that the writing of it has altogether purged my system of the issues surrounding driven grouse shooting.

Preface to the paperback edition

I have taken the opportunity of the publication of the paperback edition of this book to write a short additional chapter to bring this fast-moving story of the campaign against driven grouse-shooting up to date with events in 2015 and early 2016. Progress is being made and the issues surrounding the unsustainable nature of intensive grouse-moor management are becoming better known and understood.

This book both documents that campaign and is a part of it. If you find the case against driven grouse-shooting set out in these pages convincing, then please add your name to the current e-petition to ban driven grouse-shooting, which can be found at https://petition.parliament.uk/petitions/125003 up until 20 September 2016.

Mark Avery, Northamptonshire
@markavery
March 2015

CHAPTER ONE

The harrier harried

'The time has come,' the Walrus said, 'To talk of many things: Of shoes—and ships—and sealing-wax—Of cabbages—and kings—And why the sea is boiling hot—And whether pigs have wings.'

Lewis Carroll, *Through the Looking-Glass*

In this book we shall talk of many things, from the Game Acts to the Turner Contemporary Gallery in Margate, from sheep ticks to the Royal Family, from the discoloration of mountain streams to social media, and from the last Ice Age to the composition of the Westminster parliament. We shall discuss all these and more – but we shall start with the Hen Harrier.

Of all the birds of Britain and Ireland, the Hen Harrier (*Circus cyaneus*) is arguably the one that most strongly divides opinions – some love it and some hate it. Elsewhere in its extensive world range, covering much of Europe and Asia, and much of North America too, it is regarded either as 'just another bird of prey' or as a beautiful bird which preys, rather usefully, on small rodents. But in the UK it is a contentious bird because it eats Red Grouse, and these are often Red Grouse that someone would pay a large amount of money to shoot. If the Hen Harrier eats a grouse, the shooter can't shoot it – and that is the nub of the reason why the status of the Hen Harrier is discussed in the corridors of the Department for Environment, Food and Rural Affairs in Smith Square in London, on the moors of the north Pennines, and by groups of birders in pubs after a day in the field.

Hardly any ordinary person in the street will have heard of the Hen Harrier. They may have heard of the Harrier jump jet, whose hunting techniques can resemble those of the bird, and in the streets of Kidderminster they will know that their local football team is the Harriers. In Birchfield, Colchester, Morpeth,

Preston, Swansea and many other towns they are likely to know that their local athletics club is the Harriers, but few will know anything of the bird.

It is easy not to notice the Hen Harrier as one goes about one's daily life. They live in remote places and are fairly rare. You just don't bump into Hen Harriers that often. And so the vast majority of the British public do not know or care much about this bird, and they are unaware of the conflict that it provokes amongst grouse shooters and nature conservationists, and of how high the feelings run on both sides of the argument.

I am very squarely in the 'love Hen Harriers' camp, as are many other birdwatchers. I'm not entirely sure why I love this bird so much, and by now the reasons are so lost in the past that it's a bit like trying to explain why I love my children. I just do (most days).

I can remember the first Hen Harrier I ever saw. It was from Studland Heath on the western side of Poole Harbour one Christmas holiday when I was about 12 years old. My parents had taken me and a couple of school-friends to coastal Dorset for some bird watching. I guess we hoped to see Slavonian Grebes, divers and both species of godwits, as these were the species mentioned in my copy of John Gooders's book *Where to Watch Birds*, which was our main guide in those days. I cannot remember us seeing any of those species, but almost as soon as we stopped the car we did see a Hen Harrier quartering the saltmarsh below us.

The Hen Harrier is a Buzzard-sized bird, although a rather longer-tailed, slimmer, more elegant bird of prey. Even though we had never seen one before, and even though we were at an age and stage of our bird-watching apprenticeships at which we were apt to misidentify new birds in what now seems an excruciatingly embarrassing manner, we all knew that this was a female or immature Hen Harrier, commonly known as a 'ringtail' because both the young birds (of either sex) and the adult females have about four broad dark-chocolate bands, separated by lighter brown bands, on their tails. But the most striking feature on this generally brown bird was its square white rump.

It was a pretty good view of one, too. We watched it for a few minutes as it flew just above the saltmarsh and occasionally dived into the channels, perhaps after some prey, before it gave up on this patch of the marsh and flew strongly away out of sight. We were all delighted – the day was made.

I had to wait a good few years before I saw an adult male Hen Harrier, flying over a young conifer plantation in central Wales. This pale-grey, blueish-grey and white bird, with black wing-stips, well deserved its nickname of 'silver ghost' as it floated in the sunshine over the rows of small Sitka Spruce trees, before heading purposefully out of sight into the next valley. It was a brief view, but a treat to see such a special bird.

Every time I have seen a Hen Harrier since, be they ringtails or silver ghosts, I have felt that same thrill. It's a beautiful bird – whether it is a male sky-dancing over a moor to attract and impress a female (or sometimes more than one) and to scare away other males, a ringtail on a warm winter's day flying over the steppes of Extremadura, Spain, or the American race of the same species, (where it is known as the Northern Harrier or Marsh-hawk) crossing in front of my car in the prairies of South Dakota.

I have watched Hen Harriers coming in to roost as the light faded on winter evenings at the RSPB nature reserve of Minsmere in the mid-1970s. I have paused on a transect while studying moorland birds in the Flow Country of Sutherland to watch as an adult male flew over the Dubh Lochans and then into the plantation of young Sitka Spruce and Lodgepole Pines that was scarring the landscape. I could tell you most of the places where I have seen Hen Harriers, because each day I have seen a Hen Harrier has been enhanced by the sight of this bird.

Male Hen Harriers perform a spectacular 'sky-dancing' display that I've only seen once, and that was a rather half-hearted performance in northern Scotland years ago, but the memory sticks with me. If you are lucky enough to spend time with nesting Hen Harriers, as I hardly ever have, you may also see a food pass, where the male brings food back to the nest for the female and the chicks. The nest is the female's preserve, and she will come off the nest as the male approaches; then the two birds will fly up together as the male drops the prey and his mate catches the Meadow Pipit, Rabbit or, yes, Red Grouse chick in mid-air and settles down again on the nest. The well-known naturalist Iolo Williams described his times with Hen Harriers to me, and he said that seeing a food pass would be a sight that would stay with you all your life – even if you lived to 110 (and I do hope that Iolo does)!

I love Hen Harriers, but I am no expert on them – I've never visited a nest, seen their eggs or studied their biology. I am a consumer of Hen Harrier sightings, like many other birdwatchers. However, through my former role working for the RSPB and my continuing interest in Hen Harrier conservation, I do know more about Hen Harriers than I know about most birds, and I know more about Hen Harriers than most people do. So this opening chapter is an introduction to the Hen Harrier. More precisely, it is an introduction to the bird's biology, and to the problems it faces from humans gunning for it. Later in this book we will come to the problems it causes for some humans.

The Hen Harrier – biology

The Hen Harrier is a fairly common and widespread bird at latitudes between 35 and 70 degrees north in the Old World and New World alike. This is not a bird that hovers on the edge of extinction, nor one whose status is a matter of concern from a global perspective. No, the conservation issues surrounding the Hen Harrier are a rather parochial British issue concerning, as we shall see, a few thousand square kilometres of upland heather-clad moors.

For, in the UK, the Hen Harrier nests primarily in our uplands. This was not always so: in medieval times it was found nesting very widely in upland and lowland areas of open moor and rough grassland. It may have been its occasional depredation on free-range domestic poultry that gave it the name of Hen Harrier, but it is also possible that the name refers to one of its many wild prey species, a bird formerly called the Moor Hen or Moor Fowl, but now better known as the Red Grouse.

In winter some Hen Harriers stay on the moors on which they bred, feeding more often on the moorland edges and rough grazing, but others move south to the coastal marshes – giving rise, for example, to my first encounter in Poole Harbour. Some move further south into France, Spain and Portugal, and the UK population is augmented by birds visiting from the Continent.

Recoveries, dead and alive, of ringed birds give us some broad insights into Hen Harrier travels and longevity. The greatest distance travelled by a Hen Harrier immigrant to our shores was recorded at the end of the harsh 1962/63 winter, perhaps because the cold weather pushed continental birds, seeking western warmth, into this country: a female that had been ringed as a nestling in Finland the previous July was found poisoned near Deal in Kent in late March – over 2,000 kilometres from where she had hatched. Single birds from Germany, Finland and Sweden, all ringed as nestlings, have also been recovered in the UK, all on the east coast of England from Humberside to Kent. British-ringed birds have been recorded in winter in many European countries. A bird from mid-Wales was re-trapped by a ringer, alive, in Portugal, in the November after she had been ringed, having travelled over 1,600 kilometres to the south-southwest in just over three months, while an Orkney-ringed nestling was found dead in northern Norway in February 1961, having been ringed in July 1959 – a distance of 1,300 kilometres to the northeast.

More recently, many birds have been satellite-tagged, and this has provided much greater detail on the movement of a small but ever-increasing number of individuals. Some birds have travelled large distances (such as a juvenile male tagged in southern Scotland, which spent its first winter in northern Spain before returning to south Scotland in the subsequent May) whereas others have stayed close to where they were tagged, to within just a few kilometres, throughout the whole of a calendar year.

In winter the birds will roost together on the ground, often in marshy areas. In February and March 1976, after leaving school but before university, I volunteered at the RSPB reserve at Minsmere, Suffolk, where a close relative of the Hen Harrier, the Marsh Harrier, was the 'star' bird of prey, having hung on at this site as its sole UK breeding location. In those winter evenings, after a day of cutting reeds by hand, or erecting fences, or maybe picking up litter from the beach, I would sometimes sit in the raised Island Mere hide and wait for Hen Harriers to fly past in the gathering gloom. Sometimes they did and sometimes they didn't; sometimes we would see just an individual ringtail fly low over the reed bed with the Sizewell nuclear power station in the background, and at other times a few birds would be seen in swift succession, arriving from different directions to roost together.

Quite why Hen Harriers roost together is not really known. Can it really be that there are so few suitable roost places that the birds crowd together more through necessity than by choice? It seems unlikely, as most roost sites are flat, open boggy areas, and there must be plenty of those for Hen Harriers to choose from. We can imagine that the birds are looking for areas that are relatively fox-free, as a wandering Red Fox, in the absence of humans, would be the Hen Harrier's main threat. And at sites where they do roost, they tend to choose the same bit of a much wider area in which they all roost – they certainly seem to 'want' to be together. The roost sites are somewhat traditional, being used from year to year, and the exact same locations of trampled vegetation are used on successive nights (presumably by the same birds); it's clear that the birds travel quite some way to reach them, flying several kilometres to sit amongst the *Juncus* with other Hen Harriers sitting nearby, perhaps a few metres away. So it's not as though the birds are all cuddling up together overnight for warmth: they are more stand-offish than that, but more social than would be expected by chance. Perhaps the sites are chosen for their microclimates and lack of ground predators, and perhaps they are places where Hen Harriers start to form pair bonds ahead of the spring.

The late Donald Watson (1918–2005) wrote about Hen Harriers in his book *The Hen Harrier*, published in 1977. The book contains many personal observations of the birds roosting together, and it still forms a very good introduction to the species. Watson was a talented artist, and his book is beautifully illustrated with his paintings and drawings of Hen Harriers, other harriers and their prey, and the places where they live. Watson noted, as have others, that where food is available in sufficient quantities to support several pairs, and where the birds are left unmolested, the Hen Harrier can nest in a semi-colonial manner.

Throughout the year, whether it is nesting on heather-clad moorland in eastern Scotland or wintering on a coastal marsh in Norfolk, the main prey of the Hen Harrier consists of rodents and small birds. Voles are very important – so much so that the bird might well be called the Vole Catcher rather than the Hen Harrier if we were to start naming Britain's birds afresh. Orkney has been an important refuge for the Hen Harrier over the years, and one reason for this might well be that the Orkney Vole (*Microtus arvalis*), a continental species of large vole that has its only UK home in Orkney (it was introduced there as many as 5,500 years ago), is a favoured prey item.

Other mammalian prey in the UK includes many species of mice, small Rabbits, Brown Rats, Water Voles, Brown Hares, Mountain Hares and even the occasional Pygmy Shrew. As with many predators a wide variety of prey is taken, but small rodents are everywhere the main mammalian prey. If the Hen Harrier limited itself to taking mammals, then it would probably be lauded as a useful predator of rats, mice and voles and be considered the farmer's friend.

Small birds such as the Meadow Pipit are another favoured prey, but a wide range of species is taken, including Skylarks, Starlings, finches, buntings, chats and the chicks of waders such as Golden Plover, Lapwing, Curlew and Snipe. As with the mammals, there is probably no species of small bird that the Hen Harrier would eschew, but they take the species that they encounter the most, and so on many moorlands the Meadow Pipit is the most numerous avian prey.

Amongst all the other small birds taken by Hen Harriers are the young of the Red Grouse. And this is what gets this otherwise uncontentious bird into so much trouble, and what puts it at the top of the list of Britain's most-hated birds in the eyes of a small section of society. Where grouse shooting is king, and this applies to much of northern England and south and east Scotland, the Hen Harrier is reviled – and that has considerable consequences, overwhelming consequences indeed, for the status of the Hen Harrier in the United Kingdom.

At Langholm Moor, a site in southern Scotland where Hen Harriers were studied in great detail in the mid-1990s, a wide range of prey was fed to the nestlings. The commonest prey delivered to 22 studied nests were: Meadow Pipit, 946; Red Grouse, 261; Field Vole, 120; Skylark, 102; Curlew, 16; Rabbit, 15. In addition, a very wide range of other species was taken, including Adder, Blue Tit, Common Lizard, Merlin, Mole, Pied Wagtail and Willow Warbler.

We shall discuss the impacts of the Hen Harrier on grouse populations (rather small) and on grouse shooting (rather large), and the attempts to find a resolution to the conflict between men in tweed and this graceful bird later in this book, and in quite considerable detail, but for the purposes of this chapter let me just establish that the Hen Harrier is unpopular for the simple reason that in amongst its taking of small mammals and small birds it dares to take small Red Grouse too.

The numbers and range of the Hen Harrier have ebbed and flowed over the decades and centuries, largely as human persecution has waxed and waned. The Hen Harrier was gone from most of lowland Britain before the nineteenth century and was a rare breeding species in many of the uplands too at the end of that century. Whatever the origin of their name, Hen Harriers may well have been killed in the lowlands because of a perceived threat to domestic chickens. They would certainly be capable of taking the occasional adult and more than capable – adept, we might say – at taking small chicks. On the other hand, a Hen Harrier hunting around the chicken pens might be just as interested in the sparrows and finches attracted to the chicken feed as it would be in the chickens themselves. The female Hen Harrier, as with many birds of prey, is noticeably larger than the male, weighing about 500 grams compared to the male's 350 grams, and it is the females which are most likely to take the larger prey such as full-grown chickens, adult Red Grouse, larger Rabbits and the occasional Pheasant.

But over the last two centuries the only people who have been the least bit bothered by the Hen Harrier's feeding habits are upland gamekeepers, for whom the presence of a pair of harriers on a moorland would be a source of extreme disquiet – for where there are lots of small grouse chicks the Hen Harrier will take its share, and that share is taken before the start of the shooting season, when people pay to shoot at those grouse chicks when they are fully grown. The Hen Harrier is not the only bird of prey that takes adult Red Grouse, but it is the main species that preys upon the chicks. And its constant, methodical quartering of the ground makes it look thorough, unforgiving, and a potent threat to the grouse stocks of any upland gamekeeper.

The Hen Harrier – numbers and distribution

The status of the Hen Harrier across the whole of the UK was last enumerated by a national survey in 2010. The bald result was that there were 633 pairs. Compared with the figures for a century earlier, in 1910, this represents a remarkable recovery in numbers, since at that time there were precious few Hen Harriers nesting on the British mainland (perhaps as few as single figures of pairs, mostly on the Kintyre peninsula in western Scotland), maybe occasional pairs in Northern Ireland, and the population of the UK probably numbered only a few score of pairs, mostly found in Orkney and some of the Inner Hebrides and the Western Isles. If we guessed that the 1910 population was around 100 pairs then we might be 50 pairs too high or too low, but we would be in the right ballpark (probably).

The British and Irish population of Hen Harrier was at its lowest ebb in the century from 1840 to 1940, when it had been removed from most lowland counties and was practically extirpated as a breeding species from the UK mainland during the expansion of grouse shooting as a dominant land use in many upland areas.

In his 1976 book on British birds of prey, Leslie Brown stated that a pair nested in Inverness-shire in 1936, and that this was indicative of a recolonisation of the mainland from the birds' Orkney stronghold and refuge. There was a recovery in numbers during the Second World War, as many of those involved in waging war against the Hen Harrier were redeployed to wage war against a better-armed foe. Then, in 1954, having seen off the Nazis, the UK parliament passed the Protection of Birds Act, which gave stronger, nationwide protection to all birds, including the Hen Harrier, thus making it clearer that taking eggs, destroying nests and killing adult birds were unacceptable activities. This undoubtedly helped the Hen Harrier and other birds of prey to recover in numbers.

Hen Harriers spread to most Scottish counties with suitable breeding habitat in the 1960s and also recolonised Wales at this time. The return to England was steady but measured. Northumberland had its first twentieth-century breeding record in 1958, and as many as eight pairs nested there in the mid-1960s. Lancashire was recolonised in 1968, Durham in 1970, Yorkshire in 1971 and Derbyshire in 1997, but the populations remained small and highly persecuted. The 1970 Durham pair was discovered close to fledging and with four young. In 1971 the same site was occupied again but the male was shot. There then followed an absence of breeding records in Durham until 1983, when a single pair raised young, and then another gap until 1988, when a pair probably succeeded in nesting. It was a recovery of sorts, but hardly a sustained and rapid one.

Hen Harriers profited from the widespread planting of commercial conifer plantations in the uplands of Britain after the Second World War, as this was accompanied by a reduction in grazing pressure by domestic livestock (primarily sheep), which led to an increase in vole numbers and a reduction in gamekeeping pressure (leading to a reduction in nest losses and adult losses). Through the 1970s, large areas of land were taken out of grouse shooting and converted to young forestry plantations, which for many years, often up to ten years, remained sufficiently open for Hen Harriers to hunt in them.

In the mid-1970s three authors – Donald Watson (in *The Hen Harrier*), Leslie Brown (in *British Birds of Prey*) and Tim Sharrock (in the first formal bird atlas for the UK and Ireland, *The Atlas of Breeding Birds in Britain and Ireland*) – wrote of the Hen Harrier in a generally positive tone, as it had increased in numbers and range in recent years. All three estimated the UK population to be in the range of 400–600 pairs.

The *Atlas* map (which covered the period 1968–72) showed Hen Harriers nesting in Orkney and several of the southern Hebrides, throughout much of mainland Highland Scotland (though with very few observations in the northwest Highlands of western Sutherland, Wester Ross, Inverness-shire and north Argyll) and widely but apparently sparsely distributed in moorland areas of Scotland south of the Glasgow–Edinburgh line and into the north of England and north Wales. There was even one nesting pair, apparently, in north Norfolk.

All three authors mentioned the impact of illegal persecution from grouse-shooting interests on the bird's numbers and distribution. Sharrock suggested that 'illegal persecution continues on most grouse moors,' while Watson commented that 'in countries such as Britain, where a small but influential section of the population is intensely keen on game shooting, birds of prey are often still treated as vermin, and the Hen Harrier is apt to be placed in the forefront of this category' and Brown wrote 'without the continuing illegal persecution it receives from gamekeepers on grouse moors in eastern Scotland and no doubt elsewhere the Hen Harrier would quickly increase to well over a thousand pairs.'

These three authors also commented on the difficulty of assessing the numbers of a bird which lived at low densities in remote areas, and recognised that a formal survey would be a complicated undertaking.

The 1910 population of around 100 pairs is a bit of a guess. By contrast, the 2010 estimate of Hen Harrier numbers is based on a dedicated survey of this species, specifically designed to ascertain its numbers and distribution, and written up and published in the scientific literature. It was the fourth UK-wide national survey (the next will probably be in 2016), and before going back in time to consider the previous national surveys let us consider in more detail how the 2010 survey was carried out, and what it showed.

A national survey of a bird like the Hen Harrier is a considerable challenge – in fact it is a series of challenges: intellectual, logistical and financial. Let us first consider the intellectual challenge.

We start by knowing that there are hundreds of pairs of Hen Harriers (we know this from previous surveys and from ongoing annual studies by keen individuals) and that they live in the uplands of Britain (but not quite all of the upland areas, as they are absent from Exmoor and Dartmoor and have been for quite a while). Quite a high proportion of the population is monitored annually by keen raptor workers, amateur enthusiasts who study the birds each year, monitor their nesting success and ring the chicks in the nests in order to help improve our knowledge of the movements and survival of these birds. In some parts of the Hen Harrier range there are sufficient numbers of raptor workers, and sufficiently few pairs of Hen Harriers, that we can be reasonably sure that all nesting pairs, or the very large majority of them, will be found. This applies to Orkney (where many of the birds are nesting on RSPB nature reserves), to England (where there are very few pairs and lots of people keen to find them each year), to Northern Ireland (where there are relatively few pairs) and to a large extent to Wales (where the bird is not very numerous but is getting commoner). We can take these areas as being fully

covered, and in the 2010 survey they held 209 pairs of Hen
Harriers, as follows: Orkney, 81 pairs; Northern Ireland, 59
pairs; Wales, 57 pairs; England, 12 pairs.

In parts of Scotland, raptor study groups have very good
knowledge of the status of the Hen Harrier in their local patches
every year and simply have to be asked to contribute their data
to the national picture in national survey years (which they are
happy to do). In the 2010 survey such data were available for 135
10-kilometre grid squares distributed across Scotland (not
including Orkney, which was fully surveyed). But the key thing
is to be able to know how many Hen Harriers live in all the
areas of Scotland not covered in detail, which amounted to a
further 446 10-kilometre squares.

It might be tempting just to try to ask every birdwatcher in the
UK to look extra-hard for Hen Harriers in the years scheduled
for national surveys, and that would probably work to some
extent, as coverage would improve and records would come in to
a central place and help to build up a better picture. The trouble,
however, is that it would be difficult to get any estimate of survey
effort and so it would be very difficult to know how many Hen
Harriers were missed and how to compare this year's observed
total with any previous or subsequent totals.

So what actually happens – and this is also what happened in
previous national surveys in 1998 and 2004 – is that areas known
to be potential breeding areas for Hen Harriers are sampled by
surveyors employed for that task. It is difficult to get volunteer
surveyors to visit areas where the target bird is expected to be
absent, especially for a bird living in remote parts of the country
with low densities of human population, and it is thus a safer bet
(though quite an expensive one) to employ surveyors to make
sure all the sample squares are covered in the right way and in
the right time periods.

What is the basis for choosing the sample areas? Basically,
they are general areas known to have held Hen Harriers in the
past and/or known to hold suitable habitat. But you do need
to know, in advance of your survey, what your potential
sample area is in order to select random bits of it to be visited
during the survey, and then in order to extrapolate from your
sample to the full area once you have the data from the sample
areas.

It's not too complicated, but you do have to expend a bit of brain power on this in advance of the survey. And the Hen Harrier is in that group of species where this needs thinking through quite carefully, because the results will be scrutinised by many people and because of the challenges set by the bird's habitat and the mix of volunteer and paid effort. For many much rarer species you can just ask people for all their records and that will do the job well enough. For much commoner species there aren't volunteers already counting a high (or fairly high) proportion of the population every year, so you just do a survey of random sites and extrapolate up (that's what the BTO/ JNCC/RSPB Breeding Bird Survey does every year for a wide range of species). But for the Hen Harrier you have to have a way to capitalise on the fact that there are lots of keen volunteers who will cover maybe a third of the population (but nothing like a third of the potential land area) each year, whilst recognising that randomised sampling has to do the job for the rest of the range and population. It's not the greatest of intellectual challenges, but it is one that 'we' – the birding and conservation community – have only met in the last 30 years or so.

In 2010, therefore, surveyors were sent to 144 randomly selected 10-kilometre squares within the known range of the Hen Harrier in Scotland (out of the 446 squares that were not in Orkney and not covered intensively by raptor workers) to look for birds in the breeding season on at least two visits, but usually on three or more. A further level of statistical sophistication was added by dividing these squares into two sampling strata (essentially, places thought to be good for Hen Harriers and places thought to hold few harriers), which would improve the statistical certainty of the estimate.

The end result of all this surveying was the aforementioned estimate of 633 pairs for the whole of the UK. But I hope this lengthy explanation (and it could have been much lengthier, believe me) shows that this figure is made up of areas that are fully surveyed and a sample survey of remaining areas where there might well be Hen Harriers but there aren't enough local volunteers to be completely sure. Thus not only do we know that the population estimate is 633 pairs, but we can be 95% confident that the true figure lies between 547 and 741 pairs, because of the random sampling of potential areas. If there had been a greater rate of sampling of the random squares, then the confidence intervals for the estimate would narrow (but you soon hit a law of diminishing returns on that, which you will be grateful to know that I'm not going to go into), but if the sampling intensity had been lower then the intervals would have been much wider, and we would know that we didn't know that much! As it is, we can be pretty sure that we know how many Hen Harriers there are in the UK, give or take about 100 pairs.

Although, actually, that isn't quite right either. I've described the statistical elements of the survey so far, but clearly, if the field surveyors were incompetent (they couldn't identify a Hen Harrier correctly) or dishonest (they made up the data) then no amount of statistical sophistication would give us a good answer. And if the number of visits was too low, or if the visits were made at the wrong time of year, or if the time of day were important, then there might be other sources of error that are nothing to do with statistics.

The logistical challenge is in liaising with a disparate bunch of independent raptor workers and gaining their cooperation, whilst also recruiting good staff to do the random squares that are needed in order to establish the confidence intervals for the overall estimate and simply to cover enough ground to make the survey worthwhile. It is those paid surveyors, and the time spent in organising things (and then analysing the results and writing the papers), that cost the money. A national Hen Harrier survey can cost getting on for £100,000 to carry out, even though most of the people involved in it are unpaid volunteers contributing their time and expertise because of their love of the birds. The above-the-line costs are met by a combination of the RSPB, which has usually taken the lead in organising the surveys of recent years, and the statutory nature conservation organisations sending cheques to RSPB headquarters in Sandy, Bedfordshire.

I hope that I have explained what we know about Hen Harrier numbers in the UK in 2010, how we know it, and how well we know it. It's very different from our guess of how many Hen Harriers there were in the UK in 1910 – that's progress! It's important to hold some of this information in our heads, because it's a bit too glib to say that there were 633 pairs of Hen Harriers in the UK in 2010. And just about everything about the Hen

Harrier is contentious, so it's worth establishing what we know and how we know it.

And the 2010 survey gives us lots of other information as well. In particular, it allows us to say a good deal about the breeding habitats of the bird, and also about how much numbers had changed since the previous survey in 2004. Let's consider those changes in numbers between 2004 and 2010 first.

In 2004 there were 749 pairs of Hen Harriers in the UK, compared with 633 in 2010 – there was a 15.5% decline in numbers. Would you say that was significant? It does seem quite a lot in just six years and, clearly, if it continued for another six, twelve or more years it would lead to a much smaller Hen Harrier population, so it is not to be sniffed at. However, a statistician would look at the numbers in a different way and would remind us that the 633 was really a figure that was probably around 633 but might have been as many as 741 or as few as 547. Similarly, because the survey was done in a similar way, the 2004 result was 749 but the true figure might have been as high as 832 or as low as 675.

Statisticians live their professional lives wondering whether things are 95% sure or not, and that is the level they use for statistical significance (I wonder whether their private lives are wracked with doubt over whether they are 94% in love with someone or 95% – but I digress). In statistical terms, the 15.5% decline is not quite statistically significant; in other words, we cannot be 95% sure that there were fewer Hen Harriers in 2010 than in 2004, although the difference comes pretty close to being statistically significant. And if we include the Isle of Man population (which is not a part of the UK, which is why I haven't mentioned it so far, but was covered in both surveys, with 57 pairs in 2004 and 29 in 2010), then the total UK and Isle of Man Hen Harrier population declined from 806 pairs in 2004 to 662 pairs in 2010 – a decline of 17.9%, and statistically significant. Earlier surveys in 1988–89 and 1998 each produced UK and Isle of Man totals of around 570 pairs. Thus we can be very sure that there are a lot more Hen Harriers in the UK and the Isle of Man than there were 100 years ago, but that in the period 1988–2010 four national surveys all estimated the population as being between 570 and 806 pairs. Given the reliance of this species on voles, which are renowned for varying greatly in numbers from year to year, I think it is quite possible that Hen Harrier numbers do vary within these bounds.

Although the time trend is very interesting, the spatial variation and the habitat associations seem to me to be much more intriguing. In all the surveys carried out, the vast majority of Hen Harriers have been found nesting on moorland with heather growing on it. This land is either managed specifically for grouse shooting (the subject of the next chapter) and is easily recognisable as such from the pattern created by deliberate, periodic burning of heather to produce a mosaic of heather ages, or else it is simply moorland dominated by heather. In almost all surveys of Hen Harriers in the UK, in almost all regions surveyed, these are the two habitat types, rather similar to each other, that predominate to the tune of more than half of the nests, usually more than three-quarters of the nests, and often practically all the nests. Nests on grass moorland are a further small component, especially in Wales and Scotland, and then practically all of the remaining nests are located in young forestry plantations or in areas of old plantations where a crop has been felled and the site has been replanted with young trees.

In 2010 about a quarter of the 633 UK pairs were found on grouse moors, and about a half on other heather moors. Most of the rest were in young conifer plantations. An RSPB study that analysed the data from raptor workers spanned the years 1988–95 and analysed the success of Hen Harriers nesting in these three types of location. The study found that nesting success was lowest on managed grouse moors, at only 0.8 chicks fledged per female per year, compared with 1.4 from young conifer plantations and 2.4 on heather moorland. Interestingly, however, if one looked only at successful nests (disregarding all failed nests), then those nests that were successful on grouse moors produced as many chicks as successful nests on heather moorland not managed for grouse shooting.

It was the high failure rate of nests on driven grouse moors that made the very large difference in overall productivity. Furthermore, failure on grouse moors was often attributed to illegal human persecution, because of evidence of trampling around the nest, shotgun cartridges at the nest, the body of a shot adult found nearby, or possibly because a gamekeeper admitted to the fieldworker that the bird had been killed.

Human interference accounted for at least 30% of the failures of nests on grouse moors but very few of the failures in the other habitat categories. This study was carried out at a time when gamekeepers were more blatant about killing Hen Harriers than they tend to be now.

Information was also collected on some elements of the movement and survival of Hen Harriers by wing-tagging chicks and recording sightings of known birds through their lives. This showed that annual survival of females that nested on grouse moors (c.40% per annum) was only half that of those attempting to nest on otherwise rather similar heather moors not managed for grouse shooting (c.78% per annum). This is a massive difference and indicates the high level of persecution occurring on grouse moors.

Males moult into their grey plumage over a period of a couple of years, and often traces of brown plumage remain amongst the grey in young males, allowing males to be roughly classified as 'old' and 'young'. On grouse moors there was a higher proportion of young males each year, indicating a turnover of birds and relatively few old birds remaining from one year to the next.

Taken together, this information shows that Hen Harriers survive less well on grouse moors than on other heather moors (or young conifer plantations), and also fledge fewer chicks. The productivity and survival are sufficiently low that grouse moors act as a 'sink' for Hen Harriers, and it is only constant immigration that maintains the presence of the harriers on grouse moors in the UK. It was estimated that two-thirds of the females attempting to nest on grouse moors were themselves fledged away from grouse moors. If every heathery hill were managed as a grouse moor, then by now there would be no Hen Harriers in Britain at all, as they die so young and rear so few offspring.

The same study, and much subsequent work, shows that Hen Harriers often nest far from where they were fledged – sometimes more than 100 kilometres away, very often tens of kilometres distant. This is what we would expect from a bird that exploits early successional stages (the natural equivalent of young forestry plantations) and depends on food sources such as voles that can vary greatly in abundance from place to place; and indeed one that is not territorial. All these traits predispose the Hen Harrier to be (or derive from the Hen Harrier being) an opportunist, willing to cash in on any place where food is abundant each year. And it fits well with what was often observed in the era of large-scale afforestation of the uplands, when pairs of Hen Harriers would colonise new plantations many kilometres from any previous known pairs.

Young birds of prey of many species wander widely before settling down to breed. This is true, for example, of Buzzards, Red Kites, Golden Eagles and Hen Harriers – but in the first three species, despite wide wanderings, the young tend to settle to breed within a few kilometres of where they hatched. Natal dispersal, the distance between where a bird fledged and where it settles to breed, is low, whereas in the Hen Harrier it is much higher.

We can imagine that young Hen Harriers find themselves on grouse moors in spring, and (in anthropomorphic terms) cannot believe their luck. They are surrounded by hills with abundant Meadow Pipits and voles, and there is almost no competition, with few or no other Hen Harriers in residence, so they settle on the grouse moors – and run a high risk of being illegally killed.

Let us just suppose for a moment that Hen Harriers were more like Buzzards and settled to breed very close to where they hatched. In that situation, densities of Hen Harriers on heather moorland not managed for grouse shooting would be much higher, as that is the main habitat which has successful nests, and rather few grouse moors would have Hen Harriers attempting to nest, because rather few would be produced in the local area, particularly on grouse moors which are embedded in a landscape filled with other grouse moors. Under these circumstances, gamekeepers would not have anything like as many Hen Harriers to kill each year because they simply wouldn't turn up on the grouse moors with anything like the same frequency. It is because Hen Harriers have low natal fidelity and high natal dispersal that ridding grouse moors of them is such a hard task and one which needs to be carried out with vigour each year.

The importance of this difference in natal dispersal can be seen through this analogy. Buzzard populations are a bit like a bowl of mashed potato (stick with me on this!). If you kill lots of Buzzards in one place it is like scooping out a spoonful of mashed potato from the bowl – you can see where the hole is and the hole will only gradually fill in to some extent as the mashed potato settles in the bowl. However, Hen Harrier populations are a bit more like a bowl of soup – take out a spoonful and the whole level of the soup goes down, not just where you scoop out the soup.

Now Buzzard populations aren't quite as sticky as mashed potato, and Hen Harrier populations aren't quite as liquid as soup, but the analogy is helpful. In particular it makes you wonder how much the overall level of Hen Harrier soup is depressed by the spoonfuls taken out on grouse moors.

And that can be calculated. An analysis by the statutory conservation agencies looked at how many Hen Harriers there should be, given the available habitat, and their densities in areas where they are not persecuted, and found that the overall population of Hen Harriers in the UK should be, could be, as many as 2,600 pairs – a lot more than the 570–806 in any of the recent surveys. There is a lot of Hen Harrier soup draining away on grouse moors, which is why we refer to grouse moors as sinks. The same analysis also demonstrated that that is where the most obvious disparities were in the Hen Harrier range and population. Hen Harriers are missing in their hundreds of pairs from those parts of the country with suitable habitat that are dominated by driven grouse shooting.

Let us take Wales as an example of a part of the UK with, in recent years, little or no driven grouse shooting. The expected number of pairs of Hen Harriers, given the extent of available habitat, is around 250 pairs, which is a lot more than the 2010 figure of 57 pairs. There are about 200 pairs of Hen Harrier missing from Wales, but at least the population is increasing – and quite rapidly, it seems. Now contrast Wales with England. In England there should be, could be, 330 pairs of Hen Harriers, but the actual number in 2010 was 12 pairs – and in 2014 it was a mere four pairs. Did I hear you cry 'Give me back my Hen Harrier soup!'?

In Scotland the soup level should be about 1,600 pairs but in 2010 it was about 500 pairs. And, for completeness, Northern Ireland, instead of its 59 pairs of Hen Harriers in 2010, should have had about 150 pairs.

In the 1980s, some upland areas were designated as Special Protection Areas (SPAs) by the UK government, under the requirements of the EU Birds Directive. Such SPAs were selected on the basis of their important populations of breeding (or, in some cases, wintering) birds. And so the numbers of those SPAs designated with Hen Harriers partly in mind serve as benchmarks for how many Hen Harriers should be found in certain upland areas – they are the population levels from a few years ago in some of the areas most favoured by the birds.

Let us take the Forest of Bowland, an upland area in Lancashire that will feature several times in this book. There should be at least 13 pairs of Hen Harriers in that area (it has held many more in the past), which, as well as being an SPA, is designated an Area of Outstanding Natural Beauty (AONB) and a Site of Special Scientific Interest (SSSI) too. In 2014 there were just two pairs, and in 2012 none at all bred there, despite the AONB's logo being a beautiful Hen Harrier. These statistics suggest that a considerable part of the area's outstanding natural beauty is missing because of illegal activity.

Even more starkly, in the enormous North Pennine Moors SPA, which takes in 1,470 square kilometres of Northumberland, Cumbria, County Durham and North Yorkshire, there should be at least 11 pairs of Hen Harriers. Since 2007, there have been none at all.

In Scotland things are slightly less bad, although the Forest of Cluny SPA in Perthshire should have 28 pairs of Hen Harriers but usually holds around five.

These examples indicate the lack of Hen Harriers from those very areas designated to protect their habitat because the areas were so important for the species, along with other moorland birds. The habitat has been protected but the birds themselves have not been, and the rightful and natural inhabitants of these upland areas are absent.

Altogether, around 2,000 pairs of Hen Harriers are missing from the UK, and they are most obviously missing from land managed intensively for driven grouse shooting, because Hen Harriers colonising that type of land have low survival and appalling productivity. Furthermore, illegal persecution on grouse moors drags down the level of the rest of the population too, because Hen Harriers have high levels of dispersal. Grouse moors act as sinks into which large parts of the Hen Harrier population are lost. The Hen Harrier is unique amongst UK birds in the scale of impact which wildlife crime continues to have on its range, distribution and breeding numbers.

The war against Hen Harriers

But what, you might ask, about actual evidence of who is killing Hen Harriers? How many gamekeepers are in jail for this offence at the moment? The answer is 'none, actually' – but do not let that put any doubt in your mind that the Hen Harrier is systematically and illegally killed in many parts of the uplands of the UK, for its persecution is admitted by the very shooting community that does the persecuting, though the shooting community tends to focus on the possibility that it is a 'few bad apples' involved. Of course, people do not say that they themselves, or their gamekeepers, have broken the law, but they do admit that the law is being broken.

An early example of commendable honesty in this regard came in the opening lines of a scientific paper on Hen Harrier numbers by the then director of the (then) Game Conservancy Trust, Dr Dick Potts: 'In the UK, a full recovery of Hen Harrier *Circus cyaneus* breeding numbers is prevented by illegal culling by some gamekeepers who fear the species threatens the future of grouse moors.' This paper, published in 1998, was an early attempt to estimate how many Hen Harriers there would be nesting in the British uplands were it not for illegal persecution, and its answer, around 1,600–1,700 pairs, was a bit lower than the current estimate, but not that far short of the mark.

Since the late 1990s, considerable discussion has taken place in the pages of shooting magazines and the newspapers, as well as in rooms as widely dispersed as Fordingbridge, Wrexham, Sandy and Whitehall, over the 'Hen Harrier problem'. However, the 'problem', like all arguments, has two sides and many perspectives. Some would see the 'Hen Harrier problem' as being primarily the impact of grouse-eating by Hen Harriers on grouse shooting, but all would recognise that the depredation of Hen Harriers on Red Grouse leads to the illegal killing of Hen Harriers by grouse-shooting interests. Lots of meetings of men (mostly) in suits (often) have been entirely predicated on the fact that other men (in tweed suits, often) go into the hills with the aim of breaking the law and killing Hen Harriers in order to increase the numbers of Red Grouse that can be shot in the autumn. There is no real debate about the fact that this happens. Occasionally some newcomer to the debate starts arguing that the case against gamekeepers is unproven, but these are sporadic outbreaks of denial that rarely last long.

No, the reputable organisations funded by and close to the shooting community, including the British Association for Shooting and Conservation (BASC) and the Game and Wildlife Conservation Trust (GWCT), recognise the widespread nature of illegal raptor persecution aimed at Hen Harriers (and other raptors), and condemn it publicly.

As an example, the GWCT's director of fundraising, Andrew Gilruth, when interviewed by Charlie Moores of Birders Against Wildlife Crime in July 2014, referred to Dick Potts's paper as an early example of how his organisation had long accepted the critical role of illegal persecution in the fate of the UK Hen Harrier populations, and said about illegal persecution, 'I don't think that anyone is under any illusion that it needs to stop. I mean, the scientific literature is full of information about what the issue is. The challenge is about what to actually do about it.'

So, if there is widespread acceptance of the fact that Hen Harriers are bumped off, illegally but systematically, in the British uplands, why is it that there aren't lots of gamekeepers in prison having been convicted of these widespread crimes?

Let us imagine a plausible scenario of Hen Harrier persecution. On a remote heather moor in the north of England, a gamekeeper notices that a pair of Hen Harriers has taken up residence on 'his' grouse moor sometime in March. He hopes they will move on, maybe head north to Scotland, but anywhere will do so long as they become someone else's problem. But as time passes he sees the birds quartering the moor on a daily basis, and then, on fine sunny mornings, he notices the male sky-dancing – carrying out undulating displays to defend the area from other males and to impress his mate. Soon the female is seen spending more and more time visiting an area of long heather on a small slope, and that appears to be where the nest is located.

One morning, the gamekeeper sets off before first light to visit the Hen Harrier nest. He drives up a rough track and unlocks a padlocked gate, which has few key holders. His are the only tyres to crunch through the frost that morning. No footprints mark the track. He drives for 20 minutes into the hills, parks and walks for a few more minutes over the moors, along no track or path except the occasional sheep trail, to where he has seen the ringtail spending most of her time. He sits in the heather, watching. He is watching for the birds, but also for any walkers on the hill. It would be very unusual for anyone else to be up here at this time of day at this time of year – but you never know. Perhaps he has chosen a rather miserable morning of drizzly rain to further reduce the chances of anyone being a witness to his deed, or perhaps he has chosen a misty morning on which his knowledge of his ground won't be too hampered but any visitors to the moor will be unable to see very far. Or perhaps he is so sure that no one will be in the hills this early in the morning that he is not too bothered.

After a while he walks over to the slope where the Hen Harrier is nesting, and as he makes his way slowly, one step at a time, keeping his balance, through heather that reaches to his knees, he closes his shotgun. And then, about 10 metres in front of him, a ringtail Hen Harrier rises from the ground and flies away, her brown feathers echoing the colour of the heather, a prominent white rump acting as a target for him. He slips off the safety catch and fires one, and then two barrels of his shotgun at the fleeing bird. She is hit, and the deed is done. With a glance at the nest and its half-complete clutch of three eggs, he picks up the dead bird and stuffs her into his jacket pocket, walks away from the nest and finds a place to hide the corpse under a stone, under a loose hag of peat, or down an old Rabbit burrow.

If by chance the first shots do not kill the female, then it is likely that she will come back in a few moments to mob the intruder at her nest. Female Hen Harriers are brave to the point of foolhardiness in this regard, and raptor workers, licensed to visit nests for monitoring and research purposes, will tell of being struck on the back of the head by the clenched claws of a female harrier trying to protect her nest. Researchers protect themselves by wearing a hat, being vigilant and ducking when the female dives, but the gamekeeper is better armed and can shoot a brave, returning female Hen Harrier. If she doesn't return to offer him another shot then there is always another day – the nest site is now known and the female is tied to it throughout incubation and beyond. The gamekeeper can rue his luck in missing this opportunity, but he can take as many others as he needs, and each carries only a small risk of observation or capture.

We can only imagine what mix of emotions fills the game-keeper's thoughts as he walks back to his vehicle after killing a protected bird. As he goes about the rest of his work, maybe checking snares, burning some patches of heather or visiting crow traps, what thoughts go through his head? There may be some satisfaction that a necessary job has been carried out efficiently and with a clean kill; there will, I would have thought, be relief that there is no need to revisit the site and that there has been no sign of his being observed; there may be some shame at carrying out a criminal act and perhaps some lasting nervousness in case someone, or perhaps a hidden remote camera, was watching as the crime took place.

There are other ways of ridding your moor of nesting Hen Harriers. Frequent disturbance of the nest site is an option that does not involve killing the bird and is perhaps easier to defend in court if observed ('I didn't know they were there, m'lord'). I am told that some moors have used quadbikes or even helicopters to disturb nesting harriers. Burning of the long heather in tradi-tional Hen Harrier nesting sites may dissuade the birds from nesting, and, generally, increased burning of heather will reduce the available nesting habitat. Shooting birds away from the nest (the female is reliant on the male for food for much of incuba-tion) is also a method that is frequently used. And in the winter there is the opportunity to shoot at Hen Harriers at communal and traditional roosts.

By frequenting remote and deserted locations, by nesting on the ground, by mobbing intruders to its nest, by being an active hunter quartering large areas of ground and by roosting commu-nally in traditional sites, the Hen Harrier makes its own murder fairly straightforward.

Well, let's consider it for a moment. The man in tweed, intent on killing a Hen Harrier, can choose his moment to suit himself. There really is little chance of a party of hill walkers happening on the scene very early on a grotty weekday morning – and if they do, he can wait for them to pass or come back in the evening or tomorrow. A shot or two ringing out on a grouse moor is not going to attract attention or bring crowds running to the scene. The sight of a policeman on a grouse moor is even rarer than that of a Hen Harrier (although a number of senior police officers are known to partake of a day's grouse shooting).

The people most likely to be watching when a bird of prey such as a Hen Harrier is deliberately killed are that small band of dedicated and brave conservationists who make up the RSPB's Investigations team. I spoke to one of their senior investigators, and he gave me some insights into what actually happens out there in the real world.

Guy Shorrock, a senior investigations officer, told me that when he joined the RSPB Investigations team, as an ex-policeman and lifelong birder, he had thought that some gamekeepers killed a few birds of prey. However, over the years of dealing with hundreds of reports, picking up bodies out on the moors, and having spoken confidentially to several upland gamekeepers, he now believes that the number of grouse estates killing birds of prey is much higher. This may in some cases involve killing a 'rogue bird' that is suspected of killing a high number of gamebirds, but in other cases it amounts to systematic poisoning and shooting of raptors. On one estate, a gamekeeper told him, 'For anything that threatened a grouse, its eggs or chicks, our instructions were clear; it went.'

Another gamekeeper told Guy that on his estate, where there were four other gamekeepers, all of them were killing raptors, and he was sure the same was true of the neighbouring estates, too. That gamekeeper knew of estates where it was said that the landowner kept raptor-killing in check, but these were the exceptions rather than the rule.

A gamekeeper in North Yorkshire, on an estate in a region where Hen Harriers haven't nested for years, said that they were 'mopping up' up to half a dozen Hen Harriers each year as the birds came through in spring.

Guy also told me:

A gamekeeper came to see us from a shooting estate in the North of England. I interviewed him twice – once with a colleague and once again with a police officer. This gamekeeper had been dismissed and so you always have to be a bit careful about whether the accounts given were true or malicious, but you don't have much choice about that – the happily employed raptor-killing gamekeepers aren't going to be the ones who talk openly about what is happening.

He started giving us the data and told us that over a three-year period in the 1990s he and his fellow gamekeepers killed about 30 Hen Harriers each year.

This is a somewhat eye-watering number, but it is entirely feasible biologically, as the population was then higher and it would involve birds wandering through the north of England in winter, birds attempting to settle in spring and those heading from their southern England wintering haunts back to Scottish moors.

The same estate was killing Peregrines, too. The gamekeepers made a platform that was suitable for Peregrines to roost on, and one gamekeeper claimed he had shot nine Peregrines during the year using that one platform. It seems that once you've got it sussed out, raptor-killing isn't that difficult and becomes part of the gamekeeper's routine.

In addition there were many other raptors killed on this estate, according to the dismissed gamekeeper, amounting to 200–300 birds of prey a year – mainly Buzzards and Short-eared Owls, but also Goshawks and even, it was claimed, a rare Rough-legged Buzzard. The estate management were believed to be fully aware of what was going on. This estate was thought to be at the very top end of upland raptor-killing, and the keepers apparently took some covert pride in it. However, Guy believed that killing 50 raptors a year, each act being a wildlife crime, was and is commonplace on some upland grouse-shooting estates.

Guy was involved in investigations work at the Geltsdale RSPB nature reserve, on the border of Cumbria and Northumberland, in the late 1990s. Each year there were several pairs of Hen Harriers attempting to breed on the reserve and on the neighbouring grouse moors, but the nests had a high rate of failure. A few shot birds of prey were picked up and the occasional poisoned Raven was recovered. Guy told me:

We had received this information, so in 2000 we employed contract staff to watch Hen Harrier nests. As you know, it's a huge area. One Saturday in April one of the reserve staff was watching a Hen Harrier nest just off the reserve. He saw a man arrive and try to shoot the male Hen Harrier. We decided to keep a watch on it. So basically I did a few watches on the nest early in the morning. This involved setting off at about 03:30 in the morning; it was a 50-minute walk to the site, creeping in in the dark, hunkering down in the heather and waiting for light to see what happened. It all kicked off one weekend in mid-April when I was there and it was just getting light. I was hidden on the side of a small valley and on the other side of the valley there was a line of shooting butts about 400 metres away from where I was. The Hen Harriers were prospecting and starting to build a nest in this valley.

Just as it was getting light I saw this crouched figure creeping through the heather and into the last in the line of shooting butts. He wore a full-face balaclava, and had a telescope and a firearm. He spent quite a long time scanning the RSPB land, presumably making sure that there weren't any RSPB staff there – but he didn't spot me on his side of the fence. Then he was creeping along the line of the shooting butts trying to get an opportunity to shoot a Hen Harrier but neither of the birds came close enough to him. It was now getting quite late in the morning, relatively speaking, about 06:30, and he walked across the hillside, got into his Land Rover and drove away. That set the scene.

We thought that because the reserve was manned during the week it was more likely that something would happen at the weekend. So I was back there next weekend, and this time I had a colleague on the hill as back-up. I had crept in, in the dark, and settled down, but what I didn't know was that two other men had crept in in the dark too, and we had all settled down to wait and watch, completely unaware of the others' presence.

I'm sat there minding my own business when at 05:37, Bang! a shotgun goes off. Not too far away but not desperately close. So – I'm not alone! So I'm scanning the heather and eventually I see the man in one of the shooting butts, again with a full-face balaclava, crouched down in an olive Barbour jacket.

He eventually walked 30 or 40 metres down the hill, had a quick scan with his binoculars over our reserve and then picked up a dead bird and I thought, 'That's got to be a harrier.' He continued across the hillside and then disappeared into a ditch. So,

I'm sat there and 40 minutes pass and I see his head bobbing up and down in the ditch, wondering why he has not left. And then another shotgun blast goes off and this time it's really close to me on the other side of a dry-stone wall – and that really did make me jump. So he had an accomplice.

A short while later the two men left – my 'eyes on the hill' spotted them both leaving – so I guided my colleague to the area below the shooting butt, and he tells me, over the radio, that he can see a feather and some blood. I join him and sure enough there's a broken Hen Harrier tail feather and some drops of blood on the heather.

We looked into the ditch where the first man had disappeared and there were plenty of footprints, but I noticed two little circular plastic discs about a centimetre across. For a moment we were wondering 'What the hell are they?', but then we realised that they were studs from wing-tags and the female Hen Harrier had been wing-tagged. So we looked around more carefully and saw, half a metre down a hole, a wing tip; I reached in and pulled out the corpse of a recently killed female Hen Harrier that had been hidden in the ditch.

But even all that evidence didn't lead to a conviction, although the police did investigate and plaster casts were taken of the footprints at the scene of the crime. Local houses were searched but no evidence strong enough to secure a court case was found. Even though RSPB staff had all but witnessed the killing of the Hen Harrier and had her body, there was no court case. That's how difficult it is. And of course, there was nobody else up in the hills that Sunday morning before six o'clock, so if Guy and his colleague hadn't been there this would have been just another unexplained disappearance of a pair of Hen Harriers that had apparently been prospecting but were not known to have nested.

Later in 2000, the RSPB Investigations team had more success – the only successful prosecution of a gamekeeper (or anyone else) for killing a Hen Harrier. Guy told me:

This was a watch we started which went on for over six weeks, I think. We watched this Hen Harrier site in Morayshire which wasn't a very intensively keepered estate. The two lads who had been working at Geltsdale were sent up to Scotland and they were there that fateful day. They filmed a gamekeeper get out of his vehicle, walk up the slope and shoot one of the recently fledged Hen Harriers. He received a fine of £2,000 at Elgin Sherriff Court for shooting a female Hen Harrier.

As simple as that! Although it took weeks of covert effort to film the crime. A few years later there was one more conviction for a Hen Harrier offence. Guy takes up the story once more:

This was another Hen Harrier nest in Aberdeenshire in 2004 on land next to a shooting estate. I was doing a watch one evening when suddenly two gamekeepers appeared with firearms at the ready walking down through the heather to where I knew the Hen Harriers were. One had his hood pulled right around his face, and it wasn't for the midges that day. I knew where the recently fledged Hen Harriers had gone to roost and I could see that the gamekeepers were walking straight towards them. They must have got to within 10 metres and then they stopped and had a conversation. They seemed to be pointing in the direction of where I knew the harriers were, and I was thinking, 'Yes, you're right, they are just in front of you' and I was sure I was going to see the harriers shot. It was incredibly frustrating because it was just too dark to film what was happening, so I thought I was going to see the crime but not get good evidence. But at that moment the two men changed direction and walked back to their vehicle and drove away.

All very exciting, but I had to leave and get the train down south – but, all credit to them, the lads went back even though they'd had a series of long tough days, and one hid where the vehicle had been parked. Now this time a single keeper arrived and put on a balaclava, but unfortunately for him, he first got out of the vehicle and had a pee, and then put on his balaclava, so we had him filmed. He then wandered on to the neighbouring land and was seen trying to get a shot at a young Hen Harrier which kept flying just out of range. So that was a case where he was convicted of 'going equipped to kill a Hen Harrier' plus trespassing with a firearm, for which he was fired a total of £500.

These cases illustrate how incredibly difficult it is to see the deed being done, and to gather sufficient evidence to stand up in court, but also the extreme unlikelihood that anybody not intent on collecting evidence of wildlife crimes would be present at the relevant and telling time.

Guy believes that the techniques used to kill Hen Harriers have changed, partly as a result of the few successes that the RSPB has had in gaining evidence to convict gamekeepers of shooting these birds, but also because of the wider successes of convictions of gamekeepers for killing birds of prey. Gamekeepers used to think that they were pretty much inviolate themselves as they violated the law on remote hillsides, but now there is more of a feeling of fear that they may be being watched – and so killing birds at roosts is far commoner, as is distant rifle-shooting of birds.

Talking to Guy, I wondered how commonly gamekeepers commit crimes against birds of prey, including Hen Harriers, in the British uplands. We know that the level of wildlife crime against Hen Harriers is sufficiently high to limit the population to about a third or a quarter of what it could be in the absence of illegal persecution. We also know (as explained in Chapter 4) that the same is true for Golden Eagles and Peregrine Falcons. But is it just a few gamekeepers on a few estates that are respon- sible for this big biological impact on our natural heritage, or is everyone at it?

Not surprisingly, the grouse-shooting industry, whilst usually admitting that raptor persecution occurs and is a serious problem, tends towards the 'just a few bad apples' public view of this matter. And they might well be right. The overall biological impact of a few rotten apples (estates where many birds are killed) would be similar to the impact of very many slightly blemished ones (estates where illegal persecution is occasional).

When I asked Professor Ian Newton, a raptor expert, what he thought about this issue, he told me, 'My experience is almost entirely in Scotland, and I would agree with some of your former colleagues at the RSPB and say that many gamekeepers – maybe the ones in the uplands are worse than those in the lowlands, but many gamekeepers will be killing birds of prey habitually.'

The Hen Harrier – loved and loathed

The Hen Harrier will play a prominent part in this book not because I love it so much, but because others hate it.

Those grouse-moor managers who hate the Hen Harrier do so because they see it as a pest, as vermin, as something that harms their interests – but I was interested to explore why birders, like me, are so keen on the bird. Many birders would put the Hen Harrier near or at the top of their list of favourite birds – and that includes me. I've often played the game, with others, of choosing the half-dozen birds to take to a desert island to remind you of home, or just as your favourite birds – the Hen Harrier often features on such lists.

I think this is partly because the bird is an infrequent sight. Even where it occurs it is an occasional sight rather than ever-present. You need a bit of skill as well as a bit of luck to see and identify the bird, too. As Tim Melling of the RSPB said to me, 'Hen Harriers don't give themselves up easily.' It's a birder's bird.

When you do see a Hen Harrier it is active, it is doing something, it is hunting, it is making things happen. Of course Hen Harriers sometimes sit still, but this tends to be on the ground, out of sight, unnoticeable and unnoticed. When you see a Hen Harrier in flight it is either going somewhere, flying fast and directly with an air of purpose, or it is quartering the ground, looking down all the time, adjusting its position to search the vegetation below for prey. As a surprise predator, the Hen Harrier always has to be alert for the flight of a small bird or the scurrying of a small mammal. It needs quick reactions, like a slip-fielder in cricket, to grab its prey in its talons. It must always be alert, always on its game and always ready to pounce. It's a killer looking for prey, intent on killing, and the next death, the next meal for the harrier, may be just a wing-flap away if it is lucky and if it is skilful.

Other raptors are, of course, killers too, but there is not the same feeling of impending jeopardy when you see a Peregrine Falcon sitting on a cliff or an urban roof. Yes, it may be looking for a passing feral pigeon to attack but it may also, for all you know, be dozing off in the sun or thinking of something completely different. And even an eagle soaring high in the sky may be scanning the earth below for Mountain Hares or Ptarmigan, but you can't really tell, by looking, how intent it is on making a kill, whereas there is no doubt with the Hen Harrier that it is in killing mode. There is a sense of expectancy in watching this bird, which adds to the spectacle.

The Hen Harrier, hunting as it does at ground level, is far more a part of its landscape than other raptors. Most sightings of Peregrines or Golden Eagles are against a background of sky: these are birds of the skies. But the Hen Harrier is seen against its habitat, hugging the contours, an intimate predator, a detailed predator, where every slight rise of ground, every clump of rushes, every small winding ditch, affects the bird's flight, its approach and the tactics of the hunt. And when that Hen Harrier is an adult male it is a very special sight. The grey plumage with white rump and black wingtips makes it the cleanest, brightest predator in the UK. If you watch a male Hen Harrier in the gathering gloom it shines out at you. The clean lines of the bird's wings and tail are sharp in the failing evening light. It is a sight of beauty.

But it is also because of my background in nature conservation that the Hen Harrier captures both my intellect and my emotions. There are very few birds, or other animals, which are deliberately persecuted to such an extent that their national populations are held far lower than they would otherwise be. Most conservation issues in the present-day UK are ones where people's legitimate desires to better their lives, to make money and to prosper their businesses come into conflict with wildlife accidentally. For example, farmland birds have declined to a huge extent in the countryside where I live, not because farmers go out and shoot Skylarks and Tree Sparrows but because their farming techniques, designed to increase both profit and food supply, take too little account of the needs of wildlife. Changes in farming practices have caused big losses in wildlife, but that wasn't the intention of the farmers.

However, the problems of the Hen Harrier are driven by people who greatly dislike the Hen Harrier. There is nothing accidental about it. People stamp on the eggs knowing what they are doing, knowing that it is illegal and wanting to do it. The chicks have been kicked and trampled to death so that when x-rayed there has hardly been an intact bone left in their bodies. People look down the barrels of shotguns and pull the trigger when a Hen Harrier is in range, because they want it dead. And although the Hen Harrier does, of course, lose its eggs frequently to Red Foxes and other predators, and flies into fences and loses its life in all sorts of natural and unnatural ways, overwhelmingly its status in the UK today is determined by how much wildlife crime is directed towards it, despite the fact that it has had full legal protection for over 60 years.

Many involved with grouse shooting loathe the Hen Harrier with a passion reserved only for that species. The Peregrine Falcon is seen to be a problem species, but is admired as a hunter. The Hen Harrier is loathed, hated and despised – those words are not too strong for the emotions it conjures up. Gamekeepers refer to the Hen Harrier as a 'back door' bird because it attempts to surprise its prey rather than giving chase, and as sneaky and cunning, with neither term used in a complimentary way.

The Hen Harrier is seen as an interloper, an uninvited visitor that then proceeds to help itself to your grouse – the grouse you want to shoot later in the season.

When writing of the Hen Harrier in his 1958 book *Grouse: Shooting and Moor Management*, Richard Waddington, a grouse-moor owner from Scotland, described the Hen Harrier as:

> ... a nasty bird of evil habits. It quarters the moor a few feet above
> the ground and pounces on grouse or chicks it catches unawares.
> It must be got rid of at all cost. Whenever I see a hen harrier I
> regret that pole traps have been made illegal.

Such sentiments are rarely as honestly or forthrightly voiced these days, but there are many who practise grouse shooting who would nod in agreement when they read those words, and too many who still act in accordance with them.

Furthermore, and adding spice to the whole issue, those wildlife crimes are carried out solely by one so-called profession: gamekeepers. There are no coachloads of student nurses heading into the Peak District from Sheffield each weekend searching for Hen Harriers to kill. No band of estate agents or journalists, or even bankers or politicians, leaves Manchester to scour the Forest of Bowland for nests of Hen Harriers. No, it is one group of people, pursuing one specialised interest, that is responsible for wildlife crimes against Hen Harriers.

And yes, those gamekeepers are employed by many of the richest and most powerful landowners in Britain, which means that there is the scope for this conflict to be seen as a class issue – and it is certainly a political one. There's nothing like it anywhere else in UK conservation, and there's nothing else quite like it anywhere else in the world. The crimes against the Hen Harrier are a product of our British history, our British class system and our British politics.

You don't have to have seen a Hen Harrier to be on the side of the Hen Harrier. You don't have to want to see a Hen Harrier to be on the side of the Hen Harrier. You don't have to be a birder to be on the side of the Hen Harrier. You don't have to be a member of a conservation organisation to be on the side of the Hen Harrier. If you believe in the rule of law then you should be on the side of the Hen Harrier because its numbers are driven down in our law-abiding country by criminals who won't tolerate this protected species on their land.

And so another reason, I think, that birders like seeing Hen Harriers, and list them as among their favourite birds, is that they are on the side of the Hen Harrier. Each time you see one, you are seeing a survivor. Consciously or unconsciously, you give it a little cheer and feel glad that it has escaped so far.

*

What I would like you to take away from this chapter:

- The Hen Harrier is a marvellous and beautiful bird. If you haven't seen one then have a look at the videos of it on the internet or, better still, go and seek it out in the places where it can still be found.
- Where driven grouse shooting is a major land use Hen Harriers are not tolerated, because they eat the Red Grouse that people want to shoot. Some gamekeepers, on some grouse moors, kill Hen Harriers despite the fact that this has been illegal for more than 60 years. The level of illegal persecution is enough to reduce the UK Hen Harrier population from a possible 2,600 pairs to around 500–800 pairs.

- The Hen Harrier is loved by some, hated by some, and totally ignored by most people. There is no other species of British bird whose population is so reduced by the illegal acts of just a few people. The Hen Harrier needs more friends.

CHAPTER TWO

A short introduction to grouse shooting

If God wanted us to be vegetarians, he would have made broccoli
a lot more fun to hunt!

Anonymous

Go into the streets of Britain and engage people in conversation about grouse shooting, Red Grouse shooting, and I'd
be surprised if you find many with strong views, or informed
views, on the subject. Some will realise that it is an activity that
occurs in the hills and involves the species of bird found on the
label of 'Famous Grouse' whisky, produced by Matthew Gloag
and Son since 1886. Some will confuse it with Pheasant shooting
and believe, wrongly, that the grouse are reared by gamekeepers
and released in the hills, but rather more will have some vague
impression that the activity involves a day in the heather-clad
hills shooting a few wild, free-range and organic chicken-like
birds in pleasant scenery. Some will think that it is a sport,
pastime or industry (and opinions on what it actually is will
differ) reserved for the rich.

Today's commonest form of grouse shooting, driven grouse
shooting, is indeed an activity that is mostly reserved for the
landed, the rich, and primarily the landed rich. To buy a day's
shooting for a party of eight shooters, on a prime grouse moor
in North Yorkshire in late August 2014, would have set you
back about £35,000 (plus VAT, of course) – at least, that was the
price advertised by one agency at the Country Land and Business
Association annual Game Fair in July 2014. That puts grouse
shooting beyond the means of most of us, I guess.

Driven grouse shooting involves a line of relatively poor
people, the beaters, walking across a stretch of moorland with
flags and whistles and, by so doing, pushing the Red Grouse

that live there towards a line of relatively rich people, who then shoot at the grouse as they whizz past them at great speed (often claimed to exceed 125 kilometres per hour, although this seems biologically unlikely). A day's shooting will typically comprise a series of some half-dozen 'drives' of different stretches of moorland, each with its line of shooting butts, sunken shelters where the shooters and their loaders wait at their allocated station for the birds to be driven towards them. The shooting is fast and furious, and when the birds come, time spent reloading is time that could be spent shooting more birds, so each shooter will probably have a couple of double-barrelled shotguns and a person to reload them, to increase the firing rate.

That, then, is the essence of driven grouse shooting; that is what we would get for our £35,000 a day. For keen proponents of the sport there is nothing to rival it – a day in the hills in congenial company, and a shooting experience where your speed of reaction and accuracy are tested to the limits. Whatever one thinks of it, driven grouse shooting is a uniquely British experience, practised nowhere else in the world and rooted in our culture and history. The story behind present-day grouse shooting is a tale of money, power and politics (with a little ecology thrown in), and as such it is, of course, rooted in the British class system. But let us start with some ecology.

British grouse

Four species of grouse live in the British Isles, and each has been part of the shooting tradition over the centuries. Only the Red Grouse now plays any real part in sport shooting in the UK, although elsewhere in the world the other three species are still hunted.

In order to see all four British grouse in a day you would most likely head for the Cairngorms region of northern Scotland. In the forests to the east of Aviemore lie remnants of the ancient Scots Pine forest of Caledon, and in these pinewoods you might be lucky enough to see a Capercaillie (*Tetrao urogallus*). These large forest grouse are now very rare in Britain (*c.*1,000 individuals), having declined in recent decades; they feed on blueberries in summer, along with other forest fruits, and a rather dull diet of conifer needles in winter. The chicks feed on insects in their early days, as do the chicks of other grouse species.

Male Capercaillies are large turkey-like birds, which gather together in leks (from a Swedish word meaning 'to play' – although their gatherings are very serious) to display and establish a dominance hierarchy amongst themselves. This is where the females visit to choose their mates.

On the forest edge, you may be lucky enough to come across the next member of the grouse family – the Black Grouse (*Tetrao tetrix*). These birds also lek, and you may be drawn to the open space where the males display through their bubbling songs; there are about 5,100 males in the UK. The Black Grouse is a smaller bird than the Capercaillie; the male is glossy black with red wattles above the eyes, and a lyre-shaped tail quite unlike that of any other British bird. Because of their plumage the males are often referred to as blackcocks (not, I suggest, a term to put into an internet search engine in an unguarded moment), and the more camouflaged females who do all the raising of the chicks are known as greyhens.

Quite similar in appearance to the female Black Grouse, but distinctly redder, are both male and female Red Grouse (*Lagopus lagopus*). The UK population of this species is about 230,000 pairs, and they are found further up the hill and further away from the forest edge, on open heather moorland. The Red Grouse is territorial, with the males setting up territories in spring, defending them with their calls and fiercely fighting off incursions from neighbours and intruding non-territorial males.

Still further up the hill, above about 600 metres, is the realm of the fourth of our grouse species, the Ptarmigan (*Lagopus mutus*; *c.*8,500 pairs). Like Red Grouse, Ptarmigan are territorial, and they are quite similar in appearance, although greyer. They retain some white plumage throughout the year, and turn completely white in winter, for camouflage against the snow.

All four grouse species nest on the ground, all lay large clutches of eggs (Capercaillie 7–12; Black Grouse 6–11; Red Grouse 6–9; Ptarmigan 5–8), and all therefore have large broods of young that swell the autumn populations with their numbers to a greater or lesser extent, depending on whether it has been a good or poor breeding season. Thus in all species the autumn population is usually much larger than that in spring, and if the birds were left to themselves then the hardship of winter weather, food shortages and the attacks of predatory birds and mammals would reduce their numbers to something like the previous year's level by the next spring. In the absence of humans, year after year would pass with some good and some poor breeding seasons, and with numbers fluctuating accordingly.

Sport shooting depends on the high productivity of these quarry species. It is possible to think of there being an 'autumn surplus' of birds that will be brought down through the winter by means of the natural processes of disease, starvation and predation to a much lower spring level (and for that reason it is sometimes called the 'doomed surplus' or 'shootable surplus'). Sport shooting consists of intervening to harvest that surplus, and the basis on which the shooting is sustainable is that it is taking a harvest of birds that were 'doomed' to die anyway. So why not have the fun of killing and then eating them?

The shooting seasons for these four grouse species were set to allow shooters to harvest the autumn surplus of birds. The Red Grouse season opens on the so-called 'Glorious Twelfth' of August and ends on 10 December, as does the Ptarmigan season, whereas the Black Grouse season opens a week later but ends on the same day, and in the past, when shooting Capercaillie was allowed, its season lasted from 1 October to 31 January.

No Capercaillie should be shot in the UK these days, as this was banned by the Scottish Executive from 4 November 2001 as a conservation measure following a decade of a fairly well-honoured voluntary moratorium. Shooting certainly was not the cause of their population decline, but a combination of poor spring weather (which seems to be changing for the worse, perhaps as a result of climate change) and collisions with deer fences set inside or on the edge of the forest are the main causes. This species is in danger of national extinction in the UK, for a second time; its current population derives from reintroductions in 1837 after a previous extinction in 1785. The reintroduction was carried out mainly by large shooting estates in Perthshire.

Black Grouse were once a much commoner part of the shooting scene, but that is partly because they were once a much commoner part of the rural scene. They lived in areas of scrubby heathland and common land as far south as Hampshire, Dorset, Devon and Cornwall late into the nineteenth century. Their populations throughout the UK have declined; climate change, land-use changes and increased disturbance may all have played a part, but so too has the concentration on the Red Grouse as the preferred species for shooting, which has led to habitat management favouring Red at the expense of Black Grouse. The two species overlap in range and ecological requirements, but the best ground for Black Grouse will have rather few Red, and *vice versa*. There is little shooting of Black Grouse in the UK these days, and what amounts to a voluntary shooting moratorium is in place, as the numbers are low and declining.

Ptarmigan shooting is a niche activity that involves lots of walking, the risk of bad weather driving you off the high hills and ruining a day's shooting, and few birds to shoot at – it actually sounds like proper hunting! The average 'bag' (i.e. the number of birds killed) per gun (i.e. per person shooting) per day would only amount to a handful of birds. Few estates can offer such days, and the takers for them are few indeed.

All in all, these days, the total annual bag of Capercaillie, Black Grouse and Ptarmigan must be in the low hundreds of birds, perhaps below a hundred birds in many years. By far the predominant quarry for the grouse shooter today is the Red Grouse, which is shot in numbers of approaching half a million birds per year in the north of England and Scotland, but not, these days, in Wales.

The Red Grouse's scientific name, *Lagopus lagopus*, derives from the Greek *lagos* ('hare') and *pous* ('foot'), in recognition of the fact that its feathered feet resemble the furry feet of the Snowshoe Hare of North America – and those feet enable the grouse, like the hare, to keep warm and to walk through deep, powdery snow. These are tough birds – it's difficult not to admire them for their fortitude.

The Red Grouse is a very British bird. It was once thought to be the only uniquely British species of bird, but now that claim can be made only for the Scottish Crossbill – a bird of the pine forests also inhabited by the Capercaillie, and which is fiend-ishly difficult to separate in the field from the much commoner

Common Crossbill and the rare Parrot Crossbill. The Red
Grouse is now regarded as a 'mere' race or subspecies of a
circumpolar species that is known elsewhere as the Willow
Grouse or Willow Ptarmigan. Our British Red Grouse are at
least recognisably different in the field from the rest of the
world's *Lagopus lagopus* – our birds, *Lagopus lagopus scoticus*, do
not have white wings, as do the European, Asian and North
American *Lagopus lagopus*, which occur in 17 subspecies around
the world from Scandinavia through Siberia to Alaska (where it
is the state bird) and across Canada.

Our *L. l. scoticus* is also distinct from other members of its
species in its unique diet. All Willow Grouse are vegetarian
except that they depend on insect food as chicks, and in most
parts of their range they feed on a variety of shrubs, particularly
dwarf birch species. In the UK, however, the Red Grouse feeds
to a very large extent on heather.

There are several heather species found in the UK, which
occur in different areas, but the main species of importance to
the Red Grouse is the Common Heather or Ling (*Calluna
vulgaris*), which is the only species in its genus and is found
widely across Europe. Bunches of heather tied to a stick used to
be used as a broom, and the scientific name *Calluna* comes from
a Greek word meaning to beautify or sweep clean, *kallunein*.
Other heathers of upland habitats include Cross-leaved Heath
(*Erica tetralix*) and Bell Heather (*Erica cinerea*).

The heather–clad hills

When the last Ice Age finished, about 10,000 years ago, and the
ice sheets retreated from northern Britain, there was still a land
bridge to the continent, facilitating the colonisation of Britain by
plants and animals. Reindeer and Bison arrived and grazed the
open tundra-like vegetation. As the climate continued to warm,
the hills were colonised by Hazel, birch and Scots Pine, which
provided homes for deer and Wild Boar. Much of the uplands
would have been forested by around 8,000 years ago, and there
followed an invasion of deciduous tree species; oak, Ash and
lime. By 7,000 years before the present, the climate was at its
warmest in postglacial times, the tree line in England and Wales
was at around 750 metres, and forest cover was at its greatest

extent. Most of the uplands we now know as open hills, and where Red Grouse are now driven across the moors, were wooded, although there would have been large open spaces in wetter areas of blanket bog on the hill tops.

From about 5,000 years ago, although the changes in climate affected the composition of the woodlands on the areas now given over primarily to moorland, the increasing human population, with farming growing in importance, shaped the uplands. The forests were cleared by felling and burning, and this would have encouraged the growth of shrubs such as heather. Grazing became an increasingly important part of the upland economy, with the growing of crops being concentrated in the valleys, where the soils were better and the microclimate more benign.

By the time the Romans departed these shores in the fifth century AD, the uplands of England and Wales had been largely cleared of forests. This trend continued through the medieval period, and extended gradually to Scotland.

Today, the British uplands are largely a mixture of artificial habitats. The dominant land use over the last few centuries has been grazing. Over the years, sheep have largely replaced cattle, ponies, pigs and geese, and sheep prefer to eat grass above other woodier forage. Hill land has been enclosed, ploughed, seeded with grasses and fertilised to provide pasture for sheep, which have also roamed the unenclosed moorland at higher altitudes. High sheep numbers, and their incessant nibbling, will push the vegetation from a mixture of heather and grass to a more grass-dominated sward. Thus, in the uplands as a whole, the interests of sheep production and grouse shooting are in conflict. These conflicts have played out to the advantage of one or the other depending on the transitory economics and the interests and pockets of the landowners. Within an upland estate, the head gamekeeper and head shepherd will often have been seeking a different outcome for the land, and the balance of power may have shifted back and forth often over time.

Commercial forestry has also intervened in this landscape, largely encouraged by tax regimes and by the general lack of profitability of agriculture in these harsh climates. Large-scale afforestation, mainly with non-native conifer species, was a major change in the ecology of the uplands through the twentieth century after the formation of the Forestry Commission in 1919.

Left to themselves, the British hills would largely be covered with forests of oak, Ash and birch in the south and Scots Pine and birch in the north. Only the highest mountains (above the natural tree line) and the large areas of blanket bog (too wet for tree growth) would be open spaces. But instead of a naturally forested upland landscape we see, in different proportions in different places, the winners in a three-way fight between sheep, Red Grouse and conifers. Heather-clad hills have largely survived where grouse shooting has been prized either economically or simply for pleasure, but the open landscape it requires is no more natural than the rows of conifers or enclosed sheep pastures in the surrounding area.

First, catch your grouse

A pair of 1930s self-opening sidelocks, side by side (rather than over-under) made by the top English gunsmith James Purdey and Sons might set us back around £40,000 these days – but surely it's worth having the very best shotgun? However, before the advent of exquisite and expensive firearms there were still many different ways to catch grouse.

No doubt Stone Age people threw stones and spears at grouse in flight and on the ground. For them, however, this was not sport, but a minor way of obtaining enough to eat. And despite human ingenuity in finding many ways to catch Red Grouse for the pot over the following millennia, including falconry, snares, nets and archery, it was only the advent of firearms and their refinement that made grouse shooting a sport and a hobby.

Before the invention of the flintlock in the early seventeenth century, there wasn't much opportunity to go sport shooting, even if you had the time, money and land to make it possible. Matchlock guns, in which a lighted fuse ignites the gunpowder, were ill-fashioned for letting off a shot at a flushed bird. Even the flintlock was notoriously unreliable, as it depended on an open charge of powder being ignited by a spark from a flint striking steel – not an ideal mechanism for the rainy hills of the north. But despite the limitations of the equipment, between 1750 and 1850 there was a growing number of landed gentry and military gentlemen who took up shooting as a pastime. A walk across the moorlands with a friend or two, shooting at any game that were flushed in front of the walkers, whether Snipe, Red Grouse, Rabbits or hares, was a day out that also provided food for the table. With muzzle-loading guns, this form of exercise suited the firearms available. It was impossible to loose off several shots, unless one had several companions, so the walk between shots was an opportunity to reload, chat and admire the scenery. This form of shooting is known as walked-up shooting. It is still practised today, with modern shotguns, but is very much restricted to moorland that holds low densities of Red Grouse, and those few shooters who prefer more walking and less shooting than is now the norm.

In the late eighteenth century, a more dedicated form of grouse shooting evolved – shooting over dogs. This was similar to walked-up shooting except with the involvement of trained dogs, pointers or setters (the devotees of each argue over which is the better to this day), who were trained to locate Red Grouse and other quarry on the ground by scent, approach them closely without flushing the birds, and indicate to their human companions where the birds were hidden. The shooters could then catch their breath, ensure all was right with their guns, position themselves and flush the birds to get off a shot at them.

This form of shooting, often disconcertingly called 'dogging', was the main form of 'sporting' grouse shooting at the turn of the eighteenth century. It increased the ease with which a few grouse could be shot, because bringing the heavy muzzle-loaded guns of the time to bear on a flushed bird while walking over uneven ground through rank heather was not easy. Using dogs made the shooting much easier, although it still required a good eye. It also depended on the skill of the dogs, and owners would get great satisfaction from the success of man and dog working in harmony, as a team, to bring down a grouse or two. Much lowland shooting was also over dogs at this time.

The invention of the breech-loading shotgun, and its growing availability from the 1850s onwards, was one factor that changed the way that grouse were shot. Now, two shots could be loosed off in quick succession from each gun, and reloading only took a matter of seconds, so there was sometimes the opportunity to fire again at late-flushing birds from a covey. When shooting at a flushed covey of grouse this made it much more likely that at least a couple of birds could be killed.

The ease of reloading, with cartridges stuffed into the breech of the gun rather than charge, wadding and shot rammed down its barrel, made it possible to fire much more often. But you could still only fire your gun when you and your dogs encountered some birds, and then they flew away from you as quickly as possible. The increased popularity of grouse shooting amongst the landed gentry and the rich, and the improved rail links to the hills of northern England and Scotland in particular, created the demand for driven grouse shooting – where the shooter remains stationary and waits for the birds to come to him or her (usually him).

Driven grouse shooting, with the shooters ensconced in a line of shooting butts across the moor waiting for the line of beaters to drive a hillside of Red Grouse in waves over the butts, developed from the 1850s onwards as the main form of grouse shooting, and it remains so today. It may have developed independently on several moors, but Sir Walter Spencer-Stanhope, who owned moors in the Yorkshire part of the Peak District, is generally regarded as the first (or at least an early) adopter. He wrote that there were frequent criticisms of the practice in the newspapers of the time, until the Dukes of Devonshire and Rutland also began driven grouse shooting.

Traditionalists decried the unsporting nature of this driven shooting, where the shooter was not remotely a hunter of grouse but a mere recipient of a mass of live targets provided by the sweat and activity of the beaters. Instead of the ability to walk over rough terrain, read the ground, train your dogs and then work with them to find and shoot down a few grouse in a day, maybe 20 birds but often many fewer for a day's exercise in the hills, driven grouse shooting allowed someone who was merely a good shot, but who lacked those broader skills of understanding the habitat, to kill many more birds.

When Queen Victoria first leased (in 1848) and Prince Albert then bought (in 1852) Balmoral as a shooting estate, the popularity of driven grouse shooting was assured. Kaiser Wilhelm II shot grouse on Wemmergill Moor in Yorkshire in 1895, further sanctifying the practice. Driven grouse shooting, at great expense, is now seen as the norm, and the activity has so much snob-value attached to it that it is now the thing to do, and to be seen to be doing, amongst the landed rich and nouveau riche alike.

Those who shoot driven grouse describe it as one of the greatest thrills available. As the grouse fly over the butts they are like arrows streaking through the sky, flying at high speed and capable of changing direction in an instant. There are birds everywhere, the sound of gunfire from other butts is exhilarating, and to down each bird requires great skill and is regarded as the greatest test of a sporting gun. It's a few minutes of hectic activity with the loaders and shooters working in harmony, and then there is the calm after the storm when the dead grouse are retrieved, any injured birds dispatched and the totals are counted for that drive. And the totals of birds killed can be high. Driven grouse shooting is at its most exciting when the birds come thick and fast – and at the end of such a drive the body count can be enormous.

In the 'old days' the bags were sometimes spectacular. A party of six guns shot more than 2,000 Red Grouse on Wemmergill Moor on 20 August 1872, with the first shot fired at 08:20 and the last around 12 hours later. Frederick Milbank was responsible for a good third of these birds himself. Not tiring of the sport, the same party shot again on 21 August and 23 August and added another 2,300 birds to the total.

A few years later, Lord Walsingham had a remarkable day on 30 August 1888, when he killed 1,070 grouse on Blubberhouses Moor in Yorkshire (at a kill-rate of 70% kills to shots). He was the only shooter, using three guns (Purdeys, of course) and two loaders, and was further assisted by 40 beaters in two teams. They all got off to an early start at 05:12 with the first of 20 drives of the moor, the last of which finished at 18:45. The most successful drive was the sixteenth of the day, when His Lordship shot 94 grouse in 21 minutes – that's one every 13 seconds – and there was no sign that he was tiring physically from the effort, nor emotionally at the level of killing. In fact, the last 14 kills were made on his walk home.

Abbeystead in Lancashire still holds the record for the biggest grouse bag in a day – 2,929 birds, by eight guns, on 12 August 1915.

Peter Hudson, writing in the 1990s, recognised four periods of driven grouse shooting. The first was when grouse shooting was at its most productive in terms of bags, and ended with the First World War. In the interwar years bags declined and then recovered, only to decline again on the outbreak of the Second

World War. The third period encompassed a general recovery in bags to a peak in the 1970s, and the last of Hudson's periods was a decline to a low point in the mid-1980s. We might now add a period of recovery to the present day. Only in recent years has driven grouse shooting approached those same levels of killing, although in the interim the area given over to grouse shooting has diminished because of losses to sheep grazing, a little bit of built development, and conifer afforestation. At Wemmergill, the 1872 season had a total bag of 16,700 birds, and in 2008 it reached 16,000 birds again.

According to the Moorland Association website there are about 1200 days of driven grouse shooting in England each year – and we can expect those to have an average of eight guns involved – which would result in about 10,000 'gun days' per year. Assuming that quite a number of people, including owners of grouse moors, shoot many times a year, then maybe, just maybe, there are about 5,000 different individuals shooting grouse in England each year. Let's say there are another 7,500 in Scotland; that means that the number of shooters involved in grouse shooting each year is about the same as the crowd at the Wimbledon finals on centre court (and there may be some overlap in attendees, too) or a capacity crowd at a League 2 football match. So a relatively small number of people follow a 'sport' that dominates large areas of the uplands, but those people really enjoy shooting grouse. Here are a couple of comments that illustrate the joy felt by the grouse shooter:

> Most sportsmen fortunate enough to have hunted all British quarry have no hesitation in acknowledging the red grouse as 'King of Gamebirds' (Brian P. Martin, *The Glorious Grouse*).

> …sportsmen from all parts of the globe who gather in Scotland and the north of England every August and pay enormous amounts of money to shoot grouse will tell you, unhesitatingly, that the red grouse provides the finest sporting shooting available anywhere in the world (David Hudson, *Grouse Shooting*).

Where are the grouse moors?

In the early 1990s, Peter Hudson stated that there were 459 grouse moors in Great Britain, covering an area of nearly 17,000 square kilometres. That amounts to about a quarter of the uplands. Most of these moors (64%) and most of the area (85%) were in Scotland, but Scotland accounted for just over half (55%) of the 450,000 Red Grouse shot each year. Thus English grouse moors, which comprise only about a third of the total number, and just 15% of the total area, provide nearly a half of the total bag of Red Grouse. This reflects the greater productivity (thanks to soil, climate and altitude) of the English moors as well as their greater intensity of management. More of the Scottish estates that can offer driven or walked-up grouse shooting also offer their sporting guests deer stalking and salmon or trout fishing, and they tend to be in areas where the landscape lends itself to attracting the general tourist intent on enjoying the view. In addition, commercial forestry is more of an established part of the rural economy. This leads to a less intense focus on grouse bags; for many estates in Scotland, grouse shooting is an important part of their income but not the be-all and end-all. The best Scottish grouse moors, in terms of size of bags, are in the eastern Cairngorms and the southern uplands.

There are now something like 147 grouse moors in England, and they are mainly found in the Pennines, the Yorkshire Dales, the North York Moors, the Forest of Bowland in Lancashire and the Peak District. All grouse moors, like all grouse-moor owners, and all gamekeepers, are different, but the typical English grouse moor would be a series of dry hills, sometimes capped by wetter ground dominated by blanket bog and peat-forming *Sphagnum* mosses. The English uplands adjacent to grouse moors are less afforested than those in many parts of Scotland, partly because more of the English uplands were deforested historically, and partly because English land-owners were less tempted by the lure of money for forestry, which in turn was because their grouse shooting was always more profitable and popular, being closer to more people, including weekend visitors from London, and delivering higher grouse bags.

Thus, in the post-war period up until the 1990s, management of moors for grouse shooting, in England particularly, protected the uplands from large-scale afforestation by forestry companies attracted to the uplands by low land prices and favourable tax regimes. We owe a debt of gratitude to grouse shooting for preventing more of the uplands being desecrated by the worst of plantation forestry with exotic conifers.

Nowadays, many of the grouse moors (as well as lots of other upland areas not managed for grouse shooting) are designated either under domestic UK legislation as Sites of Special Scientific Interest (SSSIs, under the Wildlife and Countryside Act, 1981) or under European Union regulations as Special Protection Areas for Birds (SPAs, under the Birds Directive, 1979) or Special Areas of Conservation (SACs, under the Habitats and Species Directive, 1992).

Who owns the grouse moors?

There may be a few grouse-moor owners reading this book, but the majority of my readership will not own large areas of the uplands. And my own ability to go grouse shooting is greatly diminished by the fact that I am not the son of a duke.

In the eleventh century William the Bastard (who presumably preferred to be known by his other nickname of William the Conqueror) performed a spectacular land grab and announced that all the land in the kingdom was his, although he'd let a few other people have their way over some of it. Ever since then, land reform has progressed slowly in this country, and because we have never had a proper revolution a remarkable amount of land is still in the ownership of the descendants of those who held it after the Norman conquest.

Upland estates have tended to remain in the same hands for a long time. Since the main economic land uses of the uplands have been grazing, forestry and the exploitation of wild game, large blocks of land have tended to persist because of economies of scale in these enterprises. There has been a general but very slow spread of land ownership from the original noble families, particularly after the industrial revolution when 'new' money was able to buy into the uplands as 'old' money fell on hard times. This continues to this day with 'City' money and increasingly 'foreign' owners buying into the uplands and acquiring the ancient estates of the British nobility.

The Enclosure Acts, of which there were many, especially between 1750 and 1845, led to the apportionment of 'common' land, in theory by agreement, to those who had any rights over it. These Acts were parliamentary acts, and parliament was dominated by landowners. This meant that large upland areas were now fenced and divided into separate ownerships, with the owners having the majority of rights of access and land management within their own areas.

Back in 1872, there was a complete register of who owned the country. In an amazing recent book, *Who Owns Britain and Ireland*, Kevin Cahill documents the ownership of land in 2001 and finds that rather little has changed. If one looks at a prime grouse-shooting county, County Durham, then in 1872 the three largest landowners were the Duke of Cleveland (23,000 ha), Viscount Boyne (7,300 ha) and the Earl of Durham (6,000 ha). By 2001, according to Cahill, the Baron Barnard (an indirect descendant of the Duke of Cleveland) was the largest landowner (21,000 ha) with the Earl of Durham (4,000 ha) and Viscount Boyne (3,200 ha) in second and third places still.

It's a similar picture across the other grouse-shooting counties. Here are a few more examples. In Derbyshire, the Duke of Devonshire and the Duke of Rutland topped the 1872 list, and still top Cahill's list for 2001. In Northumberland the Duke of Northumberland was far and away the biggest landowner in both years. North of the border, but only just over it, the Duke of Buccleuch is the largest landowner in Dumfries, just as his ancestor was in 1872, but he has slipped from largest to second-largest in Roxburgh, ceding first place (it only seems fair) to the near-eponymous Duke of Roxburghe, who was formerly in second position. Further north in Angus, the Earls of Dalhousie and Airlie occupy the top two positions, just as they did in 1872.

The pace is certainly slow, but there is some change in terms of land tenure. The famous Wemmergill Moor, covering almost 7,000 hectares of Yorkshire, was in the hands of the Bowes-Lyon family for more than 440 years until the late Queen Mother's great nephew, the Earl of Strathmore, sold it to former poultry farmer and pub-trade tycoon Michael Cannon in 2004 (Cannon already leased the shooting). Cannon is said to have spent around £20 million on the purchase and management of this premier grouse moor.

On the North Yorkshire/Durham border, the American tycoon Robert Miller took the 13,000-hectare Gunnerside

Estate off Earl Peel's hands in 1995. Miller is an American-born billionaire (in dollars, though it's touch and go in pounds) who co-founded the Duty Free Shoppers chain. He has houses in New York, Gstaad, Paris and Hong Kong, as well as now owning one of the largest sporting estates in the UK. Earl Peel is the son of the second Earl Peel and the grandson of the first Earl Peel (for that is how it works!), and also the great-great-grandson of prime minister Sir Robert Peel. As a former president of the Game Conservancy Trust, Earl Peel is one of the most prominent grouse shooters in the land, and he still owns a smaller moor in the north of England. On 11 October 2006 he kissed hands with another moor-owner, HM The Queen, as he became Lord Chamberlain of the Royal Household, and a few years later he was invested as Knight Grand Cross of the Royal Victorian Order.

One of the moors in the Angus Glens, Glenogil (7,700 ha), was bought by 'financial wizard' John Dodd in 2004 from the Earl of Woolton. Dodd is a co-founder of the investment company Artemis, and was one of the few owners of major grouse moors to sport a diamond earring. He is an example of City money. All seemed to be going swimmingly as he worked with grouse-moor manager Mark Osborne to increase grouse bags at Glenogil. Lord James Percy, writing for *Fieldsports* magazine, waxed lyrical about the recovery of grouse numbers and the work on reducing tick numbers, adjusting grazing and exterminating vermin (more on all of these subjects later) carried out for Dodd at Glenogil by Osborne ('100% track record, failure not an option,' according to Percy) and his team. But then it all turned sour. After a string of raptor deaths on the estate, including a poisoned White-tailed Eagle in 2009, and the withdrawal of more than £100,000 of agricultural grants in 2008 by the Scottish Executive after illegal poisons were found on the estate in 2006, Dodd sold the moor in 2013, reportedly to Baron Ferdinand von Baumbach. Dodd also threatened Tayside police with legal action after the force issued an appeal for information that implicated the estate. He always insisted that his staff were innocent.

In Lancashire, the Duke of Westminster currently tops the list thanks to his purchase of the grouse moors of the Abbeystead Estate (7,300 ha) from the estate of the widow of the seventh, and last, Earl of Sefton in 1980. The fourth Earl of Sefton was the second-largest landowner in Lancashire in 1872 (after the Earl of

Derby) and built the house at Abbeystead as a 'private shooting lodge on a grand scale' in 1886. The Abbeystead Estate, which forms a large part of the Forest of Bowland, had been in the ownership of the Molyneux family (eventually the Earls of Sefton) for centuries. Major General Gerald Cavendish Grosvenor, sixth Duke of Westminster (perhaps more properly known as His Grace the Duke of Westminster, KG, CB, CVO, OBE, TD, DL, CD), is currently the only British-born member of the top ten of the *Sunday Times* rich list, with an estimated net worth in 2013 of £7.8 billion, despite the years of economic hardship and austerity that he has suffered along with the rest of us. Although he is the richest landowner in the UK his land holdings are nowhere near the largest, measuring a mere 52,000 hectares, and it is the 40 hectares of Mayfair and 80 hectares of Belgravia that account for most of that wealth. But his acquisition of Abbeystead and its grouse moor makes him and his land an important player in this tale. The Duke of Westminster is also a past-president of the Game and Wildlife Conservation Trust.

The largest private landowner in the UK is the Duke of Buccleuch (Richard Walter John Montagu Douglas Scott, tenth Duke of Buccleuch and twelfth Duke of Queensberry, KBE, DL, FSA, FRSE), with around 110,000 hectares (in 2001). Even this mighty land holding is a mere shadow of his ancestor's (the fifth duke's) holding of 186,000 hectares in 1872 (when the family was second on the list to the Duke of Sutherland). The Duke of Buccleuch's Langholm Moor will feature as the setting for the next chapter.

These examples illustrate the rather sclerotic nature of upland land ownership in the UK. The same few families have owned much of the land now shot over for grouse for centuries. The attentive reader will also have noticed that a large number of the major landowners mentioned here are dukes, earls and viscounts (and, don't worry, there are some marquises too), which illustrates the role that the Establishment has played in grouse shooting over the years, and the importance of grouse shooting to the Establishment. For the last couple of hundred years, many of the people running the country have also been running their own grouse moors. Is that too extreme a statement? I think not. And if you have some issues with the future of grouse shooting, as I do, it is just as well to know who you are up against.

The rich and the powerful usually get a disproportionate say in what happens in our lives, even in the parliamentary democracy that is the UK. And there is no doubting that many grouse-moor owners are both rich and powerful. Land ownership has always signalled power in the UK. From the time of the Norman conquest until the end of Queen Victoria's reign, the laws of England (and in the end those of Wales, Scotland and Ireland, too) were determined by the people who owned the country's land. Historically, owning land and being male have been the two main qualifications for setting the legal framework in which we all live, and to a large extent they still are. The history of power in England over the last two thousand years has largely been a story of very, very gradual trickling down of power from the monarch, through the nobility, to the landed gentry, to the common people (that's you and me).

William the Conqueror established a feudal system where the king had absolute power but consulted a band of major land-owners (whom he had appointed in the first place). In the reign of King John at the start of the thirteenth century, Magna Carta made such consultation a more formal affair, and that was the forerunner of an English parliament. Edward I (who ruled from 1272 until 1307) encouraged the petitioning of the king and parliament by the common people, and the increasing number of petitions was one small factor in creating the need for a more formal and efficient parliamentary system to address the views and concerns of the populace at large. Petitions to parliament thus have a long history – and, as we shall see later, three of them play a significant part in the recent story of grouse shooting.

Parliaments were called when the king sought advice, and they were necessary, after Magna Carta, to approve any tax-raising requirements of the monarch. By the reign of Henry VII (on the throne from 1485 to 1509) the separation of the two houses of parliament, Commons and Lords, had been established. The House of Lords consisted of Lords Temporal (the noble, rich and landed families) and Lords Spiritual (the rich and landed bishops), while the House of Commons consisted of landed representatives from each county, the so-called Knights of the Shires.

It was not until the creation of life peerages in 1958, under a Conservative government, that many people other than the old landed families (and bishops) gained access to the House of Lords. And then in 1999 a Labour government reformed the membership of the House of Lords (if not its actual members) by greatly reducing the representation of hereditary peers. For most of its seven centuries, the House of Lords has consisted of hereditary representatives of the noble families of England, Scotland, Wales and Ireland. Its membership was based on something resembling a lottery held in the Middle Ages in which only large landowners were included in the ballot, and they handed their winning tickets to their sons on their deaths.

The House of Commons evolved as an elected chamber to represent the people, and over time, because of its elected nature, it grew in influence and power until it became the primary of the two houses. Parliament became supreme in terms of power after the Act of Settlement in 1701, which established the UK as a parliamentary and constitutional democracy.

However, the franchise – those who could vote – also included a landowning criterion. For a brief period of about 170 years spanning the fourteenth century all (male, of course) householders were able to vote for their parliamentary representatives, but in 1435 this was limited to those owning land whose rental value was above 40 shillings (£2, roughly the equivalent in today's money of £40,000). The Great Reform Act of 1832 extended the right to vote to males (of course) with land ownership worth £10 (the equivalent of £35,000), which swelled the franchise to around one in six adult males and a total of some 850,000 out of a total population of men, women and children of 24 million. Following the 1867 Reform Act and the 1884 Representation of the People Act around 40% of males could vote, and the electorate had swelled to 5.5 million (out of a total population of around 35 million in Britain and Ireland). The boundaries of parliamentary constituencies had also been adjusted to take account of the fact that the population was increasingly urban.

However you look at it, political power, monetary power and actual power on the ground have long been associated with land ownership in this country of ours – and that has certainly been true during the last two centuries, when grouse shooting has been at its peak.

Who owns the grouse?

Although many of us might talk about the Robin in our garden as 'our' Robin, we do not have the right to shoot it. In most cases we do not consider wildlife to be the property of individuals: we think of ourselves as sharing the world with other living beings rather than them all being partitioned to individual human ownership.

This is, to simplify things, generally the case in British law regarding the right to kill wildlife, too. Although the birds and the mammals are not owned, the right to kill them is reserved to an individual person or entity (such as a company). Shooting rights are separate from property rights, although they often travel with each other through time. If you were to buy a stretch of moorland or foreshore the shooting rights would usually come with the land. And the quality of the shooting would affect the price you paid. In some cases, though, you might buy the land but the former owners might wish to retain the shooting rights, perhaps for their lifetime.

Before the arrival of William the Conqueror from Normandy, the hunting of game was not highly regulated in England. The Norman conquest allowed the king to assume power over a third of southern England and declare it a Royal Forest in which the hunting of noble beasts (deer and Wild Boar) was reserved to the king and, at his disposition, the aristocracy. The whole of Essex was designated Royal Forest, and Henry II made Huntingdonshire a Royal Forest too. The Magna Carta gave little to the common people of England but it did devolve a little of the powers and property that the Norman kings had appropriated to the top level of the aristocracy, and that included rights over game. Two years later, the Charter of the Forests restricted the royal hunting grounds and stipulated that 'none shall lose life or limb' for pursuing game (although such people were not necessarily treated with kindness).

After the Peasants' Revolt of 1381, Richard II restricted the pursuit of game to those who owned land. Throughout this medieval period the hunting of game on horseback or on foot was largely restricted to the aristocracy and was, as it always has been, a useful opportunity for networking and cementing the bonds of the landed classes, but it also allowed those people to practise the skills of horsemanship and the use of weapons, which were essential to success in armed combat against foreign foes, local rivals and the populace at large.

After the restoration of the monarchy in 1660, Charles II introduced a gentleman's game privilege (in 1671) based on land ownership. This was set at £100 a year, a huge amount, and 50 times the land qualification (then set at 40 shillings) that allowed a man to vote. Lords of the manor (not below the rank of esquire) were able to appoint gamekeepers empowered to seize guns, traps, dogs and such like from those unqualified to take game (i.e. most people, and aimed at the common poacher).

In the eighteenth century a series of Game Acts were introduced to combat poaching, and in some cases these included capital punishment. These established the dates of close seasons, when there was to be no shooting of game, and thus the 'sport' of grouse shooting had its season set by Act of Parliament. Mention was also made of the right of lords of the manor to appoint gamekeepers to seize guns and other equipment from anyone who attempted to take game without the landowner's permission. These acts also allowed three months' imprisonment, after a summary hearing before a single magistrate, for a first poaching offence (and public whipping and six months in jail for a second).

The 1816 Game Act introduced transportation for seven years as a punishment for poaching at night. The greatest change, though, came via the 1831 Game Act, which opened game shooting up to anyone who could buy a game certificate, and therefore removed four centuries of the need to be a landowner. Poaching by day carried a £5 fine, but thanks to amendments in the House of Lords night-poaching retained a penalty of transportation.

You and I no longer need a game certificate to go shooting, so we are free to shoot grouse provided we own or can borrow a gun and have the permission of whoever owns the shooting rights – which generally means having the money to pay for our day's sport. It certainly helps to be the son or daughter of a duke, but the bottom line is that we can all be grouse shooters now, just as we can all send our sons (though not, of course, our daughters) to Eton.

The work of the gamekeeper

The role of the gamekeeper arose long before there was a police force, and as well as carrying out tasks that were designed to protect and then enhance the shootable surplus of gamebirds, the job was also one of rural enforcer for the lord of the manor. A bunch of tough, fit, armed men was a useful thing for the lord to be able to deploy in those days – and for a long time afterwards too. But the main role of the gamekeeper in grouse shooting has been to manage things so that the grouse are as productive as possible during the breeding season, and that as many of those birds as possible are presented to the guns through the shooting season.

Gamekeepers themselves might be regarded as an endangered species – their numbers have certainly declined. In 1910 the census recorded about 6,000 gamekeepers in Scotland alone, but there were fewer than 1,000 by 1981 (and about half of these were in upland counties). However, the density of gamekeepers on areas that can be classed as grouse moors has remained pretty constant over the last century – the decline in their numbers has been driven by a loss of land to agriculture and forestry.

Poachers and disturbance

Over the years, one of the main jobs of the gamekeeper has been to prevent other people stealing or disturbing the game of his (almost always his) employer. In a situation where you own land, and you have the rights to harvest the wildlife on that land, as well as any reared Pheasants or partridges that you release, your aim will be to protect or preserve those animals as well as possible until you and your friends or paying customers get the chance to kill them. Other people who fancy taking a few Rabbits or Pheasants for the pot are free-loading on your efforts, stealing your resources and spoiling your fun.

The war between gamekeepers and poachers has been a long one, and the story is well told in Harry Hopkins's *The Long Affray*. Armed poachers and armed gamekeepers sometimes killed each other, and the law, largely written by landowners of course, was very much on the side of the shooting estates.

Man-traps were set in woods and killed many a poacher, or maimed and disabled him for life. As living standards increased and the population did too, then the work of the gamekeeper in dealing with people shifted from an armed war against the poacher to a cold war against visitors to the land who have no illegal intent. Trespass is a civil offence, and if asked to leave someone's property then you should. The owners of shooting estates, with their seats in the House of Lords, and sometimes the House of Commons, have been among the most dedicated advocates against freedom of access to open country, including moorland.

Maintenance of good habitat

Red Grouse are highly territorial, and more sedentary than most other British birds. They spend their entire lives on a small patch of land. And if one's aim is to increase the overall densities of Red Grouse occupying a hillside, then that plot of land, providing all that a pair of grouse and their chicks need, must include plenty of food and shelter from predators and the elements. The chicks eat insects, but the adults eat the young shoots and leaves of the heather plant.

Heather is a shrubby plant of dry upland areas. Around three-quarters of the world range of the relevant species, Common Heather or Ling, is in the UK and Ireland, and our race of Willow Grouse depends very heavily on this plant. The consequence is that other plants, even similar shrubby plants such as Cross-leaved Heath, are not seen as being particularly valuable by most grouse-moor managers. Ling heather does not tolerate wet areas, and so, historically, many of the wetter areas of the moor, less good for Red Grouse, have been drained and then burned to encourage heather growth.

Heather burning is the main technique by which the supply of young heather is maximised on a grouse moor. The burning season (in England) runs from 1 October to 15 April. Heather is burned on a rotation of approximately 14 years in most parts of the country. By burning strips of heather of around one or two hectares in area (though this varies between grouse moors) the required patchwork of old and young heather is produced. The young heather is more palatable and forms the main food of adult Red Grouse, and the older heather provides more shelter from winter weather and from predators, and better nest sites.

Burning heather is a time-consuming, difficult and skilful undertaking. The weather has to be just right, not too wet and not too windy, and to deliver the type of pattern that is sought, the wind has also to be from the right direction. The weather in the British uplands is not known as a particularly biddable beast.

If you were to imagine a single gamekeeper's share of the moor, perhaps an area of 2,000 hectares that needs to be burned on a rotation of around 14 years in patches that might average around one hectare, then, allowing for a proportion that should not be burned at all, the need might be for 100 individual burns each season. A team of four might be needed to do the job and to ensure that the fire does not get out of hand or spread too far, particularly onto a neighbour's land: a major logistical undertaking requiring a reasonably skilled workforce.

A study of the English uplands using aerial photography suggested that in 2000 approximately one-sixth of those uplands had been burned within the previous four years, and that the median return-time for burning (which would include areas hardly ever burned) was around 20 years. The same study found that the proportion of rotationally burned heather moorland within English national parks had doubled from about 15% in the 1970s to 30% in 2000. The management of grouse moors for shooting has intensified in recent years.

But even once a moor is drained and burned to the advantage of one species of plant and the bird that depends on it so directly, problems arise with other competing species. The main one of these is the Heather Beetle (*Lochmaea suturalis*), whose larvae can nibble away at an area of heather, even a whole hillside in the worst cases, and leave that heather stripped of its leaves.

Vermin control

I have an issue with the word 'vermin', as one man's vermin is another man's cuddly mammal or brilliant bird, but the word is still very frequently used, almost unconsciously, by the shooting community to identify those species that might eat game before it is available to be shot. The way that the word 'vermin' is used is a useful shibboleth to identify the standpoint of the person with whom one speaks.

When your aim is to produce a large shootable surplus in the autumn, then any loss of eggs, chicks or adults through the season is a problem, and a financial one at that. Because grouse lay so many eggs, the potential autumn population of Red Grouse is very much larger than the spring population, if only you can keep alive as many of the adults and their sizeable broods of young as possible. To that end any predator of eggs, chicks or adults is reducing the size of the autumn bag. The main species involved on an upland moor are crows (Hooded or Carrion), Stoats, Weasels and Red Foxes – common, widespread and generalist predators. None of these depend on Red Grouse for their living, but all of them will include Red Grouse in their diet when they are available – and of course, on a grouse moor, Red Grouse are available at very high densities.

It would be inconceivable to run a driven grouse moor without killing predatory birds (legally, birds such as crows can be shot) and mammals. The aim of the gamekeeper is to turn each pair of birds present in April into ten or so birds to present to the guns in August. Every female Red Grouse lost to a raptor at the beginning of the season brings that ten down to a single male. Every clutch of eggs lost to a Red Fox reduces the potential ten to just the adult pair. Each chick lost as it matures reduces the numbers that can be shot by one. Driven grouse shooting depends on that large autumn population of Red Grouse, and so anything and everything that takes a Red Grouse as an egg, chick or adult is, in the mind of the gamekeeper and his boss the grouse-moor owner, vermin.

Richard Waddington, in the late 1950s, wrote that:

The two great natural enemies of the grouse are foxes and hooded crows, the fox taking an easy first place. After these, in descending order of destructiveness, come the eagle, gulls, the domestic cat, the lesser birds of prey such as the peregrine, the harriers and the sparrow-hawk, and, last, stoats and weasels. The buzzard I have never known to attack grouse of any age but it has a distinct nuisance value in that it is sometimes mistaken by the birds for an eagle with the usual disastrous results in a drive.

And a little later he commented that 'in the little corner of Upper Banffshire and Morayshire in which I live, we had to kill over 2,000 foxes in three years' in order to accomplish a restoration of grouse numbers.

Earlier in the twentieth century, Lord Lovat wrote of the Fox that 'his diet must always be described as promiscuous, his morals noteworthy only by their absence' and that 'it is easy to see that every effort should be made to rid the moor of an offender with such a reputation for evil.'

This way of thinking has a long history that goes back much further than the Victorian adoption of driven grouse shooting as a country sport. As long ago as the reign of Henry VIII there were lists of predatory species that should be killed.

The largest mammalian predators were killed because they either were, or were supposed to be, a threat to human life, while the medium-sized mammalian predators (such as Red Fox, Pine Marten and Polecat) and predatory birds were seen as competitors for food. These birds and mammals would not only have been important predators of domestic stock, particularly chickens, geese and pigeons, but also competitors for species such as Rabbits (whose warrens were valuable sources of food), wild ducks and a whole range of other wild birds, whose eggs could be taken for the pot.

One of the most frequently quoted records of the scale of vermin control is that from the Glengarry estate in Scotland, an area of some 6,500 hectares, between 1837 and 1840. In those four years the estate killed only 11 Red Foxes and a couple of Magpies, but in contrast the number of Wild Cats killed was 198; Pine Martens, 246; Polecats, 106; Stoats and Weasels, 301; Badgers, 67; Otters, 48; and house cats, 78. These are phenomenal, but not unbelievable, totals. The Glengarry figures for birds include, for the same period, 27 White-tailed Eagles, 15 Golden Eagles, 18 Ospreys, 275 Red Kites, 63 Goshawks, 462 Kestrels, 285 Buzzards, 371 Rough-legged Buzzards (surely some identification error here?) and 63 Hen Harriers, as well as 1,431 Hooded Crows and 475 Ravens.

These figures make one gasp – and make one wonder – these days. They seem amazingly high in a time when naturalists struggle to see Pine Martens, Wild Cats and White-tailed Eagles, and the entire Scottish population of Red Kites has only recently passed 275 birds. Does this mean that the figures are wrong, or does it mean that the world was a different place 180 years ago?

It is clear, in fact, that the world was a very different place. Roger Lovegrove documents other Highland estate vermin records, and although others seem less comprehensive many of them outstrip the Glengarry figures for their kill-rates for particular species. And so the idea that some species should be routinely killed has a long history in Britain. When driven grouse shooting became the sport of fashion for those who could afford it there was an upsurge in the traditional culling of predatory species. There were few legal constraints up until the mid-twentieth century, and old habits and prejudices die hard.

From the grouse-moor manager's point of view, the ideal moor is one that is practically devoid of any predator that can take Red Grouse at any stage of their lives. Why pamper your grouse just for them to be eaten by the local wildlife? Huge amounts of time, effort and ingenuity are put into predator control. The critical period is in the run-up to the breeding season and through until the time when the young grouse can fly. Clutches of eggs and flightless or fluttering chicks are easy targets for any generalist mammalian predator that stumbles upon them. Foxes are the main enemy, but everything with sharp teeth will be targeted if the law allows, and often if it doesn't. Even today, it is perfectly legal to kill Red Foxes, Stoats and Weasels in unlimited numbers.

Disease and parasites

Once the habitat has been burned to suit the particular needs of the Red Grouse, and most of its natural predators have been dispatched, you might think that the job is done and your grouse moor will deliver booming stocks of flying targets each year for ever and always, but that is far from the case. Disease and parasites play a large part in the year-to-year variations in Red Grouse numbers, and therefore in Red Grouse bags.

It has long been known that Red Grouse are susceptible to a number of diseases and parasites. One of these, louping ill, is a tick-borne viral disease that affects sheep through attacking the nervous system and causing the animals to stagger, so it is well known to the upland sheep farmer, particularly in northeast Scotland. Grouse-moor owners will go to great lengths, or at least their gamekeepers will, to reduce the tick burdens on the moor. This is done these days by using sheep flocks to 'mop up' the ticks and then treating the sheep so that the ticks are killed, and also by killing other mammalian vectors of the tick that inhabit the moors, such as deer and most particularly Mountain Hares. Killing Mountain Hares, in huge numbers, is seen as good practice on many grouse moors, as it removes a food source for various predators that also prey on Red Grouse, including Red Foxes and Golden Eagles.

The major disease of the Red Grouse from the grouse shoo-ter's point of view is strongylosis, which is caused by infestations of the worm *Trichostrongylus tenuis*. This worm inhabits the caecum of birds (a dead-end in the gut whose function is not fully known). High worm burdens reduce the survival and fecundity of the grouse, and therefore can limit densities. The interactions between the worm and the Red Grouse were cleverly studied some years ago by Peter Hudson of the Game Conservancy Trust, who was able to show that the cyclic nature of Red Grouse populations and therefore of their shooting bags was caused by the timing and periodicity of worm infestations. But not only did he do some excellent science, Hudson also worked out a large part of the solution to this problem, and that has led, in part, to a resurgence in grouse densities since the 1980s.

Most grouse moors now provide medicated grit in bins on the moor, and Red Grouse will peck at the grit because it aids their digestion of the tough heather shoots. In taking in the grit they are effectively self-medicating, and worm burdens can be greatly reduced. Part of the upland keeper's routine these days is providing medicated grit at feeding sites across his grouse moor. On many moors, gamekeepers go further and catch individual Red Grouse by dazzling them with powerful lights at night, then dose them with anthelminthic drugs to further reduce the worm burden.

Grouse as food

I've eaten Red Grouse a few times, and I've not been overwhelmingly impressed by the taste of it. It's not that bad a meal, but apart from its novelty value it doesn't do much for me.

Even a devotee of cooked grouse describes it as 'almost like liver with an iron-like taste' – which may not sell the meat to all.

Young grouse, shot when they are just three or four months old, are usually served roasted, whereas the older birds, which are rather tough and quite strong tasting, can do with a longer period of cooking and are often casseroled.

I once stayed with a grouse-moor owner, and we had an excellent time talking about the issues described in this book. In the evening he invited a few friends, fellow shooters, around to dinner to make the conversation fizz along even more rapidly – and there was a hush when a plate of grouse was put in front of me. I'm not sure what they expected the 'man from the RSPB' to do, but I believe I took it in my stride and said, 'If it's good enough for Hen Harriers, it's good enough for me.'

*

That then, is grouse shooting. A legal pastime that occupies thousands of square kilometres of our country but that is practised by a few thousand people at the most. Any discussion of the rights and wrongs of grouse shooting should start from the position that the 64 million of us who do not shoot Red Grouse should let the 15,000 or so who do get on with it. After all, they are often shooting grouse on the land that they own (which has often been in their families' ownership for centuries), and shooting the grouse according to the laws that govern its shooting (which their ancestors had a large part in framing), and they are investing their own money in local communities as a result of their passion for shooting grouse.

We know, of course, that things are not that simple. As we learned in the last chapter, grouse shooting is underpinned by wildlife crime carried out by some in the industry, which affects the Hen Harrier and many other protected species. That puts this pastime on the back foot straight away. But before we come back to the wildlife-crime aspects of grouse shooting, how should we regard grouse shooting as an activity? Is it a sport, an industry, or both?

Driven grouse shooting seems to me, in sporting terms, a bit like an outdoor version of a computer game such as Pacman or Space Invaders. Yes, it requires skill, but not a skill that is these days of great advantage in everyday life. The skill of shooting grouse could easily be emulated with clays flying towards the

gun; and what it amounts to is essentially using live animals as
target practice. Much of the emphasis on the enjoyment of grouse
shooting is couched in terms of the numbers of birds shot on
each drive and on each day. Record bags, in other words record
numbers of birds killed, are the measure of the success of a shoot,
and the success of a man (and of the few women who participate)
is in how many birds he has dispatched in the day. Bag size
matters enormously – and the more enormous the better.

There is no way that the participant in driven grouse shooting
can be described as a hunter. He is a shooter and a skilled killer,
but he is not pitting his wits against the animals he kills; he
merely waits for them to be driven past or over him, and takes
his shots as skilfully and quickly as he can. I can far better understand the wildfowler who gets up early in the morning and
chooses his position to wait, hoping for a shot at some flighting
ducks, or a fisherman trying to entice a salmon or trout to take
his fly, or the stalker of a deer who needs to approach his quarry
with care and then has an opportunity to take a clean kill, than
I can the participant in driven grouse shooting. Although I
cannot imagine ever taking part in these country pursuits, if I
had to, then I'd choose to attempt fishing or deer stalking over
grouse shooting any day. As others have said, it would be more
sporting if the grouse were armed, too.

But whether or not driven grouse shooting is a sporting
sport, it is certainly a business, and it could be called an industry.
Although it is high-ticket in terms of the payments made for
the best days on the best moors, it's trivial in terms of the UK
economy as a whole. The Moorland Association website
suggests that grouse shooting in England and Wales is worth
£70 million. As part of a UK economy of £2 trillion, this is a
vanishingly small proportion. On a per-area basis the UK
economy generates about £80,000 per hectare, whereas grouse
shooting in England produces about £200 per hectare. It is
unlikely that the Treasury spends much time considering
grouse shooting as a driver for the UK economy. However, it's
rather clever how those parts of the country which have for
centuries been seen as the bleakest, least productive and least
valuable can achieve a passable value just through shooting a
rather podgy-looking gamebird, although one has to wonder,

and I will address this later on, whether this is the best use of that land.

This history and description of driven grouse shooting puts one myth to bed completely – that grouse moors are natural habitats from which a sustainable harvest is taken of a wild bird. What we have actually seen is that grouse management to provide sufficient Red Grouse for high-intensity driven grouse shooting depends on completely subjugating the land to the interests of just one species. The land is drained, grazed and burned with the intention of creating the right mix, completely artificially, of one main plant species, Common Heather, to provide nesting and feeding conditions for one species, the Red Grouse. All the top mammalian predators of this system, such as Wolves and Lynx, were removed centuries ago, and the war on the largest avian predators, be they Golden Eagles or White-tailed Eagles, continues to this day. In the absence of large and largish mammalian and avian predators, the removal of medium-sized predators, such as Polecats, Wild Cats, Red Foxes, Peregrines and Hen Harriers, continues too. The average grouse moor is as natural as the average wheat field.

Lord Lovat wrote quite plainly that:

> To speak of a restoration of the balance of nature as desirable for the improvement of grouse moors is beside the point so long as the whole object of every proprietor is to upset that balance in favour of one species only.

Natural this isn't. The management regime on a grouse moor produces Red Grouse densities that are almost always ten times what they would be in the absence of such intensive management, and it can even reach *one hundred times* those densities.

I couldn't put it any more clearly than Richard Waddington, author of *Grouse: Shooting and Moor Management*, who wrote:

> This is a book about grouse shooting as a sport. As such it concerns itself with the red grouse as a sporting bird, which is a very different matter to being concerned with the bird either as an individual or as a species. From a sporting point of view we are concerned purely with the maintenance of an unnatural number of individuals on a given area of ground.

And a little later:

> Grouse driving, in the modern sense, is every bit as 'artificial'
> as shooting hand-reared pheasants: and it is partially due to an
> attitude of mind which refuses to accept this fact that grouse have
> been allowed to decline in numbers ... over very large areas of
> Britain in the past two decades.

And that brings us back to wildlife crime. In a sport or industry
whose *raison d'être* is killing one species of wildlife (Red Grouse),
and which depends on the legal killing of many more species
whose natural activities conflict with the production of
unnaturally high densities of Red Grouse, then a bit of wildlife
crime, killing some other species, is hardly unexpected. And yet
it is illegal.

Should we imagine that most grouse moors are breaking the
law, or only some of them? It's a tricky issue, and one which is the
subject of fierce debate. The scale of illegal killing of raptors on
some upland estates, described in the previous chapter, would not
have to be replicated everywhere to result in the biological impact
of there being some 600 rather than 2,600 pairs of Hen Harrier in
the UK. If some grouse moors are doing far more than their
'share' of the illegal killing, then that means that some grouse
moors are doing rather less, and some none at all, but it is still the
case that grouse shooting is responsible for this wildlife crime.

And, unlike other crimes, the beneficiaries of the crime are
not just the criminals. If you are a grouse-moor owner then you
probably don't want Hen Harriers to nest on your land, but if
someone else is doing enough killing to make that happen then
your hands are clean and your conscience is fairly clear. The
nature-reserve manager may be in a similar position, in that no
Hen Harriers nest on his or her land, but will feel differently
about it. It is sometimes asked why no Hen Harriers nest at the
RSPB nature reserve at Geltsdale in Cumbria, and in the last
chapter we learned about the type of illegal raptor slaughter that
went on in that region in the past, but the killing doesn't necessarily have to be that local – any killing of Hen Harriers lowers
the level of the Hen Harrier soup generally, and if it is intense
enough, as it certainly is at the moment, then it deprives all
landowners of Hen Harriers because the Hen Harrier soup is so

low in the bowl. Some landowners may be spooning out the soup like nobody's business, others may be taking the odd spoonful but smiling as the level keeps dropping, some are taking none at all, and yet others are simply wishing that they had some.

By this stage, after a mere two chapters, you may be feeling sympathetic to the Hen Harrier and perhaps a little antagonistic to the grouse-moor manager and the gamekeeper. You may even be wondering whether Hen Harriers could possibly make much difference to the numbers of Red Grouse shot on a well-managed grouse moor. That is a subject for the next chapter.

*

What I would like you to take away from this chapter

- Driven grouse shooting is a fairly recent manifestation of the sport or business of grouse shooting, having been in existence for less than 200 years.
- Driven grouse shooting certainly does not represent a harvest of a natural population of birds, as the densities of Red Grouse required for the large bags that drive this form of 'sport' require intensive management of the uplands, with predators being trapped and shot (and sometimes illegally poisoned), heather being burned on a regular rotation and grouse being medicated.
- The areas where grouse are shot are usually large upland estates that have been in the hands of the same families for many generations. They are often the people who have run Britain through their wealth, their seats in the House of Lords and their grip on the voting system. They can be expected to be a fairly conservative bunch who are accustomed to getting their own way.

CHAPTER THREE

Langholm – the end of the beginning

> Now this is not the end. It is not even the beginning of the end.
> But it is, perhaps, the end of the beginning.
>
> Winston Churchill

Hen (and Northern) Harriers have been eating Red (and Willow) Grouse for tens of thousands of years. By contrast, men have been going into the hills of Britain to shoot Red Grouse for a mere 200–300 years, and driven grouse shooting has only been a major activity for about 150 years. For the first century of driven grouse shooting the Hen Harrier was not an issue – there were hardly any nesting on the British mainland, and in any case it was still legal, or largely legal, to kill Hen Harriers. After 1939 things began to change. The economics of the uplands shifted towards sheep and forestry; grouse shooting declined in extent, and with it the number of gamekeepers employed in the hills. Hen Harriers made a comeback, facilitated by the fact that after 1954 it was illegal to kill them. Grouse shooting appeared to be on the way out, through no fault of the Hen Harrier, up until the mid-1980s.

Over the past 30 years, however, grouse shooting has experienced a resurgence. This was aided by the research carried out by the Game Conservancy Trust and others, but in particular by Peter Hudson figuring out how to reduce the impact of strongylosis on Red Grouse. Grouse shooting became an increasingly feasible way to make a living off your upland estate, and it was marketed as a fine field sport, attracting rich clients not just from the UK but from overseas as well. Under these circumstances, the appearance of a hunting Hen Harrier on a grouse moor became less and less welcome. Now there was more money to be made from grouse shooting, and legal protection meant that it was harder to get rid of the bird.

Nature conservationists were, at this time, not too bothered about grouse shooting. Indeed, they saw it as an ally in preventing the worst excesses of blanket conifer afforestation of attractive, wildlife-rich and largely unprotected upland areas. Conifer plantations were seen as enemy number one, sheep as enemy number two and the grouse-moor manager often as 'my enemies' enemy' and therefore my friend. However, this happy state of affairs was not to last as the calls for something to be done about Hen Harriers became more and more strident.

Grouse-moor managers claimed that Hen Harriers ate large numbers of Red Grouse and also disrupted shoots by their very presence, and that this was imposing a serious economic cost on their environmentally beneficial businesses. Most conservation organisations were fairly sympathetic to the view that grouse-moor management did quite a lot of good, and left the arguments about birds of prey to the RSPB. Not surprisingly, the RSPB took a dim view of the level of illegal killing of birds of prey that was rumoured to be carried out on grouse moors, and also saw the anti-Hen Harrier rhetoric as worrying, particularly as it might be the beginning of a wider campaign against birds of prey in general. The grouse-moor managers spoke from their experience on the ground, but they were thought to be exaggerating greatly by many as they had never seemed the most raptor-friendly of groups.

A scientific approach

Everybody says that they approve of good science and want to base their views on it, but most people use science the way a drunk uses a lamppost – more for support than for illumination. I would say this applies to many environmental NGOs, all shooting-centred NGOs, and very largely to governments, too.

The Langholm Study, as it was usually called, more formally known as the Joint Raptor Study and now known as Langholm 1 (as there is a Langholm 2 – see the next chapter) was a big piece of science that illuminated the facts around the conflict between grouse shooting and the Hen Harrier but did not lead to any sort of resolution of that conflict. In fact, things got worse rather than better. But as far as the science was concerned it was a good study, well accomplished, and I wouldn't be without it.

The origins of the Joint Raptor Study lay in the debate that used to occur between conservationists and grouse shooters concerning the impacts of birds of prey, including Hen Harriers, on driven grouse shooting. Conservationists like me were always sceptical about claims made by grouse-moor managers that Hen Harriers and other raptors had a serious detrimental effect on grouse bags. Leslie Brown discussed the issue in his New Naturalist book on birds of prey, and clearly, although he thought more evidence was needed, was unconvinced that raptors did, or could, take enough Red Grouse to deplete stocks to a great extent. But grouse-moor managers were adamant that Hen Harriers could be a serious pest of grouse moors. In the absence of hard evidence, the debate could have gone on for ever.

In 1992 I was the recently appointed head of research for the RSPB, and I remember Dick Potts, director-general of the Game Conservancy Trust, coming to see me at the RSPB head-quarters of The Lodge, Sandy, Bedfordshire, to talk about the proposed study. The idea was to study the impacts of raptors, most likely Hen Harriers and Peregrines, on the shooting bags of Red Grouse at a number of shooting estates in Scotland and the north of England. The planning for the study was fairly well advanced by the time Dick came to see me so there wasn't a lot to influence – it was more a question of whether the RSPB was 'in' or 'out'.

The plan on the table was centred on the Duke of Buccleuch's estate at Langholm in southern Scotland, although data would also be collected less intensively from a number of other grouse-shooting estates. At Langholm over recent years there had been just the occasional pair of Hen Harriers nesting and up to three pairs of Peregrines. The proposal was to ensure that the raptors had full protection during the course of the study (as indeed the law required anywhere and everywhere) and to study what happened.

As Dick and I talked, we speculated on what might emerge. It was just possible that nothing much would happen. Perhaps raptor numbers would stay around the same level and the team of scientists could look, in more detail than had happened before, at what impact a rather low number of raptors had on a perfectly viable grouse-shooting enterprise. That was possible, but it wasn't what either of us expected.

We both thought that raptor numbers would increase a bit and that they would have some sort of impact on the grouse bags (reducing them, of course). How big an impact might it be? Neither of us really knew, and my recollection was that we talked about this and guessed that perhaps grouse bags might be halved. If we had been right then the following years would have been very different – but we were wrong.

Dick and I got on well. I admired his scientific work on the Grey Partridge and I liked him as a person. I told him I'd have to think about it, and discuss the idea with colleagues, but that I was keen for the RSPB to play a part in this important study that might well resolve some of the arguments about how big a problem the Hen Harrier was for grouse shooting as a business in the uplands.

It seemed to me, for a variety of reasons, that it was better for the RSPB to be 'in' than 'out'. Although our financial contribution would be substantial over the five years of the study (and the money would come from my research budget, on which there were always multiple claims), I thought that Langholm might lance the boil of the acrimony between grouse shooters and the disparate groups interested in birds of prey in the uplands. It might – who knows? – demonstrate that raptors had a small impact on grouse bags but suggest ways that these could be overcome. On the other hand, it might show that raptors had a big impact on grouse bags but that this was only likely to happen if raptor numbers increased dramatically – which would, in itself, vindicate the long-contested claims of the conservationists that raptor persecution was at a high level and had big impacts on the populations of birds such as the Peregrine and Hen Harrier.

If the results of the study turned out to be uncomfortable for the RSPB, then it would be better to know what was happening as it happened and to be able to prepare for the news to break, than to be ambushed by results of which one had little warning – and in which one might have little confidence. Being inside the tent brought the responsibilities of joint ownership of the study, but also the ability to contribute and influence the way that the work was done and how it was publicised.

It wasn't by any means a no-lose situation, but whatever the outcome, I thought (and this is what a head of research should think), it was better to know the worst (and it might even be the best) rather than continue to argue over things that could partly be resolved by science. So I was up for it, and it wasn't difficult to persuade the RSPB to come in behind the study.

Other organisations must have been having similar discussions, and in the end the work was funded by the Buccleuch Estates themselves, the Game Conservancy Trust, the GCT Scottish Research Fund, the RSPB, the Joint Nature Conservation Committee, Scottish Natural Heritage and Peter Buckley of the nearby Westerhall Estate. The two lead scientists were already chosen – Simon Thirgood of GCT (who died in an accident in Africa some years after the study) and Steve Redpath of the Institute of Terrestrial Ecology. The scientific steering group was chaired by one of the country's most eminent ecologists, raptor enthusiast Professor Ian Newton, whom we all trusted to be rigorous and fair.

The foreword to the report published at the end of the study, written by the Earl of Dalkeith and Ian Newton, described the situation thus:

> So far, debate on the raptor/grouse issue has been marked by a wealth of strongly held opinion, but by a distinct shortage of scientifically based information relevant to current conditions.

The Joint Raptor Study at Langholm was designed to clear away some of that unhelpful bickering, in particular to clarify whether, and by how much, birds of prey reduce the grouse bags on a driven grouse moor.

The report's authors also sought to set the scene, near the beginning of their report:

> Gamekeepers continue to kill birds of prey because they see them as a threat to their grouse stocks and, by extension, to their jobs. However, conservation bodies have argued that these birds are important components of natural communities and of

conservation concern because of their relatively low numbers. They have also pointed to the lack of convincing evidence about possible impacts of raptors on grouse stocks.

The results of the Langholm study

And so, in the spring of 1992, the Joint Raptor Study began. The objective was to 'examine the impact of raptor predation on Red Grouse numbers' – where I guess 'numbers' was meant to include both breeding numbers and wintering numbers, but also bag numbers. Between 1992 and 1996 the team of scientists studied the numbers of voles, small birds and raptors at Langholm and, far less intensively, at some other grouse moors in Scotland and the north of England.

Prior to the study, Langholm was a reasonably successful grouse moor. Throughout the research period the gamekeepers continued to kill Red Foxes (150–200 per year), Carrion and Hooded Crows (300–350 per year), Stoats (under 50 per year) and other legally killed predators. Heather burning was carried out as normal.

In 1990, 4,000 Red Grouse had been shot at Langholm. This figure was much lower than had been achieved back in the distant past (grouse bag records were available from 1913) and the decline in grouse bags was largely due to a large loss of heather moorland. Almost half (48%) of the heather-dominated vegetation of the Langholm Estate had gone between 1948 and 1988, mostly to be replaced by sheep pasture, and the losses were mainly on the lower slopes. These changes were not dissimilar to those on many other grouse moors over the years. The economic advantage of rearing sheep, subsidised by headage payments from the Common Agricultural Policy, had led to many heathery hills being 'improved'. This type of change had happened widely in Wales and in many parts of England – and had happened at Langholm, too.

However, 1990 was a good year for shooting grouse at Langholm. Red Grouse bag records here demonstrated a remarkably regular six-year cycle. In the years running up to the peak year of 1990 (c.4,000 grouse shot) much smaller grouse bags had been achieved, and previous peak years had been 1984 (c.3,000 grouse shot) and 1978 (c.5,000 grouse shot). So the expectation, based on decades of experience, was that there would be another peak year in 1996.

The long-term decline in grouse bags certainly wasn't to do with raptor numbers, as for many years raptor numbers on this estate had been 'very low'. They did not remain low, however. In the period 1992–1996 the numbers of two raptor species that were 'protected' (which we can take to be a euphemism for 'illegal persecution stopped') increased quite dramatically. Peregrine Falcon numbers rose from three pairs to five or six pairs in the latter years of the study, and the number of nesting female Hen Harriers soared from two at the start to 14 in 1996.

This represented a gamekeeper's nightmare – but that was the point of the study, after all, and so enabled the research team to investigate in quite some detail the impacts of all those raptors on the numbers of Red Grouse at all times of year.

What, then, was the impact of all those Peregrines and Hen Harriers on Red Grouse numbers? Did the science blow away the mists that enshroud this subject and put everyone on the same sound and agreed footing, at least as far as the science was concerned? Well, yes it did, in broad terms. The results were clear in many respects, although they have been somewhat lost as time has passed, and they have been misrepresented – either deliberately or accidentally – over the years.

The most important finding of the study was what *didn't* happen. There was no peak in numbers of Red Grouse or grouse bags in 1996, as would have been expected (nor was there in 1997 – it just didn't happen). Given that the Langholm grouse moor had shown spectacular peaks in numbers on a pretty regular six-year cycle for many decades, and that this was when a large proportion of the grouse were shot on the moor, this was a stunning finding. Looking back on the report from nearly 20 years' distance, it doesn't do a great job in explaining exactly why the presence of all these raptors kept the Red Grouse population low, but it did. Had it not been for all those Hen Harriers and Peregrines we would have expected a gradual increase in Red Grouse numbers in 1994 and 1995, rising to a big peak in the population, and in the numbers shot, in 1996 or maybe 1997. But no such peak occurred. The population didn't even twitch upwards. Grouse numbers remained fairly constant, and grouse bags fell a little. On two nearby moors, which had cycled in remarkable synchrony with Langholm over decades, the expected rise in grouse bags in 1994 and 1995 did occur, and both moors experienced the expected bumper bags in 1996 and/or 1997.

Whatever the exact mechanism, predation by raptors seems to have kept the Red Grouse population at Langholm in the low years of the cycle and prevented the occasional bonanza-year which, through high grouse bags, paid a lot of the costs of grouse-moor management at a site like Langholm over the entirety of the cycle. The conclusion was unavoidable: if you stick to the law and protect birds of prey, they can make your grouse moor economically unviable. That was the headline finding from Langholm, and that is the enduring truth that remains to this day, both from that study and from further research.

Now there is plenty more to say about the findings of the study at Langholm, and more to add about its consequences and implications, but let us just repeat the main finding, lest anyone thinks that it is being ducked here: birds of prey can take enough Red Grouse to make a driven grouse shoot economically unviable.

The implications and consequences of that finding are well worth discussing further, but first let us look in more detail at the science that went on at Langholm over those years in the mid-1990s. Each spring, in April and May, in the latter years of the study when raptor populations were high, raptor predation removed about a third of the breeding stock of adult Red Grouse. It wasn't known which species were mostly responsible for this toll, but it will have been a mixture of Hen Harriers, particularly the larger females, and Peregrines. Peregrine Falcons have a remarkable knack of avoiding carrying the can in all these discussions (and good for them!). They seem to be able to slip away from the limelight as Hen Harriers are put squarely into it, but many of the losses of adult Red Grouse are likely to have been to Peregrines – although, clearly, by no means all of them.

In the latter years of the study, Hen Harriers took 37% of the Red Grouse chicks (Peregrines were not implicated for the young) and these were mostly fed to Hen Harrier chicks. That is an awful lot. And imagine the expression on the face of a gamekeeper as he sees grouse chick after grouse chick being taken from his moor and disappearing down the gullets of a brood of harrier chicks.

Taken together, these two impacts – predation of adult Red Grouse and of Red Grouse chicks (and roughly speaking they were equally important) – reduced the July, post-breeding grouse numbers at Langholm by about a half. That's a sizeable impact, and not one that many grouse moors would be prepared to tolerate given the choice, but on its own it would be manageable; it was not the halving of the post-breeding population but the removal of the once-in-six-years peak in numbers that was the major blow to grouse shooting at Langholm. In a way, Dick and I had been right in our guess at the beginning of the study. The increased raptor numbers did halve the grouse bags – but if the six-year peak had merely been halved as well, then there would have been a much stronger argument for this being a manageable impact. What actually happened was the elimination of the boom years altogether.

When one hears grouse-shooting enthusiasts talking about the impacts of Hen Harriers (for Peregrines rarely get much of a mention) on grouse shooting, they often talk about the conflict between the harriers and Red Grouse. That is clearly nonsense, as Red Grouse and Hen Harriers live together in many parts of the world and have done for thousands of years. Yes, it's a somewhat one-sided relationship because Hen Harriers are the predators and Red Grouse are the prey, but these two species have co-existed for thousands of years, and still do so over thousands of square kilometres across high northern latitudes around the world, and there is no prospect of the Hen Harrier driving the Red Grouse extinct. The conflict is entirely one between Hen Harriers and grouse shooting, and Hen Harriers and grouse shooters in a few thousand hectares of grouse moor in the UK. And there is a prospect of grouse shooters making the Hen Harrier extinct in large parts of its UK range. Indeed, they have already done so in the past, and look intent on doing so again.

The long-term co-existence of Hen Harriers and Red Grouse is hardly an issue, but the results from Langholm helped to demonstrate it, too. The spring breeding population of Red Grouse hardly changed over the period of the study. In fact, even with twice as many pairs of Peregrines and more Hen Harriers than had been seen on a grouse moor in living memory, the spring densities of Red Grouse at the end of the study were not significantly different, in statistical terms, from those at the beginning. Computer modelling suggested they would, on average, be only 30% higher in the complete absence of raptors than they were in the presence of unprecedented numbers of them. So the raptors weren't wiping out Red Grouse; their impact was much more akin to wiping out the shootable surplus of Red Grouse. Of course this is the very surplus on which driven grouse shooting depends. How unsporting of them!

The other major finding of the Joint Raptor Study was, of course, that there ought to be an awful lot more Hen Harriers and Peregrine Falcons in the country. The fact that Peregrine numbers doubled in just a few years was quite impressive, and was indicative of the pressure on them from illegal persecution in normal years, but the increase in Hen Harrier numbers to 14 nesting females (there were some polygynous males) at the end of the study (and 20 nesting females in 1997) is a real eye-opener.

There were no pairs of Hen Harrier at Langholm from 1980 to 1985, and in 1986 one pair nested. From then until the study started in 1992 there were between two and five nesting females, with an average of three nesting females. The 14 females in 1996 and 20 in 1997 were, therefore, demonstrably very high and unprecedented numbers. Other nearby moors did not see such a glut of Hen Harriers – it was a localised phenomenon caused by the 'protection' of birds of prey at this site.

The increase in Hen Harrier numbers was more rapid than could be explained by the productivity of the birds at Langholm itself during the years of the project. Birds were recruited to the Langholm breeding population from far away. A male was present at Langholm which had been marked as a chick 250 kilometres distant, and two females, also marked as chicks, had travelled 115 and 172 kilometres to be part of the growing Langholm population, illustrating the large distances between the natal and breeding sites that are possible in this bird, which is adapted to colonising new sites far from where it hatched. During the years of the formal study, Hen Harriers were welcome at Langholm whatever their origins, and the numbers grew. This clearly illustrated the fact that there is a constant immigration of Hen Harriers to grouse moors that is normally snuffed out by illegal activity.

Because the Earl of Dalkeith, now the Duke of Buccleuch, had hosted this study on his land, had enabled it to happen and indeed had been an enthusiastic attendee at many meetings and discussions, as well as a generous provider of delicious lunches when we gathered together in the village hall at Langholm to discuss the progress of the study and its findings, it would have seemed a little ungenerous to bang on about how bad the criminality must have been running up to the study (though if illegal persecution was taking place, there is no suggestion that the Duke was aware of it, or condoned it). But the increase in raptor numbers suggested that person or persons unknown must have been killing quite a lot of raptors in the years before the start of the formal study. Once protection was put in place the raptors did very well, thus demonstrating the scale of illegal raptor persecution.

The wider implications

Given the dramatic findings that came out of the Joint Raptor Study, and their implications for public policy on upland management and the future of driven grouse shooting and of raptor protection, we should consider how typical Langholm is compared with other grouse moors. Would raptor numbers increase to a similar extent on other moors if they were similarly protected? And would the raptors elsewhere have a similar impact on Red Grouse bags as they did at Langholm if allowed to live without illegal persecution?

Langholm was in some ways an exceptional moor, but not, so far as we can tell, in its biology. Where Langholm *was* exceptional was in terms of its owners being prepared to host a study of this kind, which involved a large team of scientists working on the estate for many years and the eyes of the world being focused on the results. There would not be a long list of grouse-moor owners prepared to endure the attention that came with opening up their land to such a study, and the debate over the impacts of raptors on grouse shooting would have dragged on unhelpfully for years more, had it not been for the public-spirited actions of the Buccleuch family.

Langholm was a well-established historic grouse moor. It had records going back more than 80 years detailing grouse bags, and these showed that it was to some extent a microcosm of grouse shooting as a whole over that period. The overall trend in numbers of grouse shot at Langholm was one of slow and continued decline. This decline was largely driven by a loss of grouse-moor habitat to grassland for grazing – there were some areas of the estate where grouse used to be shot where now there wasn't a single sprig of heather. Agriculture, particularly sheep, had at times been a far more economically attractive option to the Dukes of Buccleuch than driven grouse shooting, and grouse habitat had been nibbled away as a result. Also, the remaining grouse moor had lost some of its heather cover as a result of what could be described as overgrazing, so that the mixture of heather and grass had shifted in places more towards grass and away from heather. These changes were fairly typical of many grouse moors in the UK – partial loss of habitat and also some degrada- tion of the remaining habitat from the point of view of a Red Grouse or gamekeeper, although habitat improvement from the point of view of a sheep or shepherd.

But Langholm was a well-known grouse moor, which in 1990 shot a lot of Red Grouse. It could be seen as a declining grouse moor in the years leading up to the Joint Raptor Study, but it was certainly not one that was at death's door. It had plenty of years of grouse shooting ahead of it. The peaks in grouse bags occurred on a fairly regular six-year cycle, as was the case with most other moors in that part of the world – the cycle was shorter to the south (in northern England) and longer to the north (in much of the rest of Scotland).

Langholm Moor is regarded as a fairly typical grouse moor by all parties, and thus its findings are taken as being broadly indic- ative of what would probably happen at other grouse moors if raptors were protected as the law demands.

Another finding of the Joint Raptor Study, coupled with some work that occurred after the study ended, also backs up the idea that Langholm was fairly typical. Data collected during the study showed that, in the absence of human persecution, the numbers of Hen Harriers settling on an area each spring were primarily related to the densities of voles, which cycled from year to year (a little like Red Grouse numbers), and to the numbers of small birds, principally Meadow Pipits. Hen Harriers do not seek out areas rich in Red Grouse, although some of their favoured areas are packed with them, but they home in on areas rich in their main prey of small birds and small mammals. The Langholm study also established that vole and pipit numbers were highest on those moors that were a mix of heather and grassland – in other words, ones that had often experienced overgrazing in the past and where heather cover was rather reduced. Overgrazed moors with lots of pipits and voles attracted the largest numbers of nesting Hen Harriers.

Subsequent studies by GWCT showed that Langholm was just about in the middle of the distribution of Meadow Pipit numbers across grouse moors in the UK, suggesting that some moors might attract much lower densities of Hen Harriers than Langholm, whereas others might attract even higher densities. Langholm could not be regarded as exactly similar in all respects to all other grouse moors, but it could be regarded as typical of many of them and in the middle of the range of grouse moors across the UK. And that has been the take of conservation organisations on this subject ever since. I wonder, though, whether Langholm Moor is in fact so typical.

Langholm is a grouse moor of around 8,000 hectares, and thus represents less than half a percent of the total area of grouse moor in the UK (said by Hudson to be 1.7 million hectares). If one simply multiplies up the peak Hen Harrier numbers at Langholm, achieved just after the end of the formal study, that yields a potential UK population of around 4,000 pairs, which is considerably higher than the current estimate of a potential Hen Harrier population of 2,600 pairs.

The Joint Raptor Study included data from a few other grouse moors, although not very many, as there were few other moors where the owners were prepared to protect breeding raptors in the same way, and there weren't, anyway, the resources to study the situation in detail at other sites. However, at Moors 'F' and 'G', not far from Langholm but in Cumbria, where the authors of the Joint Raptor Study stated that there was suspected illegal control of raptors, in the presence of low densities of raptors driven grouse shooting remained feasible. And at Moor 'C' in

Scotland, where it was claimed that no illegal persecution of raptors took place, Hen Harrier numbers never reached Langholm proportions and 1,400 Red Grouse were shot in 1996. These data confirmed what we all already knew, that driven grouse shooting was possible at low raptor densities. They also suggested that some moors, such as Moor C, might never attain densities of raptors as high as those at Langholm.

There is still a lot of misinformation and rumour perpetrated about the results of the Joint Raptor Study. At one point this became so bad and so corrosive that the GWCT and the RSPB produced a joint statement on the agreed findings of the study just so that there could be no hint of any difference in the interpretation of what the scientific study actually found – although of course opinions still differ as to what the follow-on actions should be as a result of the science.

After Langholm, where next?

You might say that devoting a whole chapter of this book to the Joint Raptor Study is a little excessive. It is, after all, just one study among many. However, it was an explosive event at the time, and it also, I believe, lit a slow-burning fuse that will bring an end to driven grouse shooting in the not-very-distant future.

With its publication, the Langholm study fatally undermined the idea that driven grouse shooting as it was carried out at the time and the legal protection of wildlife were possible bedfellows. The aftermath of the Joint Raptor Study was marked by more strident calls for raptor control and lots of muttering that 'something should be done about it'. The grouse-shooting industry had presumably got the result that it wanted, and was vindicated in its view that raptors were a big problem for the grouse manager. Nature conservation organisations, particularly the RSPB, though they had never claimed that raptors could not reduce grouse bags, were certainly put in a new position. They now had to face the fact that there was a real conflict here between protecting nature and an industry that occupied a significant part of the rural landscape (both literally and metaphorically).

The RSPB, as the major non-governmental organisation (NGO) on the conservation side of this debate, was in a slightly uncomfortable position – partly of its own making. By being a partner in the study it had to 'own' the results too. It couldn't say, 'interesting – we'll have to look at this more carefully', as would have been possible in other circumstances; it had to have a view. There were three ways that it could go, and two of them would look rather churlish.

First, the RSPB could have said something like 'too bad! Yes, raptors ruin your industry if they are protected, but you'll just have to put up with it, grin and bear it, and be quiet.' That would be a line that other NGOs might have taken on other issues of similar trickiness, but it's simply not how the RSPB operates. The RSPB engages with issues, conflicts and dilemmas, and tries to find a workable way through so that wildlife doesn't suffer too much and nor do people's commercial interests. So saying 'we don't care!' wasn't really in the RSPB's repertoire – although maybe it should have been.

A second, even more contentious response would have been along the lines of 'Wow! You've been killing a lot of raptors, and the increase in raptor numbers at Langholm over the years of the study proves it. That's illegal, you know, and we're on the side of wildlife law. We can't see a way out for you, so we think it is time to realise that driven grouse shooting is an unsustainable activity that harms wildlife, and you should stop doing it. There's a conflict – the law is on the side of the Hen Harrier and the Peregrine Falcon, so your strange pastime is doomed and we will henceforth seek to hasten its end.' Now that would have been a very bold thing for the RSPB to say, and I don't recall anyone ever seriously suggesting that we should (although, as Head of Conservation Science, I wasn't privy to all discussions on this matter).

For one thing, the RSPB is in a particular position with regard to its Royal Charter: its position is that it won't take a position on shooting of gamebirds, or field sports in general, either in favour or against, except where those activities affect the charitable objectives of the RSPB (which are clearly nature conservation). In other words, it won't take a stance for or against field sports just because some of them involve killing birds for fun, but it is not constrained from commenting on aspects of field sports that are illegal or unsustainable.

If there had been a conversation on these matters, I know the RSPB well enough to know that it would have gone a bit like this:

A: 'Well that's it then, if you can't shoot Red Grouse without breaking the law when it comes to raptors, we'd better come out against grouse shooting.'

B: 'Hang on, it's not the grouse shooting that's the problem, it's the illegal killing of raptors, so we can be against wildlife crime without being against grouse shooting.'

A: 'But the Joint Raptor Study shows that they go hand in hand.'

B: 'No it doesn't. It shows that at Langholm they couldn't co-exist. But surely there are lots of other moors where the owners and managers are good guys, and we shouldn't tar everyone with the same brush. And anyway, let's see whether diversionary feeding works. And let's see in more detail how typical Langholm is compared with other moors – maybe it's the worst-case scenario. And let's remember, this isn't all about raptors, it's about the overall impacts of grouse shooting on wildlife, and we'd have to admit that there is a lot of good mixed up with the bad. So let's not be hasty.'

And the view of 'B' prevailed, as 'B' was putting forward the RSPB's wholly sensible and wholly rational way of looking at the world. It's a way of looking at things that serves it well in so many issues, and has done for decade after successful decade.

And so it was the third, unchurlish option that prevailed. The RSPB would work with grouse-moor managers to try to find a solution to this conflict, while always maintaining its position that killing raptors was illegal and there was no excuse for it.

On the other hand, the grouse shooters had a field day, and I don't really blame them, saying, 'I told you so! The Joint Raptor Study is proof that raptors are a pest! Let us kill them.' It wasn't the organisations that represent shooting interests that said this – although had the Countryside Alliance been in existence then I suspect it would have said something very like it – but the chattering in the press, and the shooting press in particular.

More than a decade after the end of the Langholm study, David Hudson wrote in his book:

> There is an almost unanswerable case for giving special status to moorland keepers and allowing them to control raptors within properly agreed and defined limits. I find it difficult to see such a sensible move ever being allowed, though.

This demonstrates how Langholm had made it respectable in shooting quarters to question the legal protection given to birds of prey, in a way that was rarely done before the study proved that there was a real conflict.

Langholm could have led to a parting of the ways between the non-governmental nature-conservation movement and grouse shooting, but it didn't. The results of the Joint Raptor Study had to be poked, thought about and elaborated on. But from this point, it felt almost unavoidable that grouse shooting and nature conservation (but most particularly bird conservation) would be at loggerheads. One side saw birds of prey as 'the problem' for their industry, the other saw the grouse-shooting industry as 'the problem' for many protected species.

We'll see how the issues played out and how the two sides played their cards, but the next stage included a growing realisation of the wider impacts of grouse shooting on the economy, the ecology and the social fabric of the uplands. The future of driven grouse shooting would no longer be a tug of love and hate over Hen Harriers. The issues were going to broaden considerably.

Langholm was just one study, but nothing was the same afterwards. The genie of raptor impacts on driven grouse shooting was out of the bottle, swooping around the political and policy world in a way that could not be ignored. Many wondered whether we were all better or worse off as a result; many still do.

A summary of the Langholm study conclusions

It seems appropriate to end this chapter with the conclusions of the Joint Raptor Study as set out on the Langholm project website:

Historically

- From 1948 to 1988, there was a 48% reduction in heather cover, which resulted in a long-term decline in grouse bags of 3% per annum after the Second World War.

During the course of the Joint Raptor Study

- The changes in grouse bags at Langholm during 1992–96 could not be explained by changes in habitat or population cycles.
- Raptor predation at Langholm reduced autumn grouse abundance by 50%, leading to the cessation of driven grouse shooting.
- Since they were based on 1995 data, the calculations in the report are likely to have underestimated the total raptor impact compared to subsequent years when raptor numbers were higher.
- The unprecedented build-up in harrier numbers at Langholm was probably a consequence of complete raptor protection, the grass/heather mix, the stage in the vole cycle and possibly the control of other predators (although this was not looked at explicitly in this study).
- Any moor with similar characteristics to Langholm may suffer the same fate; however, some of the factors above might be manipulated through habitat management to reduce this effect.
- The cyclic nature of grouse bags means that most Langholm-like moors will be vulnerable during low points in the grouse cycle.
- The link between heather cover, pipits and harrier settling-density suggests that not all moors are necessarily like Langholm.

*

What I would like you to take away from this chapter:

- Driven grouse shooting and compliance with wildlife laws were shown to be in conflict at Langholm Moor.

This had been what many had thought and feared, but it was now known to be true. Whereas there were some on either side of the debate who had hoped that compliance with the law would be compatible with driven grouse shooting, this was now known to be very difficult.

- When the law was respected, raptors, including Hen Harriers and Peregrine Falcons, increased in numbers and removed the shootable surplus of Red Grouse on which driven grouse shooting depends.
- Langholm seemed to be a fairly typical grouse moor, and so this study exemplified the conflict that is playing out on grouse moors across England and Scotland.

CHAPTER FOUR

The battle lines are drawn

You may have to fight a battle more than once to win it.

Margaret Thatcher

This chapter deals with the period after the Joint Raptor Study up to the end of 2013. In those 17 years the issue of grouse shooting moved from being a little local difficulty between birds of prey and those who wanted a day's shooting in the hills to an argument about the sustainability, legitimacy and acceptability of a field sport and the management on which it depends.

Although, of course, it didn't feel like that at the time. It is only now, looking back, that one can see how increasing knowledge and evidence, changes in policies and politics, and changing societal norms came together to shape the way that we should regard grouse shooting. This chapter describes many of the important events and studies in chronological order and ends with an account of why, entering 2014, I came to take a harder line on grouse shooting than I ever had before.

1997: Formation of the Countryside Alliance

In July 1997 the British Field Sports Society, the Countryside Movement and the Countryside Business Group merged to form the Countryside Alliance. Although it would claim that its aim is to raise all rural issues to parliamentarians, the media and the public, the Alliance's major activity would be seen by many as promoting field sports. And many would say that it does so in a very uncompromising way.

Although the organisation has campaigned on broader issues, such as the closure of village post offices and the availability of broadband in rural areas, its main focus appears to be on hunting, shooting and fishing. It promotes wild-shot game as a healthy food through its Game to Eat campaign, fishing through its Fishing4schools campaign, and falconry and deer stalking.

The founding of the Countryside Alliance was prompted by the arrival of a Labour government after 18 years of Conservative rule. Labour came to power with a manifesto commitment to allow a free vote in parliament on banning hunting of foxes with hounds. Perhaps mindful of a need to demonstrate cross-party support, the president of the Countryside Alliance is a Labour Peer, Anne Mallalieu, its vice-president is the Duke of Westminster and its chairperson is the Labour MP Kate Hoey, in whose decidedly un-rural Vauxhall constituency the Alliance has its headquarters. Its former chief executive (2004–2010), Simon Hart, was elected Conservative MP for Carmarthen West and South Pembrokeshire at the 2010 general election.

For many years, the Countryside Alliance has been a bunch of rebels without a cause, or actually with a lost cause – fox hunting. The 'Liberty and Livelihood March' in London in 2002, which attracted getting on for half a million people, was the largest demonstration on London's streets until the anti-Iraq war rally in 2003. But this greatest success was also the Countryside Alliance's greatest failure – as hunting with hounds was banned in Scotland by the Protection of Wild Mammals Act (2002), and in England and Wales by the Hunting Act (2004).

On fox hunting, it will surprise many readers of this book to hear that I had some sympathy with the views of the Countryside Alliance, although the strident way in which they were put forward was enough to put anyone who was undecided into the 'anti' camp. At the time of the furore over the Hunting Bill I was working for the RSPB and helped to make sure that we kept completely out of the debate (as it was largely an animal welfare rather than a conservation issue), but my personal view was that fox hunting was not a matter of sufficient importance, in the greater scheme of things, to warrant the angst and divisiveness of legislation. The Hunting Bill looked like an urban Labour Party having a go at a rural Conservative Party in a mean-minded way. Alternatively, one could say that it was because Labour received considerable funding from animal welfare supporters that a ban on fox hunting came to the top of the political agenda.

Opponents of the hunting ban campaigned against it on a wide range of sometimes somewhat self-contradictory grounds, and in many ways the campaign resembled the opposition to a banning of driven grouse shooting. First, fox hunting was 'traditional' – as though a perfectly respectable response to the question 'Have you stopped beating your wife?' might be 'No, I've done it for ages.' A second line of argument was that fox hunting was economically important to rural communities ('I can't stop beating my wife because the sticks I buy to beat her with are crafted by poor local people who would otherwise go out of business'). The third argument was that foxes are an economic pest and needed the incredibly inefficient method of chasing them around the countryside on horseback to keep them under control, and that without the hunts fox populations would explode to plague proportions (they haven't). Simultaneously, it was also argued that hunting was good for the foxes themselves and that their populations would wither and decline without being kept healthy by hunting (they haven't).

We will see varieties of all these arguments being trotted out in favour of grouse shooting too, and in favour of Hen Harrier killing. There are many similarities and many differences, but the parallels are clear. The biggest differences are that fox hunting was legal whereas Hen Harrier killing was not and is not, that a pack of hounds tearing a fox apart is a more distressing thing to observe than a bird being shot, and that fox hunting was a far more visible element of British life than are grouse shooting and its furtive companion, raptor persecution.

The Countryside Alliance gave field sports the campaigning organisation that they lacked, and it shook up the established organisations that dealt with field sports: the Game and Wildlife Conservation Trust (GWCT, at that time known simply as the Game Conservancy Trust), the British Association for Shooting and Conservation (BASC, formerly known as the Wildfowlers Association of Great Britain and Ireland – isn't it interesting that shooting organisations are so keen to get words like wildlife and conservation into their titles?) and the Moorland Association.

These three organisations had divided up the pro-shooting NGO world as follows: the Moorland Association represented big landowners in the English and Welsh uplands who owned grouse moors; the GWCT was a science-based organisation with a fine history, though a less distinguished present, of research into the ecology of gamebirds, their habitats and thus the value of game shooting to the wider countryside; and BASC had its roots in wildfowling for ducks and geese on inland waterbodies and coastal marshes and estuaries.

The Hunting Bill proposed a threat to field sports that these three existing organisations weren't set up to oppose, and the growth of the Countryside Alliance brought together a group of people who gained support and respect from their own community of supporters whilst alienating many opponents and those who had previously been undecided. The arrival of the Countryside Alliance provided a radical campaigning voice that had been lacking, and after its spirited but failed attempt to counter a fox-hunting ban, it was at the disposal of other field sports under threat. Indeed, perhaps to gain more support, the Countryside Alliance talked up the threats to field sports and more generally to a rural 'way of life' that would not be familiar to many people who live in rural areas.

The emergence of the Countryside Alliance, particularly after the Hunting Act was passed, dragged all debates about the countryside to the political right. The Countryside Alliance said stirring things about threats to the countryside that the established, staid organisations could not say, but that their members wanted to hear. If you were a supporter of grouse shooting you might see the Countryside Alliance as being of more use to you than decades of research by the GWCT. As a result, the sensible members of the field-sports industries have become somewhat side-lined, and have seemed almost happy to be so, whilst more exciting voices have tended to take their place.

The Countryside Alliance has helped to cause, and at the same time has been a symptom of, a widening division in UK society, between town and country. There is no Urban Alliance, and the very name Countryside Alliance suggests very strongly that it represents one group of people against another – this is no Rainbow Alliance, that's for sure.

In a small, crowded country like the UK, where the nearest area of farmed land is easily within reach of any urbanite who has a car or the cash to make a short train journey, it is rather strange that so much debate is dressed up as a 'rural *versus* urban' issue. The aim of many supporters of the Countryside Alliance is to protect their own particular interests, often described as those of the 'real countryman', from 'townies', lefties', 'veggies', 'antis' and any others bent on destroying the country 'way of life'. In essence, it is a conservative view of the world – conservative with a small 'c', and often with a large 'C', but increasingly with a large 'U' for UKIP, the United Kingdom Independence Party. It advocates that everything is fine as it is, and that any proposed changes to field sports in particular are designed to see an end to those sports by people who don't understand the countryside because they live in towns.

There is, of course, some truth in this – we have become a much more urban society and there is a surprising number of urban children who have no idea where the milk that goes on their cornflakes comes from – but it is in essence the opposite of the truth. The real threats to 'the country way of life' spring from the fact that people, both in town and in the country, are getting to know and understand some aspects of it far better. And that was the case with fox hunting. It became an issue not because non-fox-hunting people knew little about it, but because the advent of modern media and modern communications made it more and more difficult to hide the less savoury aspects of the practice.

1998: Political devolution

The establishment of the Scottish Parliament in 1998 meant that nature conservation policy on both sides of the Scottish/English border could be different in future. Nature conservation is a devolved matter, and from this point on it would be elected politicians in a Scottish government, elected by voters in Scotland, who determined Scottish laws and policies. Likewise the situation in England would be determined by a Westminster parliament (which, however, does have MPs from all other parts of the UK sitting in it and capable of voting on English-only issues, at the time of writing).

Devolution meant that in the case of driven grouse shooting, as with any other nature conservation matter, the debate could become more localised. It would be the experiences, prejudices, local circumstances and world views that occurred or prevailed in Scotland and England that would, somewhat separately,

influence the future of driven grouse shooting, and through it
the future of wildlife living on land currently managed for
driven grouse shooting, on either side of the Scotland/England
border (and in Wales and Northern Ireland too, but they figure
to a much lesser degree in this tale). It also allowed the possibility that progress in one part of the UK could be made
independently of the others.

1998–1999: Diversionary feeding

The Joint Raptor Study at Langholm demonstrated, for the first
time and convincingly, that Hen Harriers, coupled with
Peregrines, really can make driven grouse shooting economically
unviable. It also confirmed that the killing of Hen Harriers is a
rational action for the grouse-moor manager, as who would
want to have their Red Grouse, worth £175 a brace, disappearing
into a brood of Hen Harriers for no financial return?

The foreword of the report of the Joint Raptor Study
contained this wish from the Earl of Dalkeith and Professor Ian
Newton:

> [The] collaboration between scientists, conservationists and
> landowners that has marked the Langholm study proved invaluable
> and fruitful. We hope that it will continue into the future, enabling
> some of the issues that arise from the present study to be addressed
> and resolved.

The first continuing collaboration was a study of diversionary
feeding, which also took place at Langholm. The idea was pretty
simple, even though it was quite ground-breaking: if Hen
Harriers are fed other food during the critical period when they
are feeding their own young, then they will take far fewer Red
Grouse chicks and their impacts can be lowered, perhaps to an
acceptable level. The idea that the future role of an upland
gamekeeper might include daily provisioning visits to Hen
Harrier nests, rather than the more traditional one-off visits to
kill the birds, was certainly novel, and seemed as much to
gamekeepers who were consulted about it.

However, in the breeding seasons of 1998 and 1999 a proper
trial of artificial feeding, using day-old chicks and white

laboratory rats, was carried out at half of the Hen Harrier nests at Langholm. Food was delivered to a feeding point close to the nests, and the birds soon cottoned on to the fact that they were being offered a rather easy life. From the point of view of technical proficiency the trial worked. It also worked from the point of view of reducing substantially the number of Red Grouse chicks delivered to Hen Harrier nests – by up to 86% compared with unfed nests at Langholm in the same years.

But, rather strangely, the diversionary feeding did not lead to there being many more Red Grouse to shoot in those years. Perhaps this was because there were still 8–12 Hen Harrier pairs at Langholm and only half of them were fed, or perhaps it was because there were other factors, in the absence of Hen Harrier predation, limiting the shootable surplus of Red Grouse.

Despite the lack of an upturn in Red Grouse numbers for shooting at Langholm, this trial has to be seen as highly successful. On a more regular grouse moor, which might have experienced the occasional pair of Hen Harriers nesting in the past, the deployment of diversionary feeding could have dramatically reduced any impact of that pair of Hen Harriers on the shootable surplus (which for one pair of Hen Harriers would be quite small anyway).

The scene was set for upland estates to show that they wanted to stick to the law and therefore to tolerate pairs of Hen Harriers that would otherwise have been killed, by feeding them through the summer months. Was this a price that grouse-shooting estates were prepared to pay in order to avoid the stigma of illegality? We would see.

2000: The Countryside and Rights of Way (CROW) Act

This legislation came about after a major campaign by conservation, access and environmental organisations. It had two major impacts on the countryside of England and Wales, both of which were important for grouse-moor owners and managers.

One of the major impacts of this Act, and probably the one that enthused the Labour government the most, as it had been a manifesto commitment before the 1997 general election, was the establishment of a right to roam in open country such as downland, heathland, moorland and registered common land. This was seen as unfinished business by the Labour Party, which had introduced the National Parks and Access to the Countryside Act, with a fair degree of cross-party support, in 1949. The last of the 12 potential national parks identified in the Hobhouse report of 1950, the South Downs, was designated as recently as 2009, but nearly all of the others, almost all in upland areas of low agricultural productivity, and most of them having at least some grouse shooting within their borders, were designated in the 1950s.

The Acts of 1949 and 2000 were both partly inspired by the Kinder Scout mass trespass of April 1932, in which more than 400 people trespassed on private land owned by the Duke of Devonshire in the Peak District, in defiance of the civil law. Five of them were arrested and sentenced for public order offences, involving scuffles with gamekeepers. A fuse was lit in 1932 which caused a bang in 1949 and an even larger bang in 2000.

Upland landowners, some of them with seats in the House of Lords, were unenthusiastic, to say the least, about a right to roam being given to the people. Some of this would have been a natural resistance to change, but also one can see why someone would be reluctant to grant access rights to all and sundry over land that had been in the hands of the family for centuries. The impacts on wildlife of opening up the hills were often brought into the debates. Large upland landowners said that hordes of people would destroy the wildlife interest of vast areas of the country, and some of us believed that there was something to be said for this. The RSPB argued for access to be given through linear rights of way rather than completely open access, but the eventual Act took the simpler and more radical course of freeing up access to unenclosed land as a whole.

Grouse-moor owners were particularly against the access provisions of the Act, and this was thought to be for two reasons. The first, unsurprisingly, was that allowing people to walk across the moors might lead to high levels of disturbance of ground-nesting birds, of which the Red Grouse is one. The second, many of us thought, was that open access would make it more difficult for gamekeepers to go about those aspects of their work which are illegal, as the public would be much more likely to witness them, and to come across poison baits and illegally set traps or snares. Both fears were probably true to some extent, but grossly exaggerated during the debates over the Act, and neither has come to pass to a very large extent since.

The other main change introduced into nature conservation by the CROW Act was that sites designated for their wildlife interest as Sites of Special Scientific Interest – under, again, the 1949 National Parks and Access to the Countryside Act – needed to be properly managed to retain that interest. The 1949 Act had led to the designation of a network of what were supposed to be representative examples of sites of high nature-conservation value. Those designations protected, to a great but not complete extent, those sites from physical damage such as cutting down the trees in an ancient wood, or building a supermarket on a wetland. Those provisions had worked pretty well, to the extent that, rather than being a few examples of sites of high conserva-tion value, the SSSIs tended to become the last remaining sites, but the Act was far better at preventing bad things from happening to such sites than it was at encouraging good things. Regular assessments of SSSIs showed that many of them were declining in their quality for wildlife, either because they weren't receiving enough management (e.g. grasslands scrub-bing up because of lack of grazing) or because they were being too intensively managed (e.g. grasslands being overgrazed by sheep). Although the 1949 Act and its successor, the 1981 Wildlife and Countryside Act, were doing a good job at protecting England's threatened wildlife from a catastrophic loss of impor-tant sites, too many of those sites were losing their value through neglect or over-harsh treatment. If the SSSIs were supposed to be the jewels in the crown of British wildlife, they were losing their sparkle.

The CROW Act included provisions that would allow the statutory nature conservation agency (at the time called English Nature, later to become Natural England) to assess the quality of habitat, and require landowners to get their SSSIs into good condition. One of the greatest achievements of this legislation was that it galvanised both government and statutory agencies into action on wildlife sites that they owned or managed, and thus the SSSIs on Forestry Commission, Ministry of Defence and Crown Estate land were rather quickly assessed and led the

way in reinvigorating SSSI management – and wildlife benefitted as a result. Charities such as the National Trust, the RSPB
and the wildlife trusts, all major landowners, also had to get
their act together at this time, and they did. All in all, it was a
good example of government leading the way and working in
partnership with other organisations to achieve its aims.

Progress on SSSI quality was made through setting national
targets for the proportion of SSSI land by area that should be in
good nick by 2010. Although the definition of good condition
was a bit of a cheat, since your SSSI could either be in favourable
condition or in 'unfavourable recovering' condition to count as
OK, this target galvanised many landowners into action and,
generally speaking, had a very positive impact on the ground.
Some, however, resented the government having a say in how
they managed their land. These issues were particularly keen in
the uplands, where the question of heather burning became
fiercely contentious. What was 'over-burning' from a general
wildlife point of view, and what were the impacts of heather
burning on the full range of plant and animal species of conservation concern on areas managed primarily – some would say
solely – for driven grouse shooting? These issues were played
out at a time when intensification of grouse-moor management
was occurring and when more frequent burning was thought by
many, probably rightly, to be one way to increase their grouse
bags and income (and thus the capital value of their land).

All in all, the CROW Act was unpopular with grouse-moor
owners and managers.

2001–2002: Foot-and-mouth and the Curry Commission

Rather ironically, the second summer after the introduction of
a right to roam, the countryside was closed to a great extent by
foot-and-mouth disease. This affected upland areas considerably
and brought home to many that it was visitors to the countryside,
rather than farming, that were the mainstay of rural communities.

As a result of the foot-and-mouth outbreak, and after the
2001 general election that was delayed by it, the returning
Labour government created a new government department,
Defra, from the old Ministry of Agriculture, Fisheries and Food
and the Department for Environment, Transport and the

Regions, and appointed Margaret Beckett its first secretary of state. That department also set up a commission, chaired by Don Curry (a farmer and businessman, now Lord Curry), to look at the future of farming. His commission reported in 2002.

The Curry Commission provided an opportunity to scan the whole agricultural scene after the shock of foot-and-mouth disease, and to address some of its ills. Looking back on it now, it was a well-written and quickly produced report which is still well worth reading. However, it did not really change how farming in both the uplands and lowlands of England, was carried out. There were certainly some changes to the structure of payments to farmers, but it was hardly an earth-shattering change of direction.

The report did, for those who read it, make clear how much public money goes into the countryside, mainly through the complex structure of the EU Common Agricultural Policy (CAP), which pays £3 billion per annum to English farmers. This is sometimes described as EU money, or as government money; it's sometimes even described by farmers as their money. But what it is in fact is *our* money – taxpayers' money. Now, £3 billion from a nation of 60 million folk is around £50 each per annum, or about £1 each a week. That isn't a huge amount – I'd be happy to buy some of my local farmers a cup of coffee each week, and that would cost me far more – but multiplied up by the whole population it comes to a large sum of money, and when that sum is divided between the rather small number of farmers and landowners in the UK (let's say roughly 100,000) then it looks like a worthwhile cheque arriving through the post. It averages out at around £30,000 each.

This is not the place to go into the byzantine complexities of the CAP (hardly anywhere is the right place to do that), but in simple terms (though the details vary from one UK country to another, and from time to time) two-thirds of the money you and I give to farmers is a hand-out with practically no strings attached and is paid to every owner of every bit of farmed land. The basis for payment was changed on the recommendations of the Curry Commission, and the reference years of 2000–2002 were used to set a baseline for payments. This approach lasted until 2014.

The other one-third of your £1 a week is spent on helping farmers do a better job of farming. In England, most of the money goes into two pots for environmental payments. These are voluntary schemes which farmers and other landowners can enter through choice. Up until very recently (2015), in England there has been a 'broad-and-shallow' Entry Level Stewardship scheme, which has been open to any farmer who wants to do a few useful things for wildlife on his or her land, and a more complicated and demanding scheme that delivers more for wildlife. Most of the money (again, about two-thirds) goes into the simpler, less demanding scheme.

That's how your money is spent. In my view, about seven-ninths of your £50 each year is simply income support for landowners, some of whom are dukes, earls and viscounts, and some of whom are not short of a bob or two. Again, in my opinion, only the other two-ninths deliver any environmental benefit for your money – that's roughly £10 of your £50. We can all thank the members of the Curry Commission for making sure that this ratio of income support to environmental good is not even worse than the current situation, as they stressed the importance of taxpayers' money delivering public benefits, such as wildlife, clean water, storage of soil carbon, nice views and so on – things that the market will not deliver. Through the period considered in this chapter, it is also worth noting that an increasing proportion of the public funding available to farmers was directed at improving the management of SSSIs, which was made necessary by the requirements of the CROW Act concerning better management of these sites.

The payments to farmers through the CAP are not easy to understand, nor are they especially easy to justify. If the EU were to emerge anew, fully formed in its current shape of 27 member states in the age of mid-2010s austerity, then the payments in the CAP would not be as they are now. They would be much smaller, and much better directed at delivering identifiable public goods. But the CAP system we have now emerged under a European Economic Community of six member states and has evolved through time, with farmers' and landowners' representatives understandably using every trick in the book to keep every euro that has at any time been deemed suitable to be given to them.

At various times the CAP has been seen as a means of encouraging agricultural production, as a mechanism for supporting rural communities, and as a way of encouraging more ecologically friendly land-use practices. This system of public support to agriculture applies to the grouse moors of the hills of Britain as well as to lowland arable farms, but it was not specifically designed to subsidise large upland shooting estates, where the shooting of a few thousand birds each year is the main aim, where most of the landowners are absentee (and some are amongst the richest in the country), and where protected wild-life is killed illegally.

The take-home message for the reader of this book is that there is a lot of (your) money going to landowners, some of it to upland landowners as they cover a high proportion of the country (whether that be the UK, England, Northern Ireland, Scotland or Wales), and that the aim of giving them that money is shifting over time to become more directed at delivering good value to the taxpayer through supporting landowners in doing things that the market will not pay them to do.

2002: English Nature/Natural England Hen Harrier study

Natural England (initially under its old name of English Nature) began a study of harriers as part of its Hen Harrier Recovery Project. The work involved liaison with moor owners and managers, and monitoring the fate of Hen Harriers nesting in England. Wing-tagging and radio-tracking of birds was carried out to a larger extent than had been done in England before. This study was an indication that the statutory sector, a government agency, was becoming concerned about and more involved in issues of raptor persecution in the English uplands.

2006 (and 2007): *Peak Malpractice 1* (and *2*)

In March 2006 the RSPB published a hard-hitting document called *Peak Malpractice: What's Happening to Wildlife in the Peak District National Park?* which brought together information on suspected and known wildlife crime in the area of the Peak District National Park known as the Dark Peak. We described the Dark Peak as a 'no-go zone' for protected wildlife and called for more adherence to, and action to enforce, wildlife laws.

Raptor workers in the area have long known the Dark Peak as a persecution hot-spot – since at least the year 2000. Before then it was a favoured area for Goshawks, but in succeeding years the population fell (from around 16 pairs each year in the mid-1990s to under five pairs in the early 2000s), and so did the nesting success of the remaining few pairs, to a level that was not only much lower than in earlier years in the Peak District but also considerably below that of other similar UK Goshawk populations.

In 2002 two local gamekeepers were interviewed by police, and their houses raided, over the destruction of a Goshawk nest in this area. One of them was convicted. A few years earlier a clutch of Goshawk eggs had disappeared from an active nest. Other incidents in the area included a Buzzard that was poisoned with strychnine, and another that was found with two broken legs, consistent with having been caught in a leg trap. Peregrine chicks were found dead in a nest that showed signs of human interference, and in another case where a Peregrine nest eventually failed a man with a rifle was chased off from its vicinity earlier in the year. Illegal poison baits were found, and a whole range of encounters with men in balaclavas near nests suggested to raptor workers that the pressure on birds of prey in this area was intense.

One particular example strikes me as very telling. This was a case, in January 2005, when a pigeon lure was set up on a moorland. These lures are used in lowland arable farmland to attract pigeons to areas where they can be shot. Each consists of a model pigeon, resembling a Wood Pigeon, which rotates in the breeze on a plastic frame. It is difficult to imagine what the purpose of using such a lure would be in an upland situation except to attract birds of prey such as Goshawks or Peregrines to places where they could be shot.

Survey work by the South Yorkshire Badger Group suggested to them that Badgers might have been trapped or poisoned in areas close to where driven grouse shooting was practised – they couldn't check the actual moorland area because they were refused access permission. A wounded, snared Badger, showing injuries consistent with having been caught previously in a snare too, was found in this area, and several dead snared Badgers were found not far away.

These examples, all from the same area, indicate the sort of activities carried out to persecute protected wildlife and the impacts they can have both on animal welfare and on the population levels of the wildlife. These incidents all took place in the part of the Peak District still given over to driven grouse shooting, and the only successful prosecution in this area was of one local gamekeeper. One of the purposes of the RSPB report was to highlight to the public and decision-makers the scale and impact of wildlife crime within a national park, which was set up to protect natural beauty.

This first report was published in March 2006, but events in the summer of 2006 prompted an update (*Peak Malpractice, Update 2007*) the next year.

There was good and bad news to report from 2006. The bad news was that no Peregrines or Goshawks nested in the part of the Dark Peak known as the northeast Peak moors. Further wildlife crimes, either proven (such as a shot bird) or suspected (such as birds disappearing from established pairs at nest sites) occurred involving Peregrines, Ravens, Goshawks, Short-eared Owls and Buzzards.

The good news, though it wasn't all good news, was that two pairs of Hen Harriers nested in the Dark Peak, in the Derwent Valley, and raised ten chicks to fledging. These were only the second and third known successful Hen Harrier nests in the Peak District in nearly 140 years. That sounds like great news, but it wasn't a completely joyous event as both the males disappeared, strangely, during the breeding season and it was only because the chicks were fed by volunteers that any young fledged at all from these nests.

English Nature showed that between 2002 and 2006 nearly 60% of Hen Harrier nesting attempts in England away from their stronghold (at the time in the Forest of Bowland) failed because of adults disappearing from nests. By contrast, no adult Hen Harriers disappeared from 52 nesting attempts in Bowland in the same period. How odd!

2006–2012: Environment Council dialogue

It's good to talk, and for more than six years a group of organisations (BASC, Countryside Alliance, Country Land and

Business Association, GWCT, Moorland Association, National Gamekeepers' Organisation, RSPB, Hawk and Owl Trust, Northern England raptor groups) sat around the table several times a year, under the auspices of the Environment Council, and tried to find a solution to the conflict between Hen Harriers and driven grouse shooting. I attended a good number of those meetings myself and used my best endeavours to find a way through the impasse. It always seemed that some grouse shooters simply wanted to be allowed to carry on with their crimes with our blessing rather than meeting us halfway. I'm sure it felt differently to them.

Just about all the organisations involved were paying for the conciliation and arbitration services of the Environment Council staff, so the whole business wasn't without the costs of time and money, but I felt that it was certainly worth the effort. I realised that it would look bad if the RSPB pulled out, so even towards the end of my involvement, when I was losing hope of a break-through, I kept us in the process. And I made sure that I personally attended as many meetings as possible, to signal RSPB commitment at a senior level. During this long process the players got to know each other better, swapped jokes, argued with passion but almost always with politeness and explored options such as quota schemes that would allow grouse moors to 'cap' the number of Hen Harriers on their land, diversionary feeding, translocation schemes, reintroductions to the English lowlands, and many more.

I've often wondered what it would have taken to find a solution. And sometimes I have thought, since I believe that everyone would much rather have had a solution than not had one, that maybe there is no solution out there that will keep both 'sides' grumpy but neither side feeling as though they had completely won or lost.

I wouldn't say that the process left me jaded, but it didn't make me feel optimistic about the future. In the summer of 2012, about a year after I left the RSPB, the organisation left this dialogue, having decided that it wasn't getting anywhere – after seven years of talking, that seemed fair enough. And soon after-wards the Environment Council itself folded, and with it its website and the rather cryptic records of our off-the-record discussions.

Whenever anyone new comes onto the scene of the conflict between Hen Harriers and grouse shooting with high hopes of finding a solution by 'getting people round the table', I think back to many tables over many years. We tried, all of us – we really did.

2007: Langholm 2

Scientists and land managers returned to the site of the original Langholm (Joint Raptor) study for a second major project, envisaged to last for ten years. The partners this time around were the Buccleuch Estates, Scottish Natural Heritage, Natural England, the Game and Wildlife Conservation Trust and the RSPB.

This project, which is planned to last until 2017, aims to demonstrate how driven grouse shooting and nature conservation can live together in harmony. Recognising that the heather moorland at Langholm had declined in extent and was not in entirely good condition, the project aims to extend and improve heather cover, to increase Red Grouse numbers to levels where driven grouse shooting could resume, and to maintain Hen Harriers as a viable component of the Special Protection Area which had been established partly on the basis of their numbers.

This study will provide a further test of the viability of diversionary feeding of Hen Harriers.

2007: The Heather and Grass etc. Burning (England) Regulations

The heather and grass burning code, produced in 2007, carries the logos of Defra, Natural England, the Moorland Association, the Country Land and Business Association, the National Farmers Union, the Heather Trust and the National Gamekeepers' Organisation.

In paragraph 10, the document clearly states that:

There should be a strong presumption against burning sensitive areas. Doing so may permanently damage the environmental interest of the land and may be unlawful. In special circumstances, the advantages of burning on sensitive areas may outweigh the disadvantages. If you feel a sensitive area on your land falls into this category, you may wish to contact Natural England for advice.

The code goes on to make it clear that peat bogs, including blanket bogs and raised bogs, should not be burned unless in line with a management plan agreed with Natural England.

The Defra website sets out the regulations that back up the voluntary code and prescribe in a certain amount of detail when and under what conditions heather (and other) burning is allowed and how it should be carried out.

2007: Sandringham

The royal estate of Sandringham is in lowland Norfolk, almost at sea level, and is therefore not a location one would expect to be involved in the Hen Harrier debate. However, in late 2007 the fate of two Hen Harriers, reported to have been shot at Dersingham Bog National Nature Reserve near Sandringham, was much in the news, as was the certainty that Prince Harry had been out shooting in the area at the time and even the possibility that he was present when the birds were killed.

It's probably best not to rake over these old events too much, and I did write about them in an earlier book (*Fighting for Birds*), but there's no getting away from the fact that it was a big story at the time, and many of us regard it as a major unsolved wildlife crime.

The bare bones of what is alleged to have happened are as follows. A Natural England warden was with two companions looking specifically for Hen Harriers coming to roost, as they often did at that site. While they were watching two Hen Harriers, both ringtails, shots rang out and the two birds were seen to fall out of the air. They fell to ground out of sight of the astonished observers, and the shots had come from an unseen location.

Some of the details of how events unfolded are available from three internal Natural England emails that emerged under Freedom of Information Act requests. Each was sent on the night of 24 October, the night of the events at Dersingham Bog.

At 20:15 this email was sent (the names of staff were redacted by Natural England before sharing the email, and I have removed another name, as these details do not matter):

Thank you for getting back to me tonight. As promised, here is a short statement of the events as an update and as a recorded statement of events:

At 5 pm, xxx went onto Dersingham Bog NNR with two members of the public to look for Hen Harriers coming in to roost. They went up onto the escarpment overlooking the bog at TF675289. A volley of 10–12 shots were heard just before 1800 h. At around 1800 h, xxx saw a 'ring-tail' Hen Harrier approaching the flight pond off the reserve on the Royal Sandringham Estate from a NE direction at tree top height. He then heard a shot and saw the Harrier immediately fold and drop out of sight behind cover.

Within seconds he saw a second bird appear to the SW heading NE at tree top height, heard another shot and the harrier fold and drop immediately. There was a pause of approximately 30–40 seconds before another shot was heard. Shooting was then heard further to the SW. This volley continued for at least twenty minutes. The people shooting were out of sight, behind trees. Visibility was good and, despite being c.500 m away, the harriers were easily recognisable through binoculars.

xxx rang me at 1802 h in the office to say what had happened. I rang Shaun Thomas's mobile, but could not get an answer, so rang Sarah Wilson's mobile and left a message, before ringing the Operation Compass hotline number to Mark Thomas at the RSPB. Mark passed on the call to the WLO at Norfolk Constabulary. An officer then rang xxx and suggested that they would check it out in the morning. I rang Mark Thomas again to say that I was not satisfied with the course of action taken and he rang the WLO who had been in discussion with the Chief Inspector who had advised that he contact the Royal Sandringham Estate and ask for entry in the morning.

xxx has made a written record of the events.

Possibly while that email was being sent, I was on the phone to my former colleague from the RSPB, Guy Thompson, who was now working for Natural England. I'd been briefed on the events, as much as we knew them at the time, by Mark Thomas, who was mentioned in the email above. I thought it wise to contact Natural England at a fairly senior level to make sure that they knew that we knew that things were afoot. Guy emailed his boss, the Natural England chief executive, Helen Phillips, at 20:29 that same evening:

> I've just received a phone call from Mark Avery to inform me that there's likely to be a police investigation of a Hen Harrier persecution incident on the Sandringham estate tomorrow morning. Apparently a member of Natural England staff together with a Sandringham employee tonight watched two Hen Harriers coming into roost and getting shot from within the Sandringham estate. The police have been notified of the incident and are likely to request entry onto the Sandringham estate to investigate tomorrow.
>
> Mark was fishing for how we might respond and tried to draw me on how this was an opportunity to demonstrate our credentials as a 'trenchant champion'. I think we can work on the assumption that RSPB will be going public with this asap and will want to make hay with it. There's not going to be a huge amount to be gained from jumping proactively on their bandwagon but clearly, if asked, we'd want to respond along the lines of 'Natural England condemns the illegal persecution of wildlife. We understand that the matter is subject to a police investigation.' I've asked Julian to ensure that someone gets back to Mark tomorrow to let him know who will be leading for Natural England and what our response will be and to get onto developing a line to take first thing.

Helen Phillips replied to Guy at 22:50 that night with the following:

> Tx, think we should go in very hard, once we have evidence – perhaps xxx cld activate Richard Brunstrom link on this for us.

Richard Brunstrom was the chief constable of North Wales and the Association of Chief Police Officers' lead on wildlife crime.

At this distance in time it is reassuring to see that Natural England took this matter seriously and did not back off on what could be a contentious case (which it was!).

The crime was reported to the police (and to the RSPB), and was investigated. It emerged that the only people known to be out shooting on the estate that evening were Prince Harry, a friend and the gamekeeper (with ducks their quarry). After an investigation by the police, the Crown Prosecution Service decided that in the absence of any Hen Harrier bodies (none was found) and in the absence of any witness evidence of who fired the shots, there was no case to be taken forward. Let's be quite clear, they did not say, and there is no evidence that they thought, that no crime had been committed. And that's why many of us regard this as the most high-profile unsolved wildlife crime of all time.

Sir Martin Doughty, chair of Natural England, said his staff were disappointed there would be no conviction, and that this form of illegal persecution was 'the greatest threat' to the bird's long-term survival. He also said:

> Every year Hen Harriers are killed illegally ... but successful prosecutions are incredibly rare. Natural England will redouble its efforts to build a future for this rare and beautiful bird of prey. We want to try to find ways to bring back Hen Harriers while having viable countryside pursuits.

Sir Martin also felt moved to correct speculation that the whole event was made up or represented a mistake in bird identification, with a letter published in the Independent on 13 November 2007. In the letter he pointed out that the Norfolk Crown Prosecution Service had stated on 6 November that *'there is insufficient evidence to prosecute anyone over the shooting of two hen harrier birds, a protected species, at Sandringham on 24 October 2007'*. Sir Martin went on to add that the CPS did not question that the birds were shot; nor did they challenge the credibility of the Natural England witness.

The Countryside Alliance website still says, 'The notorious incident in question was at Sandringham and turned out to be a work of fiction discounted by the police.'

This unsolved case helped enormously to promote awareness of the problems faced by the Hen Harrier and caused by illegal persecution, even though it took place many miles from the nearest Red Grouse.*

2007: *The Uplands – Time to Change?*

This RSPB document, quite a short one, drew attention to some of the issues for people and wildlife in the uplands. It wasn't the first to do so, but it made the case that was becoming increasingly recognised, that the uplands had greater value for society than was currently recognised or than was currently being delivered. Some quotes illustrate the report's approach, and its findings:

Many protected areas are in poor shape, with 36% of all the special features designated as part of the upland SSSI/ASSI network in unfavourable condition, principally caused by inappropriate grazing, poor burning practice and water management issues. Important habitats have declined in extent. Upland heath and upland semi-natural oak wood have declined in extent by more than 25% since the late 1940s and blanket bog by 21% between the 1940s and 1980s. Upland hay meadows, such a characteristic feature of upland valley bottoms, are now reduced to 1,000 ha in the English uplands.

It is estimated that peatlands in England and Wales could absorb 41,000 tonnes of carbon per year if pristine, but release 381,000 tonnes carbon per year if damaged by practices such as excessive burning, drainage and overgrazing.

The uplands are treasured and unique areas, but despite significant public subsidy, the potential public benefits are not being delivered. Habitats, wildlife, natural resources and businesses

---

*Because Prince Harry, a friend and a gamekeeper were in the area at the time, the police asked whether they had any information that could help. Unfortunately, they had no knowledge of the alleged incident.

have all declined. The vast potential of the uplands could be husbanded better than now.

2008: Analysis of wader numbers at Langholm

The Joint Raptor Study of the mid-1990s had not looked in any detail at the numbers of most other birds or mammals present on Langholm Moor – the focus was on Hen Harriers, Peregrines, voles and Meadow Pipits. But other data were collected, and even in the absence of published data rumours circulated about the trends in other species. One of the rumours was that the populations of other ground-nesting birds had plummeted during the period of high raptor numbers at Langholm. If this were so, it would further strengthen the argument for some form of raptor control.

Many years after the end of the Joint Raptor Study, a scientific paper was published containing data from that period and also from a few years after the end of the formal study but when legal predator control was still being practised at Langholm and when raptor numbers were high. Its results were in stark contrast with the rumours. The study found no evidence that the numbers of Golden Plover, Curlew or Lapwing were limited by raptor predation, and the numbers at Langholm changed more or less in synchrony with changes at other nearby estates with low raptor densities. Nor was it the case that there was a decline in all three species, as maintained by the rural myth that was circulating: Golden Plover declined a bit, Curlew increased a bit, and Lapwing increased too.

2008: Golden Eagle conservation framework

In 2008, Scottish Natural Heritage, the statutory conservation organisation in Scotland, published a 'conservation framework' for Golden Eagles, which assessed whether the status of this bird in the UK (almost completely limited to Scotland, although Golden Eagles have nested, and should still be nesting, in northern England) met the requirements to conserve it under the EU Birds Directive. This assessment was built on years of study by the likes of the late Jeff Watson (the son of Donald Watson, who studied Hen Harriers), Phil Whitfield and a large number of volunteer raptor workers. The conclusion was that the Golden Eagle population is held well below its natural capacity, and that the main constraint is illegal poisoning of birds associated with driven grouse shooting.

There should be around 700 pairs of Golden Eagles in Scotland, and yet the last national survey, in 2003, found only 442 pairs (and previous surveys found 424 pairs in 1982–1983 and 422 pairs in 1992). Some of the increase in the 2003 survey, in the remote Western Isles, was thought to be due to increased survey coverage, and a figure of 434 pairs was considered more comparable with the assessments of the previous two surveys.

The main areas where Golden Eagles are missing are those eastern and southern areas where driven grouse shooting is a dominant land use. Golden Eagles feed on a wide variety of prey, including Mountain Hares and Ptarmigan, but they will also scavenge at carcases where they are available – and indeed, a large part of the diet of Golden Eagles in western Scotland is made up of sheep and deer carrion. This habit makes them susceptible to illegal poisoning, and an analysis of illegal poisoning incidents in the uplands of Scotland shows a remark- able correlation with the incidence of heather burning for the main areas where poisoning remains a big problem (having declined in incidence in other upland areas of Scotland).

The small overall increase in Golden Eagle numbers concealed some large regional variations. Generally speaking, Golden Eagles increased in numbers in some western areas, where grouse shooting is absent or a minor land use, and declined in the eastern areas that are dominated by grouse moors.

Young Golden Eagles are recognisable by their plumage, and in stable populations most breeding pairs consist of birds in full adult plumage. Where they are not persecuted, Golden Eagles can live for 20 years or more and first breed at around four years. In Scotland, particularly in areas where driven grouse shooting is common, young birds are often seen in pairs, indicating an unusually high turnover of the breeding stock due to illegal persecution.

Thus in Highland Scotland, Golden Eagles are most numerous in the west (for example on the Western Isles) and least numerous in the east (for example on Deeside and Donside), and yet the breeding success of the eagles is much higher in the east, if they survive persecution, than in the west. It is ironic that these birds are not allowed to survive in those parts of Scotland where they would actually fare best.

South of the Glasgow–Edinburgh line, there are very few pairs of Golden Eagles, and this has been an eagle no-go area for many years. The Southern Uplands are probably less suitable for Golden Eagles than areas such as Perthshire and the Cairngorms National Park, but there still should be many pairs of eagles present.

Essentially, this SNH study found for the Golden Eagle the same state of affairs as already described for the Hen Harrier in Chapter 1: the bird is largely absent from grouse-shooting areas due to illegal persecution of a protected species.

2008: Natural England Hen Harrier report

Six years after the start of their study, Natural England issued a hard-hitting report on the results of their monitoring (which continued). The report's title – *A Future for the Hen Harrier in England?* – is important, and the most significant part of that title is the question mark at the end. Political devolution had focused the attention of all the constituent UK administrations on their own corners of the country, and in England this resulted in more attention being paid by an English government agency to the fate of this bird than might have happened, and indeed had happened, under the old Nature Conservancy Council. It was clear that south of the political line that separated England from Scotland, the Hen Harrier was in a fairly perilous state and was under assault from upland grouse-moor managers. The maximum number of Hen Harriers nesting in England during the study to date was 23 females.

One of the key findings of this report was that 'persecution continues to limit Hen Harrier recovery in England', which was not ground-breaking but was one of the clearest statements of this fact that had come from the statutory sector rather than from raptor workers or the RSPB.

The report highlighted that few Hen Harriers attempting to nest on English grouse moors succeed in raising young. Where nests on grouse moors are successful, they raise good numbers of young, but overall breeding success is low on grouse moors (as had been shown much earlier for Scotland by RSPB studies). The

Forest of Bowland was the stronghold of the English nesting population, holding around two-thirds of all nesting attempts, the majority on land owned by the utilities company United Utilities rather than on the adjacent grouse moors. In this small corner of upland Lancashire the nesting success on the United Utilities land was 1.96 chicks per attempt, whereas on the nearby grouse moors the figure was 1.22 chicks per attempt. These differences were reflected across the rest of the English uplands: overall, on grouse moors the nesting success was 1.05 chicks per breeding attempt, whereas away from them it was 2.08.

The study showed that levels of persecution were relatively low in the Forest of Bowland, on both grouse moors and moors not managed for grouse shooting, compared with the rest of the country, which explained how the Hen Harrier had hung on in this area in greater numbers than elsewhere. On grouse moors away from Bowland, persecution was the main cause of nesting failure. For the first time, the study also clearly highlighted the fact that adult birds often went missing during the breeding season in areas of high persecution. This was something that practically never happened in the Bowland nesting areas, where the RSPB had a strong presence on the ground with volunteers guarding nests around the clock, and Natural England staff carrying out radio-tracking studies of adults. Away from Bowland, but not on grouse moors, the percentage of nests failing because one or both parent birds had disappeared during the nesting attempt was higher, but still much less than 10%, whereas on non-Bowland grouse-shooting areas, over 60% of failed nesting attempts were associated with disappearing adults.

The studies of radio- and satellite-tagged birds indicated that the Hen Harriers reared in the north of England tended to stay on their natal moors to feed through the autumn until November and then dispersed more widely, with some staying on the northern English moors, others moving to the lowlands or coastal areas, and some travelling long distances abroad, as ringing recoveries had, over many years, also established.

Tracking the tagged birds was also 'raising questions about their ultimate fate', and Natural England were:

looking into the disappearance of six Hen Harriers at an autumn roost known to us in the northern uplands. The anecdotal evidence of deliberate persecution given to us in confidence by a local land manager correlates with the information provided by the last known location of a number of birds.

In the same way, a number of birds, including six birds fitted with satellite transmitters, have been tracked from the Bowland Fells into parts of the North Pennines managed principally as driven grouse moors, and have not been recorded subsequently.

In addition, the Natural England study had witnessed destruction of Hen Harrier nests through illegal burning of heather, deliberate disturbance of nesting birds, and cases of illegal killing of other species of raptors in the study areas.

None of this information was unexpected, although the scale of difference in nesting success between contiguous areas which are and aren't managed for grouse shooting, and the frequency of adult birds disappearing, is always an eye-opener. But it added up-to-date hard data to the story that had emerged from earlier studies in Scotland. And because the English Hen Harrier population was so much smaller, the information seemed much more personal and intimate.

2009: Natural England *Vital Uplands* document

On 12 November 2009, Natural England launched its vision for the English uplands in 2060. This contentious document examined 'how the uplands could be sustainably managed over the next fifty years to secure the food production role that they have played in recent decades while delivering a wide range of other public benefits'.

Martin Doughty's successor as chair of Natural England, Poul Christensen (a farmer from Oxfordshire) said:

Our Vision is the starting point for a dialogue we want to have with upland stakeholders up and down the country about how we can all work together to shape the future of the uplands. The uplands provide society with a huge range of services – they are vital for food production, carbon storage and climate regulation, flood management, and water supply, as well as providing inspirational landscapes for recreation and homes to many rare and important species.

The document included a variety of arresting facts and figures about the uplands – such as the fact that the uplands cover around 12% of England, and yet only 1% of the population lives there; 53% of SSSIs lie within the uplands; 3% of the uplands are covered by native woodlands; 75% of uplands have been designated as national park or AONB; 70% of the UK's water supply is collected from upland catchments; and there are 70 million day visits to upland national parks each year.

Looking back on it, the vision seems pretty reasonable – as time has moved on we have become more familiar with some of the concepts it embraced, such as landscapes and habitats delivering 'ecosystem services' such as carbon storage and flood alleviation, and not just market goods.

It now seems rather tame and sensible to suggest that the uplands might be better for all of us with a bit more native forest and with restored blanket bogs that are actively sequestering carbon. However, it did not find favour with some 'stakeholders', who found it difficult to embrace the possibility of change, particularly to their own ways of doing things. The secretary of the Moorland Association, Martin Gillibrand, was quoted as saying:

> It is good that Natural England is taking time to consider the optimum state of the Uplands in 2060. It would be better if it recognised what a fantastic asset we now have in our managed heather moorland, and committed itself to building on that asset in cooperation with the Moorland Association.

The rough reception of this document was an indication of how conservative the grouse-moor owners, in particular, are, and how single-mindedly they pursue their own objectives (on their own land, they might point out – but I and others would remind them that it is not wholly at their own expense, or without consequences for society as a whole).

In March 2012, Poul Christensen said at a conference that Natural England's *Vital Uplands* document had let his organisation down badly, due to its controversial nature. 'We told rather than listened and I'm very sorry how people perceived it' – an amazing thing for a chairman of an organisation to say about a document that he himself had launched. The document has disappeared from the Natural England website but can still be found on the John Muir Trust website – good for them!

2008–2009: Forum articles in *Journal of Applied Ecology*

An article by Thirgood & Redpath in 2008, which analysed the conflict between grouse shooting and raptor predation, suggested that a trial should be undertaken implementing a 'ceiling' on Hen Harrier numbers in grouse-shooting areas, such that a grouse-moor manager would be allowed to manipulate Hen Harrier numbers once they had reached a certain level to stop them from rising further. This would, of course, be tantamount to saying 'we can't stop you wiping out Hen Harriers but if you allow some to survive we'll let you wipe out the others.' No consideration was given to other forms of shooting, such as walked-up shooting or dogging, as a replacement for the current intensive form of driven grouse shooting.

The authors, rather even-handedly, described both sides, 'hunters' and 'conservationists', as having entrenched positions, which in my view means that the hunters are entrenched in breaking the law because there is little chance of getting caught, and the conservationists are entrenched in wishing the current laws to be implemented and not broken. GWCT scientists replied by suggesting that a fall in the number of Red Grouse that were shot would jeopardise the whole economic system for grouse-moor management. Basically, without the large numbers of Red Grouse that were currently shot, there would be no incentive for grouse-moor owners to manage the land with gamekeepers, and much conservation value, for example the breeding wader populations that grouse moors supported, would be lost. They were against a move to the less profitable walked-up shooting largely on the grounds that it wasn't economically viable, although the evidence for this depended entirely on the current values attached to different forms of grouse shooting.

A different view was held by RSPB scientists, who followed a line much closer to the one taken in this book when they wrote:

> It is incumbent on grouse moor owners to demonstrate that their stewardship of large tracts of the UK's uplands is founded on sustainable principles capable of delivering multiple benefits. Given the levels of public funding directed to managing the uplands, many areas of which are of European significance for their biodiversity, the public and a range of other stakeholders

have a right to be involved in deciding how they are managed in the future. Managing the land for shooting will continue to be important, but only if the grouse-shooting sector is prepared to co-exist with birds of prey.

And also, as a rather pithy summary, 'If driven-grouse shooting is only viable when birds of prey are routinely disturbed and killed, then we question the legitimacy of driven-grouse shooting as a sustainable land use.'

Thirgood & Redpath and the GWCT concentrated on the maintenance of driven grouse shooting as an aim, in some shape or form, and its economic viability despite, as the RSPB pointed out, there being 'no evidence that driven-grouse shooting is critical to the delivery of economic or environmental benefits in the uplands'. The RSPB was prepared to accept that other forms of grouse shooting might be sustainable, and drew attention to the growing evidence that the management of grouse moors for driven grouse shooting caused wider environmental harm.

2010: Lead Ammunition Group

In October 2009, Dr Debbie Pain, director of conservation of the Wildfowl & Wetlands Trust (WWT), and I (as RSPB conservation director) wrote to the Secretaries of State for Environment and Health to alert them to relatively new scientific information about lead levels in the flesh of animals killed with lead shot. Lead is a poison, which is why we have been busy removing it from petrol, paint, water pipes and fishing weights – but we still use lead ammunition, even though many countries, and several states of the USA, have banned it wholly or partially on the grounds of human and wildlife health.

The last Labour government brought in a partial ban on the use of lead ammunition for shooting wildfowl in England, and the Scottish government banned it over wetlands, but lead is still used in all other shooting.

The new findings related to the fact that small fragments of lead flake off a lead shot pellet or a lead bullet passing through the flesh of a shot bird or mammal. These small fragments are not normally visible to the human eye and cannot be removed from the carcase by butchering as they are so small and spread so widely through the flesh. The lead is therefore ingested when predators or scavengers eat the carcases of birds or mammals shot with lead ammunition, and the same happens if we eat lead-shot game.

In 2010 the Labour government set up a group to look at these issues of wildlife and human health. The report is due in 2015, and my expectation is that it will recommend the withdrawal of lead ammunition from use in England.

The move away from lead ammunition has been resisted with incredible vigour by the shooting industry. It's not exactly clear why, given that many other countries have moved away from lead and that wildfowlers have been using non-toxic ammunition for more than a decade. Although there are lots of arguments about whether non-toxic shot is as good ballistically as lead, the truth of the matter is that it is perfectly serviceable, as shown all over the world, but it does take a bit of adjustment for the shooter.

A move away from lead ammunition would give grouse shooters some extra problems, in that old and valuable shotguns, for example those Purdeys, are less able to withstand steel or other shot and may have to be adjusted to cope with alternative ammunition. This may seem inconvenient, it may even seem to some like the state interfering in their liberties, but it certainly can't be a big issue to spend a few hundred quid on a pair of Purdeys that are worth £20,000 or more.

A more serious reason for the opposition to the removal of toxic lead ammunition, and the opposition is fierce, is that shooting organisations have been promoting wild-shot game as a healthy source of food – and so the evidence that lead-shot game has high levels of poison in it is inconvenient to their cause.

Research by WWT and RSPB on lead levels in game meat sold in supermarkets and game dealers in the UK showed that all species tested (e.g. Pheasant, partridges, Red Grouse, wildfowl, Rabbit) occasionally had very high lead levels. For other meats, such as beef, pork and chicken, there is a set level of lead above which the meat cannot be sold. That level is 100 parts per billion wet weight. The research showed that around half of game meat on sale to the public, when cooked in the normal way and after any visible lead pellets had been removed, had higher lead levels than would be legal in meat from domestic animals. Why there is no statutory level set for lead levels in game meat, which is traditionally shot with lead (for heaven's sake!), is a matter of some perplexity to me. I suspect that the shooting lobby had someone in the right place at the right time in the distant past.

The human health impacts of ingesting lead are serious if you eat enough of it, or if you belong to a susceptible group. The Food Standards Agency revised (i.e. strengthened) its advice on ingestion of lead through game meat in October 2012, when it said on its website:

> The Food Standards Agency is advising people that eating lead-shot game on a frequent basis can expose them to potentially harmful levels of lead. The FSA's advice is that frequent consumers of lead-shot game should eat less of this type of meat.

FSA director of food safety Dr Alison Gleadle elaborated:

> To minimise the risk of lead intake, people who frequently eat lead-shot game, particularly small game, should cut down their consumption. This advice is especially important for vulnerable groups such as toddlers and children, pregnant women and women trying for a baby, as exposure to lead can harm the developing brain and nervous system.
>
> It's important to remember that not all game is shot with lead. Generally, the large game sold in supermarkets is farmed and will have no or very low lead levels. Our advice is not applicable to consumers of such meat.

Scientists and the medical profession state that there is no agreed safe level for lead intake. Independent expert groups across the European Union advise that exposure to lead should be reduced as far as possible. Putting together the lead levels found in game sold to the UK public and the impacts of lead on humans means that for children, eating lead-shot gamebirds around once a fortnight would lead to a whole point reduction in IQ, and for adults anything over one meal of lead-shot game a week could have critical impacts such as increasing the risk of heart failure.

This announcement made it difficult to maintain that wild-shot game really is a healthy meat, given that its lead levels would prevent it being sold if it *wasn't* game. The Countryside Alliance website still says that game is a 'tasty and healthy alternative to lamb, chicken, beef or pork'.

2010: Raptor petition

On 3 February 2010, the RSPB handed a petition numbering 210,567 signatures to the minister of state at Defra, Huw Irranca-Davies, calling for the maintenance of full legal protection for birds of prey. The petition was, at the time, the most successful ever organised by the RSPB in terms of number of signatures, and it had been deliberately set up as a marker of public support for the protection of raptors, given the prospect of an incoming Conservative, and less raptor-friendly, government arriving in May 2010.

2010: A new government

I worked at the RSPB for just over 25 years, and that period spanned governments led by Margaret Thatcher, John Major, Tony Blair, Gordon Brown and, from 6 May 2010, David Cameron. My early years at the RSPB were spent, in a way, with my head down working as a scientist with little interest in politics (although I recall making sure I was working away from the office the day that Mrs Thatcher visited The Lodge). I became conservation director in 1998, and so the events of May 2010 led to my first very close experience with a non-Labour government.

The electorate voted for more Conservatives and fewer Labour MPs and got them. Although the Liberal Democrats' share of the vote increased, fewer LibDem MPs were returned, but there were still enough for them to hold the balance of power in a coalition government with the Conservatives. The need to find some cabinet and other ministerial posts for Liberal Democrats changed what must have been plans that had been well thought-through by the incoming prime minister, David Cameron.

Everyone had expected that the shadow ministers would simply move into Defra and start implementing the policies they had been thinking about and shadowing for years. This would have resulted in a Defra ministerial team led by Nick Herbert (former press officer of the British Field Sports Society, one of the founding organisations of the Countryside Alliance) and including James Paice (farmer, shooter and council member of the Game and Wildlife Conservation Trust), Richard Benyon (landowner, grouse-moor owner, shooter and council member of the Game and Wildlife Conservation Trust) and Lord Taylor of Holbeach (farmer). There would rarely have been such a pro-shooting collection of government ministers – not just temperamentally, socially and ideologically pro-shooting, but active participants in the industry.

However, the intervention of the Liberal Democrats, via the electorate, changed some of that, and Caroline Spelman, the shadow local government minister, was the surprise arrival as secretary of state at Defra; Nick Herbert had to be content (or malcontent) with becoming a minister of state at the Department of Justice. This was still a ministerial team embedded in the farming and shooting industries, but with a secretary of state who spoke several European languages and felt that she could make a positive difference to biodiversity during her tenure.

Spelman made a lasting and constructive contribution, through her own personal efforts, at international biodiversity talks in Japan and raised the standing of the UK to levels unknown since John Gummer's time in office. But she made the mistake of following government policy over forestry privatisation and left the government in 2012, to be replaced by the climate-change sceptic, EU-sceptic and pro-Badger culling Owen Paterson – possibly the least sympathetic minister that the PM could have found for the role at Defra from the point of view of the environmental movement (a movement that Paterson described acidly as the 'Green Blob' in an extraordinary article published on his departure from Defra). Paterson was sacked from Defra in July 2014 and replaced by Liz Truss, who kept a low profile throughout her tenure. James Paice left at the same time as Spelman and was replaced by Liberal Democrat David Heath. Richard Benyon stayed in the post until October 2013 when he was replaced by Liberal Democrat Dan Rogerson, and at the same time David Heath was replaced by Conservative George Eustice.

The upshot of all this was that Defra had ministers who were very close to the shooting community, and indeed the grouse-shooting industry, for much of the five years of the Conservative–Liberal coalition government.

2010: The Otterburn study

This study, carried out from 2000 to 2008 and published in 2010, looked at the impacts of predator control on breeding wader populations from just four sites in the north of England. The Pennine chain stands out as a breeding wader hot-spot in the national bird atlases that have been published over the years, and previous work has demonstrated that the densities of breeding waders are higher on areas managed for driven grouse shooting than on similar areas that are not managed in that way. This is a slightly inconvenient fact for anyone who wants to take a position that is determinedly anti-driven grouse shooting – but facts are facts and they have to be lived with. There is no doubt that the shooting industry makes the most of this one, as it is rather a convenient one for them.

The aim of the Otterburn study was to look at the role of predator control in helping breeding waders, through an experimental approach. This is not an easy task. Four study areas were chosen in the north Pennines, and on one of them (Ray Demesne) predator control was carried out through the eight years of the study; at another (Emblehope) no predator control was carried out, and at the other two sites predator control was practised either in the first half (Otterburn) or the second half (Bellshiel) of the study. Thus the experimental aspects of the study relied on just two areas where predator control was switched on or off. It is not a large sample, but that is understandable considering the logistics of the task.

Nesting success of the three wader species studied (Golden Plover, Curlew and Lapwing) was higher in places, and in years, when predators were controlled than when and where they weren't. Some of these differences were quite dramatic in scale. There was a tendency for population levels to increase in the years of (or following) predator control and to decrease when predator control was absent.

This study provided further substantiation of the view that legal predator control makes an important contribution to the high densities of ground-nesting waders on land managed for grouse shooting in the north of England.

2011: UK National Ecosystem Assessment

The concept of 'ecosystem services' has grown in prominence over recent years, and in 2011 an assessment of 'what nature does for us' was published by the UK government. Its relevance to this debate was that it highlighted the economic importance of the British uplands in a different way – their importance as a carbon store and water management resource.

Much of nature conservation is rooted in a feeling of love and respect for the other millions of species with whom we share this planet. There is considerable overlap between animal rights supporters, animal welfare supporters and nature conservationists. All approach animal (not necessarily plant) issues from somewhat similar, and certainly emotionally overlapping, perspectives. I suspect there is not a very large overlap between the memberships of the British Trust for Ornithology and Animal Aid, but I am fairly sure there must be some. If they ever sat down together, a BTO scientist and an Animal Aid activist would often look confused and bewildered at each other's ways of expressing themselves, but a long conversation would in the end persuade both parties that they were, more or less, on the same side, even if pursuing notably different objectives using notably different methods.

One thing that would bring these two people together (and I have two particular individuals in mind as I write this) is that they would both see a bird, say, as a sentient being, a fellow creature, a beautiful fellow inhabitant of the earth and as a species of value in its own right (in some complex way) rather than being 'useful' or 'useless' to our species. Such a view, some would say loaded with sentimentality and anthropomorphism, is more easily adopted with respect to animals than plants, and to vertebrates (particularly mammals) than invertebrates, and to species rather than habitats. It's easier to feel passionate about a Red Fox suckling her cubs than it is about a peatbog storing carbon.

Much of nature conservation is thus grounded in empathy with nature, and it is easier to feel empathy with those elements of nature that most closely resemble yourself, your children and your friends. This may explain the relative weakness of plant conservation in the UK and globally, and the hugely greater support for organisations whose focus is on mammals and birds rather than on the equally beautiful butterflies or fish. This approach to nature sees it as separate from and having value separate from ourselves – after all, if our species went extinct tomorrow the rest of nature would carry on regardless (and with rather greater prospects in many cases). This world view looks at nature as being special in its own right.

There is another approach that looks at the ecological roles that species, and those collections of species in particular places that we call habitats or ecosystems, play as they go about their daily lives. An example would be that plants produce oxygen through photosynthesis, which accumulates in the atmosphere, filters out the sun's ultraviolet light, and is the gas on which all animal (and plant) respiration is based. Plants aren't producing oxygen 'for' anyone or anything, but without that product of the way plants build up carbohydrates from carbon dioxide and water this planet would be very different. It would be uninhabitable by creatures such as ourselves, and so it is sometimes convenient to see oxygen production by plants as an 'ecosystem service' provided for free but of great value to all life on Earth.

Plants are pretty good at delivering ecosystem services without thinking about them at all. Trees are very important carbon stores, locking up the carbon that would otherwise enter the atmosphere and contribute to climate change, but so too are peatbogs, formed of the preserved bodies of moorland plants, particularly mosses. The UK is rich in peatbogs, and they are mostly found in the uplands, and often in those very areas where driven grouse shooting is carried out.

In a parliamentary answer on 22 July 2010, biodiversity minister Richard Benyon pointed out:

Peat soils provide a wide range of 'ecosystem services' or functions for society, including carbon storage. UK peat soils are estimated to store around 5.5 billion tonnes of carbon, equivalent to 31 times the UK's total annual greenhouse gas emissions if it were all lost to the atmosphere.

Peat soils also support valuable wildlife and biodiversity and a range of peatland habitats in both upland areas (for example, blanket bogs and moorland) and lowlands (for example, raised bogs and fens). The importance of peatland habitats is recognised by the designation of 68% of English upland blanket bogs as Sites of Special Scientific Interest (SSSIs) ...

Mountains, moorlands and heaths (including relatively small areas of lowland heaths) cover about 18% of the UK land surface and yet they are of disproportionate importance in carbon storage (40% of UK carbon stores) and are the source of most of our drinking water (70% of which falls in the uplands).

The assessment carried out for the UK government in 2011 put the uplands of the UK in a different light from that in which they are generally seen by most of us. The report was clear in describing the uplands as important carbon stores, providers of clean water and managers of hazards (particularly flood risk). These benefits to society are not market benefits, and they aren't marketable benefits, but they are benefits, and as such they could have a notional 'financial benefit' ascribed to them.

This is a useful way of thinking, even though it is somewhat unfamiliar to us all. The traditional way of viewing the uplands is that they are wonderful places to get away from it all (and that is something that can be evaluated too, once one starts thinking of ecosystem services in the round) but that they are very difficult places to make a living. Because of their poor soils and harsh climates the best that you can do in the uplands is rear a few sheep or grow a few trees for timber, and even these land uses are pretty marginal. Trees and sheep both grow better in the lowlands, but as ways to make money they are outcompeted there by cattle, wheat and building houses. Rightly, therefore, we don't think of the uplands as being a powerhouse of the British economy, nor even of the British rural economy, but we should be developing a new perspective that sees them as a powerhouse of ecosystem services.

There is another change of perspective needed to get one's head around this way of looking at things, too. Growing sheep or trees delivers a financial benefit to the landowner or manager who grows them and sells them. Growing peatbogs does not.

You can't easily sell the carbon in your peatbog. This means that if ever there were a conflict between growing sheep that you could sell and growing peat that you could not sell, most land managers would be more tempted by the sheep option than the peat one. And that would be true whether or not an economist had valued the peat, notionally, as of higher or lower value than the sheep. If you cannot pocket the cash then it doesn't really count. So if there are any conflicts between private profit and public goods (such as carbon storage, water quality or flood alleviation) then private profit is likely to win – at least as things are structured at the moment. Therefore, the way we farm and manage our uplands may not be delivering as much to society as a whole as perhaps it might.

Where this way of looking at the uplands, or at life in general, leads is to the idea that perhaps government, which ultimately means you and I (provided that, like me, you pay your taxes), should maybe pay for peat. If there is no market for peat, but peat is of 'value' to society, to us, to the world, then let's rig the system to reflect that value. And more generally, should government intervene in markets, through regulation or incentives, to persuade upland landowners to manage their land in different ways?

For the grouse-moor manager, this is a new game with very new rules.

For the conservationist, this is also a new game, and one that many conservationists are disinclined to play. The very idea of monetising (a ghastly word) nature is a hideous prospect for some. It clashes with their belief systems and opens up the possibility that some aspects of nature might be traded away, or sold down the river, if they aren't seen to measure up to other financial estimates. What price do you put on the sight of a male Hen Harrier sky-dancing across a moorland in this way of thinking?

And if we should value our uplands and our blanket bogs for their peat, do the management regimes associated with driven grouse shooting add to or take away from those values?

2011: IUCN UK Commission of Inquiry on Peatlands

A report from the UK Committee of the International Union for the Conservation of Nature examined the evidence relating to the state of peatlands in the UK. Although peat habitats are found in at least 175 countries, the UK is among the top ten nations of the world in terms of its total peatland area. We have between 9% and 15% of all the peatland in Europe (46,000–77,000 km^2) and about 13% of the world's blanket bog – one of the world's rarest habitats.

The study found that 10 million tons of carbon dioxide are emitted from the UK's damaged peatlands each year, and that the UK is among the highest emitters of carbon dioxide from damaged peat, largely through drainage, burning, agriculture and forestry.

Julia Marton-Lefèvre, IUCN's director general, described peat-land conservation as 'a prime example of a nature-based solution to climate change', and commented that 'we urgently need to switch from aspiration to action to secure the benefits that peat-lands provide'. Achim Steiner, UN under-secretary general and executive director of the UN Environment Programme said that 'restoration of peatlands is a low hanging fruit, and among the most cost-effective options for mitigating climate change'. However, the commission's findings were that:

> It is of great concern that the Inquiry found that much of the UK's peatlands have been damaged, with severe consequences for biodiversity and valuable ecosystem services. A significant amount of carbon is leaking into the atmosphere from drained and deteriorating peatlands. This is particularly alarming as a loss of only 5% of the carbon stored in peat would equate to the UK's total annual greenhouse gas emissions. On the other hand, healthy peatlands and those that have been restored and enhanced can make a positive contribution to tackling climate change.

In other words, the UK is important for blanket bogs on an international scale, and blanket bogs are important for the UK as they store carbon (if treated well), maintain important wildlife populations (if treated well), regulate water flows off upland areas and therefore regulate flood risks (if treated well), provide clean water supplies (if treated well), and look rather pretty too. This report was a wake-up call to the UK, and to Defra, to do a much better job on peatland restoration and conservation. Since much of the land in question was managed for driven grouse shooting, it put the ball firmly in the grouse shooters' court. Grouse moor management now had to demonstrate its acceptability on a much wider range of ecological criteria.

2011: Study of Peregrine Falcons in relation to driven grouse shooting

A study of Peregrines and driven grouse shooting was published in 2011, based on data collected by raptor workers in the north of England between 1980 and 2006. The findings were similar to those relating to Hen Harriers and Golden Eagles. The locations of areas managed as driven grouse moors were derived from satellite imagery of strip burning of heather, and then the Peregrine dataset was analysed according to whether the traditional nest sites were in areas of grouse shooting or not.

For a dataset of 1,081 nest histories, it was shown that nesting success was 50% lower in those areas managed for driven grouse shooting. As with Golden Eagles and Hen Harriers, clutch size and brood size of successful nests were just as high in grouse moor areas as away from them, strongly suggesting that the overall ecology of the areas, especially food supply, was equally suitable for nesting Peregrines, if only they were allowed to survive. In addition, there were many data collected in the field pointing clearly to the likelihood that criminal human interference was the main factor determining this difference in nesting success.

Modelling showed the usual scenario, that the populations on grouse moors acted as a sink population; the productivity of nests in these areas was not sufficient to maintain the population, which only persisted because of ongoing immigration from areas where Peregrines were not illegally killed.

2011–2012: Vicarious liability – Chrissie Harper's e-petition

Chrissie Harper is a raptor enthusiast who manages Chrissie's Owls, a family-run concern which, among other things, rescues sick and injured owls. I met Chrissie at various shows and events, and hers was a name that occasionally cropped up criticising the RSPB for our stance on raptor issues in the past. But I got to know Chrissie through these meetings and found her a true lover of wildlife, though with a different take on things, sometimes, from my own.

In November 2011 Chrissie launched an e-petition on the Westminster government's website, calling for the introduction of vicarious liability for wildlife crimes. Here is the text of that e-petition:

Introduction of offence of vicarious liability for raptor persecution in England

Responsible department: Department for Environment, Food and Rural Affairs

Scotland, recognising that those who persecute birds of prey frequently do so at the direction of their employers or others with vested interests, has introduced an offence of vicarious liability, the purpose of which is to bring those parties to justice.

This petition calls on the government to introduce an offence of vicarious liability to bring to justice those who direct or turn a blind eye to raptor persecution in England.

As an indication of how bad things are, in the last year only four pairs of Hen Harriers successfully reared chicks in England, fourteen Peregrine Falcon territories failed on grouse moors in Lancashire's Forest of Bowland, and only one successful Goshawk nest was recorded in the Derwent Valley, Derbyshire.

Current legislation is not enough to deter those who break the law and destroy our heritage; the introduction of vicarious liability would hit those directing the slaughter.

The way that these e-petitions work is that UK citizens can register their support for them over a period of, normally, 12 months. Unlike other e-petition sites on the internet, this official government site is only open to UK voters, and it requires information from each signatory to limit the possibility of multiple signatures. As a result, it is taken a bit more seriously than other e-petition sites, and if the number of signatures passes a threshold of 10,000 then the relevant government department has to make a formal response to the petition.

Fewer than one in a hundred petitions on the government website generate the 10,000 signatures necessary to trigger a response from government, but Chrissie's easily passed the threshold; it ended up with 10,908 signatures, which was something of a triumph given that the very phrase 'vicarious liability' is complicated and off-putting, and, more crucially, that the petition received no burst of support from wildlife conservation bodies such as the RSPB, which had been a keen supporter of the introduction of vicarious liability in Scotland.

Vicarious liability, to put it simply, is the idea that people higher up a management structure should take responsibility for the illegal actions of their subordinates, so that junior staff do not take the blame and carry the can for organisational failings. An example outside of the environmental sphere would be in health and safety legislation, where the chief executive of an organisation might find him- or herself in the dock if junior staff cause injury or death through ignoring or breaking the law. The senior manager might be asked questions along the lines of 'What training was in place for all staff? How did you monitor compliance? What information was available to staff on the requirements of the law?'

The logic of taking this approach to wildlife crime is clear. The person laying a poison on a moor or approaching a Hen Harrier nest with harmful intent is unlikely to be the duke who owns the land but his gamekeeper, who, at least in theory, does what he is told. Is a gamekeeper who kills birds of prey a rogue employee, or is he carrying out what he suspects, or absolutely knows, are the wishes of his ultimate employer (and probably landlord too)?

No doubt Chrissie thought that the RSPB would come in behind her and support the e-petition, given that the RSPB had been so active in lobbying for this measure and had been so fulsome in praising the Scottish government when it proposed vicarious liability for wildlife crime.

The Hawk and Owl Trust formally supported the e-petition (as early as December 2011) and Martin Harper, my successor as RSPB conservation director, wrote in his blog in support of the introduction of vicarious liability for wildlife crime in England to follow that in Scotland, and asked readers to sign Chrissie's e-petition. But, in all honesty, not very many of the RSPB's one-million-plus members read the conservation director's blog.

In the end, although the RSPB never did put much effort into asking its members to sign the vicarious liability e-petition, the work of Chrissie Harper and others ensured that it was one of the most successful e-petitions ever, and it elicited the following response from Defra:

As this e-petition has received more than 10 000 signatures, the relevant Government department have provided the following response:

Defra is aware of the Scottish Government's decision to introduce a vicarious liability offence under the Wildlife and Natural Environment Act (Scotland) 2011, which came into force on 1 January 2012. The new offence is targeted principally at addressing the persecution of raptors. The new offence will mean employers or agents may be prosecuted where an employee is found to have illegally killed a bird of prey (or other wild bird) – in effect they may be prosecuted for the same offence. There is, however, a defence that an employer or agent can rely on, this being that they did not know an offence was being committed and that they took all reasonable steps to prevent an offence being committed.

It is unclear whether in practice the new offence will result in successful prosecutions of employers or agents. There are no immediate plans therefore to introduce a similar offence in England but Defra will look carefully at how the offence works in practice in Scotland. The development of our future wildlife crime policy will include consideration of how effective the new offence in Scotland has been in helping to address raptor persecution.

2011–2012: The Glenn Brown case

One of my last duties as RSPB conservation director, in April 2011, was to sit through one day of the trial of gamekeeper Glenn Brown in Chesterfield Magistrates Court. A few days later I had left the RSPB and was driving across the USA watching birds and seeing scenery. Whilst I was failing to see a Greater Roadrunner in the Joshua Tree National Park, Glenn Brown was sentenced. However, by the time I returned to the UK he had appealed against his conviction – and so the story was only fully resolved in January 2012, when the appeal failed.

Glenn Brown was convicted of a variety of offences under the Wildlife and Countryside and Animal Welfare Acts, involving taking a Sparrowhawk and operating a trap with a live pigeon as bait (some would call this a hawk trap). He received 100 hours of community service and was ordered to pay £10,000 costs. On losing his appeal he was ordered to pay a further £7,000 costs.

The relevance of this event is that it occurred in the Peak District National Park in the area identified and commented upon in the *Peak Malpractice* reports of five and four years earlier, and on land owned by the National Trust (which describes itself as one of Europe's leading conservation organisations).

Brown was employed by the National Trust tenant, Geoff Eyre, whose work on re-establishing heather on overgrazed moorlands has been recognised by several awards, including the Purdey Award (there is no suggestion that Eyre knew of or authorised Brown's criminal conduct). Brown was the second gamekeeper in this small part of the Peak District to be convicted of a wildlife crime in just a few years.

2011: The RSPB Skydancer project

The RSPB's Skydancer project, which started in October 2011, aimed to raise awareness of the Hen Harrier and its plight in the communities of the north of England where Hen Harriers live, and in so doing to promote the bird's conservation. It has been a bottom-up approach to the conservation of the species which has engaged thousands and spread awareness of the bird and the problems it faces.

The Skydancer project was initially opposed by the shooting industry, who described it as an RSPB 'vanity project'. When it received funding from the Heritage Lottery Fund the Countryside Alliance chief executive, Alice Barnard, commented:

> I am surprised that money from public funds should be put towards research by a wealthy organisation … that has a one-dimensional approach to Hen Harriers.

And again:

> There are many smaller charities that could have put such a substantial grant from public funds to much better use, rather

than a Royal Society doggedly pursuing a one-eyed agenda to the detriment of thousands of other land managers, wildlife and countryside users.

That was an interesting reception for a bridge-building project.

It would be wrong to assume that in rural, moorland-edge human communities all the people know about this bird – they don't. The project found that many local residents had never seen a Hen Harrier and many had not heard of it, although those who had heard of it often had strong views on one or other side of the 'debate'.

The Skydancer team visited primary and secondary schools and also colleges such as Newton Rigg, Askham Bryan and Myerscough, where gamekeepers are trained. Schoolchildren were captivated by the beauty of a bird that lived on nearby hills, or that ought to live there, and many carried the message home to their parents, grandparents and other relatives. One girl's parents said 'she won't stop talking about Hen Harriers – even when we go to the supermarket we have to look out for them', and a 12-year-old wrote of what she took home from the session thus: 'How lucky we are to have these birds on our doorstep.'

After all the years of argument, a key aim of the project was to win some trust and understanding in discussions with game-keepers and trainee gamekeepers. One gamekeeper, approached at an agricultural show by Skydancer project staff to talk about Hen Harriers, asked, 'Why? Are you wearing a wire?' – fearing that he was being entrapped by the smiling young lady who engaged him. Later in conversation he described his attitude as being that Hen Harriers were vermin and that we all had to choose between Hen Harriers and other wildlife. He clearly felt that his fellow gamekeepers were doing a public service by killing Hen Harriers.

Despite the initial aggressively negative response from the Countryside Alliance and others in the shooting industry (who tried to persuade the Heritage Lottery Fund not to fund the project), Skydancer won the Best Education Project in the National Lottery Awards in 2014, beating six other finalists in a public vote for the favourite project. The project is due to end in September 2015.

2012: Walshaw Moor

In 2002, millionaire businessman and grouse shooter Richard Bannister bought the 6500-hectare Walshaw Moor estate, near Hebden Bridge in West Yorkshire, from Lord Savile (in whose family it had been for 150 years). Walshaw Moor forms part of the South Pennine Moors SPA (designated under the EU Birds Directive), the South Pennine Moors SAC (designated under the EU Habitats and Species Directive) and the South Pennine Moors SSSI (notified under domestic UK legislation). It's a moor in the south Pennines with just about every nature conservation designation that it could feasibly have.

Walshaw Moor became the scene of an unprecedented dispute over moorland management between Natural England and the estate which, as we shall see, ended rather abruptly. It was a dispute over whether the management of the moor for driven grouse shooting was compatible with maintaining the nature conservation value of the site.

Natural England was clearly of the view that the estate was managing the land poorly, indeed illegally, as they had taken the very unusual step of pursuing a legal case against the estate, as well as the more routine one of seeking to modify the existing management agreement for the site, which had been in place since 1995.

An email from the chief executive of Natural England, Helen Phillips, to the Defra minister Richard Benyon, dated 9 November 2011 (made available under FoI, the Freedom of Information Act) sets out the case pretty clearly and is reproduced below in full. It is clearly not just a routine communication but is a detailed briefing on, and justification of, the Natural England position.

Richard

Further to our meeting yesterday, a summary of current position: Walshaw Moor Estate Limited There are two regulatory proceedings currently being dealt with in relation to Walsaw [sic] Moor Estate – criminal proceedings for illegal works on the Moor; and an appeal by the Estate against the modification of a consent. Whilst the two actions relate to the same Moor and Estate there is in fact no overlap between the issues dealt with in either set of proceedings.

(i) The Prosecution

Natural England initiated prosecution proceedings against the Estate for carrying out damaging activities on the SSSI without consent which is an offence contrary to the provisions of the Wildlife and Countryside Act 1981. [Sentence blocked out here by Defra] In deciding to prosecute Natural England took account of both its own Enforcement Policy and the Code for Crown Prosecutors and was satisfied that this was a matter that was suitable for prosecution. There are a number of reasons for this:

(i) the scale of the damage and the sheer number of breaches;
(ii) the Estate has a previous conviction for similar offences; and
(iii) there was no offer of mitigation in the form of voluntary restoration.

We are satisfied that we have robust evidence to support this prosecution nevertheless the Estate has decided to plead not guilty. The judge at the recent pre-trial hearing questioned whether the Estate decided to plead not guilty. The judge at the recent pre-trial hearing questioned whether the Estate actually wanted to change their plea but at the moment their position remains that they will plead not guilty. The trial will be heard in the Crown Court on 17 September 2012.

A successful prosecution will allow Natural England to secure restoration orders via the court to ensure that the significant damage caused can be restored.

(ii) The Appeal against a Notice of Modification

The inquiry relates to the modification of a consent issued in 1995 which referred to the maintenance of existing infrastructure. The dispute as such is over the burning regimes being used by the Estate on sensitive protected areas. Put simply, it is Natural England's contention that the Estate is not maintaining existing infrastructure but is in fact carrying out a burning regime far different to that previously maintained and that this new regime is damaging protected habitats.

Natural England served the Notice of Modification of the consent in March 2010. There then followed a period of negotiation whilst both sides tried to reach a common position that would have allowed the Estate to undertake certain activities as part of an HLS [Higher Level Stewardship] agreement. These negotiations were unsuccessful and the Estate appealed against the Modification in December 2010. It is worth noting the Modification does not take effect whilst the appeal is in progress and if the Modification is upheld by the Inspector the Estate will be entitled to statutory compensation for any loss suffered. The appeal will be dealt with by way of an inquiry which is listed to take place for 3 weeks commencing January 2012.

Both parties are in the process of preparing their evidence for the appeal proceedings.

For your information only:

It is also worth noting that the Estate has made approaches to Natural England with a proposal to settle both the criminal and the appeal proceedings. Their initial proposal was not acceptable to us and we have made a counter-offer. Nevertheless we are mindful of the cost to the public purse of pursuing these proceedings and the risks to both parties if a conclusion is reached that is unsatisfactory to either. We have therefore organised an internal review of Natural England's case to understand better the risks and to see whether there may be scope to reach a resolution that is acceptable to the Estate whilst ensuring that we have met our statutory duties and that this sensitive environment continues to be protected.

If you want anything further, please let me know.

Helen

In essence, then, there were two lines of attack being pursued against the land manager. The first was that the estate had breached the existing agreement by carrying out damaging activities on the designated site. These, it emerged through FoI requests much later, were as follows (in Defra's words):

WMEL [Walshaw Moor Estate Limited] were charged with 45 offences. This consisted of 30 incidences of moor gripping [installing drainage channels], the construction of 5 tracks, the construction of 5 car parks, the creation of 2 ponds by peat extraction, the construction of earthworks (shooting butts) in 2 locations, and 1 incident of using vehicles likely to damage the site.

In Natural England's view, restoration of the alleged damage
would include the removal of damaging infrastructure from the
site, the filling in of moor grips and ponds and re-profiling and
re-vegetation of the affected areas.

The Walshaw Moor Estate denied any criminal activity.

The second was that increased burning of the moor was
damaging the blanket bogs, which were a major reason why it had
been designated under domestic and EU wildlife protection laws.

The meeting on 8 November 2011 and the subsequent email
briefing to the minister may well have been at Natural England's
suggestion, given the potentially sensitive nature of the case,
although it may also have been prompted by lobbying by the
Moorland Association (which we also learn of through FoI
requests). On 28 September 2011 the secretary of the Moorland
Association, solicitor Martin Gillibrand, had emailed the
minister Richard Benyon as follows:

Dear Richard

Natural England

We had a very useful meeting with Natural England under the
aegis of Peter Unwin, and tackled the issue of the need for Natural
England's consent for very minor works. We had originally sought
to resolve this by agreement as to a general consent for these
works but the more I think about it the more certain I am that
consent is neither necessary nor appropriate, particularly given the
assurances that were given to owners when the land was designated
that they should continue as hitherto and only significant changes
would require notification/consent.

'Significant', which is the requirement of the Habitat
Directive, seems to have gone by the board and the process is now
substantially gold plated, or bound in red tape.

I suspect that it will require firm guidance from your office
as to just what is appropriate in the circumstances, although we
discussed this at some length. I am not sure how the outcome is
going to be achieved.

We also discussed burning rotations where Peter suggested
that Natural England should involve the Moorland Association
in the internal discussions at an early stage, which would

be very welcome, but again I think it may need a rather firmer direction.

You mentioned a little time ago that you might be able to find a slot in your diary for a brief meeting when you're up north for the Party Conference, and if that is still a possibility Edward Bromet and I would very much like to follow that through with you. I would also welcome a chance to update you on the position in the hen harrier discussions through the Environment Council, and the possibility of obtaining derogations to cover the entire proposed process.

Martin Gillibrand
Secretary, Moorland Association

The requested meeting clearly took place, and rather more quickly than most NGOs were finding their meeting requests being met, as Benyon replied to Gillibrand as follows only two weeks later (again, as revealed through FoI requests):

10 October 2011

Thank you for your letter of 28 September. I was pleased that I was able to meet both you and Edward Bromet last week while I was in Yorkshire and discuss the issues set out in your letter.

I undertook to look into the issues you raised about heather burning, the Fire Index, hen harriers and CROW and I will come back to you with a substantive reply in due course.

Thank you for dinner. I found it interesting and illuminating!

Yours sincerely
Richard

The Moorland Association was clearly unhappy about the Walshaw Moor case and what it could mean for intensive burning of moorland for driven grouse shooting across many other grouse moors in the north of England. Gillibrand's email helpfully pointed out to the minister, a grouse-moor owner himself (though in Scotland), that he might like to look into the issues.

As the date for the public inquiry (mentioned in the email from Helen Phillips) approached, the Moorland Association increased its lobbying of the minister. On 22 December 2011

Edward Bromet, chairman of the Moorland Association, emailed Richard Benyon at his private email address as follows (again, from a FoI request):

> Dear Richard,
>
> We spoke yesterday but I can do no better than send over the attached by way of information. What Natural England are doing is complete madness. Suggestions of readdressing the basis of existing agri-environment schemes and whether heather burning should be allowed on blanket bog and wet heath has the potential to destroy 2/3rd of heather moorland in England and with it all the mammoth economic and environmental benefits!! It would make the management of moorland, most of which is privately funded, completely impossible. It is a ridiculously shortsighted move and has the ability to destroy cooperation or constructive discussion.
>
> I look forward to hearing further from you.
>
> Best wishes
> Ed

So the minister was being told by fellow grouse shooters that the actions of his agency, Natural England, in attempting to limit heather burning on heather moorland sites of high nature conservation importance could 'destroy two-thirds of heather moorland in England'. The minister was being lobbied very hard by grouse-shooting interests, and it is clear that Defra has only disclosed some of the correspondence that passed between the minister and his fellow grouse shooters. It is likely that Richard Benyon felt somewhat torn, or maybe somewhat squashed between a rock and a hard place, but we have no documented insight into how he felt, nor as to how he may have acted in this matter.

The criminal court case was scheduled for the summer of 2012, but first there would be the public inquiry. Everything was set up for a long inquiry that would investigate the pros and cons of the burning regime used by the Walshaw Moor estate to deliver its shootable surplus of grouse. The case could have implications for other grouse moors across northern England, and it could become a test case for whether intensive burning of moorland, particularly of blanket bog, was compatible with the conservation of sites designated for their nature conservation value. Just as events at Langholm Moor had shown that grouse shooting and raptor protection were in conflict, perhaps events at Walshaw Moor would demonstrate that driven grouse shooting and blanket bog protection were in conflict.

One can hardly say that the nation held its breath to see what emerged from the public inquiry, but around a thousand people – the grouse-moor owners of northern England, the involved staff of Natural England, and a few academics, journalists and nature conservation organisations – waited with great interest to see how things would play out.

But the expected 'Bang!' never came to pass. Instead there was something of a whimper when, in March 2012, Natural England reached an agreement with the Walshaw Moor Estate, which looked to some to be a euphemism for caving in to intense pressure from grouse-shooting interests over the proper management of designated blanket bogs. And so the public inquiry fizzled out and the criminal case was dropped.

The joint statement from Natural England and the estate, which reads to me as though it was made through clenched teeth, was as follows:

> Walshaw Moor Estate Ltd and Natural England are pleased to confirm that they have resolved their ongoing dispute regarding management activities conducted on the Moor, and confirm that they have entered into a new management regime which is considered beneficial to the environment and biodiversity of the Moor as well as the economic interests of the Estate.
>
> Walshaw Moor Estate Ltd and Natural England look forward to working together in a constructive partnership to further the interests of both conservation and the Estate, to the parties' mutual benefit, and in the public interest.

It is still unclear exactly why this agreement was reached. Was there some great flaw in the science that Natural England was using? Was there some flaw in the legal procedure which had led to the case? Was pressure put on Natural England to come to an agreement? It really is a case still shrouded in mystery, and although the Walshaw Moor estate was presumably reasonably happy about its outcome, the value of the case as a test case for the future of upland high-intensity management for driven grouse shooting was lost.

The agreement (we discover from further FoI requests) included paying the estate £2.5 million over ten years through agri-environment payments. In an email to Defra officials, sent on 9 March 2012, Natural England director Jim Smyllie confirmed that the total legal expenditure in relation to the appeal, the judicial review and the criminal proceedings was £1,022,000. He also wrote as follows:

> It has taken the litigation including a 5 week public inquiry relating to the notice modifying the consent, a threatened judicial review and the instigation of criminal proceedings to allow Natural England to have a productive conversation with the Estate about future management of the Moor.

And that might have been the unsatisfactory end of the Walshaw Moor case, had it not been for the fact that on 15 October 2012, following six months of investigation, the RSPB sent a complaint to the EU Commission over the case and its wider implications. The RSPB suggested that Natural England had contravened European environmental legislation in its dealings with the Walshaw Moor estate. Mike Clarke, RSPB chief executive, said:

> The decision to lodge this complaint has not been taken lightly, but this is a vitally important issue which centres on the Government's statutory duty to protect our natural environment.
>
> Natural England – the Government's wildlife watchdog – has dropped its prosecution without giving an adequate explanation and without securing restoration of this habitat. It has also entered into a management arrangement which we consider has fundamental flaws. This combination of actions is probably unlawful and will do little, if anything, to realise the Coalition Government's stated ambition to restore biodiversity.
>
> Natural England has an excellent record but at Walshaw it has not fulfilled its duty to protect wildlife. This has happened in the year that the Government seeks to review its environmental

agencies. We think this case is a timely reminder that we need a strong independent champion of the natural environment.

This is just one of several protected areas in our uplands, and this case may set an important precedent for how these sites are managed in the future.

The complaint to the EU is still running, and correspondence is still passing behind the scenes between the UK government and the EU Commission as the Commission investigates whether the UK is carrying out its obligations under EU-wide environmental legislation. Thanks to another FoI request we learn that Defra thinks that 'even though some of the alleged damage may not ultimately be restored, the management agreement ensures that the overall ecology integrity of the site is secured and moving towards favourable condition.'

By the end of 2013 there were still many unanswered questions about the Walshaw Moor case (which were to rumble on into 2014 – see next chapter – and beyond). What we knew was that Natural England had taken the major step of seeking to prosecute an upland landowner on 45 charges of damaging protected habitat, which was managed as a driven grouse moor. The minister involved in Defra, Richard Benyon, himself the owner of a grouse moor (in Scotland), had been lobbied by the Moorland Association, and the legal case had ended rather mysteriously (although there is no suggestion that Benyon acted improperly). It was by no means certain that the alleged damage to the designated site would be repaired in full, and the taxpayer had paid over a million pounds in legal costs, which appeared to have delivered nothing except an agreement between Natural England and the estate to the effect that the taxpayer would continue to pay large sums of money to the estate for the management of a damaged nature conservation site.

Without knowing every detail of this case – and Defra and Natural England have been unwilling to explain exactly what went on – it is difficult to understand how and why events unfolded as they did. But at the end of 2013 one was left wondering why Natural England had dropped its case, why the damage to the SSSI and SPA wasn't going to be fully restored, and to what extent the situation at Walshaw Moor might be replicated across many other upland estates in the north of England.

2012: The Uplands Stakeholder Forum Hen Harrier Sub-group

The Uplands Stakeholder Forum Hen Harrier Sub-group was set up in 2012 to address the decline in Hen Harriers, but largely so that this issue did not dominate wider discussions about the future of the uplands. Its members included Natural England, the Moorland Association, the National Gamekeepers' Organisation, the Game and Wildlife Conservation Trust, the National Parks Authority and the RSPB, so its membership overlapped quite considerably with that of the group that had spent years talking over the same issues in the failed process coordinated by the Environment Council. Would this body get further than the Environment Council had?

2012: Bowland Betty

A female Hen Harrier raised in the Forest of Bowland in 2011 and fitted with a satellite tag was found dead, having been shot, on the other side of the Pennines in the Yorkshire Dales, near a grouse moor, in July 2012.

This bird, named Bowland Betty, had been followed through her wanderings via the satellite tag, and the RSPB staff member on the Skydancer team, Jude Lane, wrote movingly about helping to tag the bird and putting her back in the nest in the previous summer, and then following her movements through the wonders of modern technology.

Bowland Betty had spent her first, and only, winter on the other side of the Pennines from her Lancashire home, in North Yorkshire, before heading back home to the Forest of Bowland in mid-March. But she was back in Yorkshire for the first 11 days of April, and then on 12 April 2012 she briefly visited Langholm Moor. She returned to the Pennines for a while before venturing further north to Scotland, this time to near Dornoch in Inverness-shire, but by 21 April she was back in Bowland again, where she was seen displaying. But by 6 May she had travelled even further north, to the Flow Country of Sutherland, where she passed through the RSPB nature reserve at Forsinard and on almost to the coast of Caithness south of Thurso, in the area around Loch Shurrery.

On her southward journey she spent time in the Cairngorms, travelled to the west coast near Arisaig and then visited Loch Tay before returning to Bowland, where she stayed briefly before heading once again to the Yorkshire Dales. But after several days of the tag sending a signal from the same locality her body was recovered in early July by Steven Murphy of Natural England. Bowland Betty had been shot and had bled to death.

The intimate details of this young bird's travels made her seem like a real 'personality' in a way that other Hen Harriers, the details of whose lives we know very little about, do not. What was the motivation for all that travel? Where would she have settled to breed in spring 2013 had she survived? Would she have laid eggs back in Bowland, or would it have been in the Yorkshire Dales, where she had spent a lot of her time and where she met her death. Or might she have settled in one of the places in Scotland that she had visited? Might she have become part of the Langholm 2 study by nesting there? Perhaps, had she survived, she would have nested somewhere to which her wanderings had not yet taken her. We'll never know.

Bowland Betty exemplified the fluidity of the Hen Harrier's life – the ability to travel long distances quickly and to visit many of the suitable areas of the total UK range. Bowland Betty was a very mobile particle of Hen Harrier soup. And she visited many areas where we know that grouse interests predominate. How often had she been seen by gamekeepers on her travels? How many of them had waited to see if they could get a shot at her?

2013: Licensing of sporting estates – John Armitage's e-petition

John Armitage worked for the RSPB, latterly as the regional director for the North of England, for more than 20 years. The Forest of Bowland was one of the sites in his area, and he lived through the debates and arguments over the fate of raptors in this area. He was steeped in the issues and the personalities.

Following the success, in terms of signatures, of Chrissie Harper's e-petition on vicarious liability, John launched his own e-petition in February 2013, calling for licensing of sporting estates as a way to regulate their behaviours – through the possible withdrawal of licences if the estates can be shown to have misbehaved. The text of the e-petition was:

Licensing of upland grouse moors and gamekeepers

Responsible department: Department for Environment, Food and Rural Affairs

Given the continuing levels of illegal persecution of birds of prey the Government is called upon to introduce a system of operating licences for upland grouse shoots. Following any proven offence of persecution on the shoot concerned, i.e. illegal trapping, use of poisons, shooting or the interference with or destruction of nests, the licence would be revoked for a period of not less than two years and commercial shooting activity cease.

Linked to the above the Government is called upon to introduce an accreditation scheme or licensing system for all gamekeepers, be they employed in a full time or part time capacity. If an individual then has any proven involvement with raptor persecution, the licence would be withdrawn for a period of three years along with the right to hold a gun licence. Any repetition of an offence would result in the licences being withdrawn for life.

This e-petition picked up the baton of better and greater regulation of shooting estates from Chrissie Harper and carried it on into 2014, as it was due to end in February of that year. We will meet it again in the next chapter.

2013: The first Hen Harrier Day

Alan Tilmouth, a birder and writer based in Northumberland, should be credited with starting the first Hen Harrier Day, which was a 'virtual' day. He suggested that people change their Facebook photos to ones of Hen Harriers to mark the opening of the grouse shooting season in 2013. Scores of people followed Alan's lead, and this initiative showed that there was at least a small number of active supporters of the Hen Harrier who could be relied upon to take some action on social media.

2013: National Trust vision for the High Peak

The National Trust is a significant owner of upland land. It owns large areas of the Peak District, and in fact it owns large areas of those very parts of the Peak District where raptors are too rarely found nesting, and where, when they do attempt to nest, adults often disappear from nesting sites. The National Trust owns much of the land covered by the *Peak Malpractice* reports, and Glenn Brown was in the employment of one of the National Trust's tenants, Geoff Eyre, who managed a grouse moor.

For some time the National Trust had been reviewing the management of its upland estate and pondering the way forward. It had done a lot of work on ecosystem services – carbon storage, water quality, flood alleviation – and had looked to reduce its carbon footprint in its properties and managed land.

On 20 September the National Trust issued this press release, which began to set out their vision for their upland estate in the High Peak. I can do no better than quote it in full, as it covers a wide range of issues that were becoming more and more prominent in discussions about the future of the uplands. Also, the press release had clearly been given a great deal of thought, as the National Trust knew full well that it would not be popular with many of its own tenants. It marked a clear statement of how the future of upland management might be changing.

50-year project aims to breathe new life into the uplands

The National Trust's 'biggest and most ambitious' landscape-scale nature conservation initiative is being launched in the Peak District today.

It aims to inspire people and involve them in restoring a landscape of healthy peat bogs, diverse heaths and natural woodland rich in wildlife.

With input from a wide range of people and organisations, the Trust has mapped out a bold new 50-year vision for 10,000 hectares (40 square miles) of land it looks after in the High Peak moors.

They cover boulder-strewn landscapes of rocky tors, dramatic valleys and cloughs, and mile upon mile of wild and remote bog and heath. The iconic Kinder Scout and the spectacular Upper Derwent Valley are perhaps the best known parts, essential elements of the much loved Peak District National Park, which is visited by more than 10 million people each year.

A remarkable landscape is made all the more special by the fact it is nestled between Sheffield and Manchester, close to the homes of millions of people.

Jon Stewart, National Trust General Manager for the Peak District, said: 'This dramatic, beautiful and fragile landscape is the ideal place for the biggest and most ambitious work that the Trust has ever undertaken to develop a clear road map for one of its upland estates.

'Whilst there is much to celebrate about the moors and their valley-sides there are massive management challenges such as eroding peat, drying out bog, lost woodland, suppressed heathland vegetation and maintaining good access. We want to work with those who care for and have a stake in their future to address these challenges.'

Conservation work will restore habitats such as bogs and heaths on the moor tops and heathland and woodlands in steep valleys, known as cloughs.

The blanket bogs, rich in peat, on the moors are of national and international significance. It's vital that this fragile habitat is maintained because severe erosion can release carbon into the atmosphere and have a knock-on effect on the quality of drinking water from peat ending up in reservoirs.

The peat found in the uplands of the UK has as much carbon as the forests of Britain and France combined and the High Peak moors alone store the equivalent of two years carbon emissions from the city of Sheffield.

A priority for the vision will be to keep the bogs wet through for example blocking gullies that have eroded the landscape and making sure that there is plenty of vegetation cover. Work has already begun on this on the plateau of Kinder Scout.

Work will also begin to increase the spread of trees and shrubs – both naturally and through planting – in the valleys to help restore lost wildlife habitat and a key part of the landscape, improve water quality and help conserve soils.

By creating the right conditions it will be possible for valued species such as birds of prey, red grouse and mountain hare to call the High Peak moors home in the decades to come.

One longer term measure of the success of the vision would be creating the right conditions for the black grouse to return to the moors; an upland bird that disappeared from the Peak District in the 1990s.

Jon Stewart added: 'We have learnt a huge amount about how managing these moors to boost their wildlife and restore the landscape can also have massive benefits for our drinking water quality, flood management, carbon storage and people's enjoyment, health and well-being.

'They are in effect a life support system. Managing the moors in tune with these benefits we believe provides the best way forward for those making their living from the moors as well.

'So this vision is all about working with people to care for the land whether our farm tenants, partners or the many people that passionately love the Peak District to restore the landscape and habitats, provide fantastic access to a wild place, deliver better water quality and care for the carbon in these upland soils.'

This statement came after a public consultation (which I helped to publicise on my blog), and there is no doubt in my mind that men in tweed were strongly lobbying for these plans to be ditched. In essence, the National Trust was moving away from driven grouse shooting, or at least the management on which it depends, restating its opposition to wildlife crime, and emphasising the importance of ecosystem services.

This was an important statement from a respected, and hardly radical, upland land manager, one that had to consider the public good rather than private profit in its management decisions. It signalled a move away from the intensive moorland management on which driven grouse shooting depends.

2013: *State of Nature* report

This review of the state of UK wildlife, habitat by habitat, published in May 2013 by a wide variety of wildlife NGOs, stated that 'of 877 upland species for which we have information, 65% have declined and 35% have declined strongly' and 'Although some species thrive from intensive grazing and burning regimes, most species and habitats benefit from less intensive grazing and habitat management.' One of the conclusions from this important report, then, was to emphasise that intensive management of the uplands is a cause of biodiversity loss.

2013: Hen Harrier populations in England

The national Hen Harrier survey carried out before the start of the first Langholm project, in 1988–1989, recorded 18 pairs of Hen Harriers nesting in England, and the 1998 survey, a little after Langholm reported, enumerated 19 pairs. By the time of the 2004 survey there were just 11 pairs, and when I left the RSPB in spring 2011 it was shortly after the 2010 survey had found 12 pairs of Hen Harriers in England. Over the following years, those numbers dropped steadily: four pairs nested successfully in 2011, just one pair in 2012 and two pairs, both unsuccessful, in 2013. Remember (from Chapter 1) that there should be about 330 pairs in England. Things were not going well for the Hen Harrier in England.

In early August 2013, Martin Harper, the RSPB's conservation director, was quoted as saying:

> We are only a few days away from 'the Glorious 12th' – the traditional August start of the grouse shooting season. My challenge to those who run grouse moors is simple: respect the law and allow Hen Harriers and other birds of prey to flourish again.

This struck me as being somewhat limp, and that issuing a challenge to the enemy just as they vanquished your troops perhaps wasn't a very realistic proposition. For despite all the talking, and despite its full legal protection, and despite the promising nature of diversionary feeding, the Hen Harrier was heading to extinction as a breeding bird in England.

How I felt about it all

The period sketched out above, from the watershed of the Joint Raptor Study to the end of 2013, covered about a third of my life so far, and as far as I was concerned it certainly wasn't dominated by the issue of driven grouse shooting. It spanned the period of my two children passing through secondary education, gaining places and then good degrees at university, and growing into young adults. I lost my father, we moved house (but only shifted by 100 metres), the mortgage was paid, holidays were taken, cars were bought and driven into the ground, and life went on.

In 1998 I moved from head of conservation science at the RSPB to conservation director, and I spent almost 13 years in that role before leaving the RSPB at the end of April 2011. Professionally, too, my life was not dominated by the issues discussed in this book, except for short periods. I spent far more time on the declines of farmland birds, on climate change and its impacts on wildlife, on planning the RSPB's land acquisition strategy and on a host of other issues, than on grouse shooting and what should be done about it.

However, although the issue was not a dominant one, it was never completely absent. There was always a conversation, or a death of a raptor on a grouse moor, or a piece attacking the RSPB in the shooting press, to remind me of the issue and its stalemated, unresolved impasse. It was, I guess, an impasse wrapped in a stalemate, wrapped in a conundrum – a complicated and knotty problem that I wished would be solved but that, with the best will in the world, was beyond the wit of man to resolve (though perhaps more progress would have been made with fewer men and more women).

When I left the RSPB in April 2011 the fate of driven grouse shooting wasn't top of my agenda either, and a valedictory piece I wrote for the *Guardian* was mostly about farming, making no mention of Red Grouse or Hen Harriers. From late summer until the end of the year I was busy writing my book *Fighting for Birds*, which discussed the current state of nature conservation through the experiences of my 25 years at the RSPB. One chapter, which turned out to be a favourite of many readers, was named 'The raptor haters'. It dealt with raptor persecution, and in it I tried to spell out the options for nature conservationists to deal with driven grouse shooting. I suggested that one option would be simply to ignore the wildlife crimes committed by the grouse industry and let them get on with it while tackling more important or more tractable issues. The second option would be to carry on talking and discussing solutions, with diversionary feeding being a leading possibility, and the third, which I dubbed the nuclear option, would be to go for an all-out ban on driven grouse shooting by forming a coalition with anti-hunting organisations. As I re-read those passages I am taken back to when I wrote them, and I remember feeling torn at the time. Was it already time for the 'nuclear option'? Did the whole issue need a good shaking up in order to make progress? I was undecided, but from the way I wrote about the issue in *Fighting for Birds* you can tell, I think, that I was quite drawn by the nuclear option, but not yet ready fully to embrace it.

At the end of 2013 I looked back to the results of the Joint Raptor Study and took stock. The conflict whose biological basis had sharpened with the results of that study had simply deepened. The hope expressed in the foreword to the report of the work at Langholm, that people would work together, had been satisfied for a while but had come to nought. As time went on the evidence for raptor persecution had hardened and the impacts of that wildlife crime had increased. From the Hen Harrier's perspective things had got quite a lot worse.

But there had been other changes too – significant ones. The Langholm study was quite a big bit of science, and good science at that, but it was looking at a small part of what now seemed to be the full extent of the issue. Back in the 1990s it was perfectly possible to see driven grouse shooting as a problem simply because it put grouse shooters in conflict with the conservation of a few species of birds of prey. An important issue, one that fired me up personally, but hardly the biggest deal in the world. And that's why the RSPB alone, and no other wildlife NGO, was involved in the Langholm study and in campaigning on the issue of birds of prey being illegally killed. To many it seemed like a very bird-centric issue.

But over the years it became clear that intensive grouse-moor management was having many much wider impacts. First there was the impact on designated sites. Natural England had rattled some cages over the condition of SSSIs on grouse moors. Was heather burning good for all wildlife? It seemed not. Was heather burning compatible with maintaining blanket bogs that were a rare world resource, for which the UK had a significant responsibility? It seemed not. So, on wider nature conservation grounds it was becoming easier and easier to feel uncomfortable that so much of the British uplands were managed in this way.

Then there was the scale of legal killing. You don't have to be a vegan to feel a bit uncomfortable about a sport which is about killing things, and which depends on killing a lot of predators such as Foxes and crows before you even get on to the real business of killing Red Grouse. This is obviously a personal decision, but I had moved from not really thinking about killing animals as being a big issue to feeling a lot more sensitive to the view that it was a rather strange and mildly unpleasant 'sport' (I know that some reading this will raise a quizzical eyebrow at my use of the word 'mildly' there). The glorification of big bags in the shooting press and the shooting literature also made me feel much less tolerant towards grouse shooting as a whole, not just annoyed that 'they' kill 'our' Hen Harriers. My position had changed: I felt more against grouse shooting than I had previously been.

And then there were the wider environmental issues wrapped up in the term 'ecosystem services'. Through this period, our understanding of these grew considerably. If management of land for grouse shooting really did increase greenhouse gas emissions, increase water bills and increase flood risk, then it began to look even more like a case of private enjoyment for a few imposing public costs on too many people. That affronted my sense of social injustice.

That irritation grew because we taxpayers are all contributing large amounts of money to what goes on in the uplands through farm subsidies and payments for management for nature conservation. Were we really getting good value for money for our investment? These thoughts were running around in my head at a time when Natural England was making large numbers of staff redundant and the whole country was feeling the massive pinch of austerity, and yet I was giving my taxes to grouse-moor owners. Hang on a minute!

There was nothing particularly personal about my growing antagonism to driven grouse shooting. I have always got on rather well with most grouse-moor managers I've met. I guess we have tended to share the same educational background, laughed at the same jokes, read the same books, listened to the same music and used the same language. I cannot say that some of my best friends are grouse-moor owners, but I can say that on a personal level they have tended to be more my sort of preferred company than many of the people whose politics, for example, I more fully share. So, let's be straight about this, my growing disquiet with driven grouse shooting is not because I don't like toffs – because I *do* quite like toffs.

However, I have grown to dislike the way that the shooting industry conducts its advocacy. I just don't think they have been entirely honest and straight, and that gets a bit wearing and unpleasant after a while. I've noticed that this element of the 'debate' has really activated lots of others too. Many raptor workers have started from a position of neutrality or vague unease about grouse shooting and have then moved to a more 'anti' position as they have seen issues misrepresented and ignored. There is a danger that shooting is losing the respect of many of us because of the way its proponents behave; not simply that they shoot living things (although that is certainly enough for some people to make up their minds) but because the shooters too often appear to be hypocritical. A nastiness has crept in, possibly on both sides of the debate, but it is certainly there and it does nothing to endear one to the other's case.

Grouse shooting seemed to me to be an industry that was entrenched, perhaps because it felt beleaguered, and was prepared for a fight to maintain its position in society. Its proponents had backed themselves into a corner. If you sell your sport on the basis that it is natural and traditional, and people find out that it is anything but natural and causes ecological harm, then calling it 'traditional' just means that you have been doing the wrong thing for a long time. It seemed to me that a pastime that was based on the enjoyment of killing wildlife might be well advised to take a less bullying and more friendly approach to its critics and the ills that it knew it harboured in its midst. There was never any acknowledgement that grouse shooting should clean up its act, only a repetition of the 'just a few bad apples' excuse and a denial of the evidence when the truth was inconvenient. That's how it felt to me.

So I had moved, gradually, from a position which was largely 'live and let live' (with a desire for grouse shooting to clean up its act) because I thought that the only issues of harm were the killing of some marvellous protected birds of prey, to a harder position where I would be quite happy to see driven grouse shooting disappear from our hills.

I was convinced that the issue of driven grouse shooting did need a damn good shaking, although I was still wrestling in my head with whether a call for an all-out ban was a good idea or not. But it did seem to me that the issue needed more public exposure in order to increase the pressure on the criminals to mend their ways and give ground, or at least give Hen Harriers, and for better future management of our hills in return for the taxpayers' investment in them.

At a time when the evidence that driven grouse shooting caused considerable ecological, social and financial harm, as well as some good, the government in power seemed completely deaf to these issues. The Conservative-led coalition was just over halfway through its five-year term in power and had done precious little to address any of these issues – perhaps because many of the ministers in Defra had come, through the prime minister's choice, from the very community of people who were causing the problems. The government had been dismissive of Chrissie Harper's e-petition on vicarious liability and had shown its real colours by its pathetic handling of the Walshaw Moor case.

Natural England, once an environmental watchdog, was now more akin to a mistreated pet, muzzled, caged and neutered, and unloved by its Defra owner. There were real fears that in the early days of the coalition government Conservative ministers might move to a complete abolition of Natural England, and upland landowners contributed greatly to the clamour for that to happen. Gone were the days when, led by strong personalities such as Martin Doughty and Helen Phillips, Natural England would 'go in hard' on the issue of raptor persecution, and in came the days when Natural England's own rather moderate upland vision was, in what was seen by some as a craven act, repudiated by its own chairman, seemingly under pressure from upland landowners (and maybe from Defra itself).

The shooting industry, as represented by organisations such as the Countryside Alliance, the Game and Wildlife Conservation Trust, the British Association for Shooting and Conservation and the Moorland Association, was not giving an inch. It appeared that they were going to make the most of the fact that they felt that they had broad government support for grouse shooting (and how could they not think that?). Far from giving any ground, they were taking more and more against a weakened Natural England that was now little more than an arm of Defra.

In addition, the personalities had changed over the years. There were – and let's put this as politely as possible – fewer and fewer people in senior positions in the shooting organisations with whom nature conservationists and environmentalists could have a pleasant chat about life, the universe and everything after a robust conversation over Hen Harriers or heather burning. There were now two sides, and the grouse-shooting side was winning.

Grouse shooting is a vested interest. It's an industry that makes money and employs people. Under those circumstances it is easy to see that it will fight tooth and nail to maintain the status quo and to oppose any changes suggested by wider society that it finds inconvenient. And in this case there is no strong opposing vested interest. The victims of driven grouse shooting are dead Hen Harriers, dead Foxes, a slightly higher level of greenhouse gases in the atmosphere, less blanket bog, higher water bills for many people and an increased risk of flooding. The losers in this issue either don't have a voice, because they are plants and animals, or they might have a voice but are unaware that they are being disadvantaged, in the case of the general public. It's a classic case where the victims need to be heard, and that is often done via charities and other non-governmental organisations.

It seemed to me that the RSPB was the main voice questioning the legitimacy and value of grouse-moor management, and that it was trying to get its messages across with lots of other, arguably much more important, things on its plate, and in a political context that was not very receptive. Perhaps this was an area where a reasonably knowledgeable but independent campaigner could make a difference to the debate by being outspoken in a way that a wildlife charity finds difficult. I resolved to spend my spare time in 2014 trying to make a difference to the way that the uplands of Britain, particularly of England, are managed.

*

What I would like you to take away from this chapter:

- Between the end of the Joint Raptor Study in 1996 and the end of 2013 the gulf between grouse-shooting interests and nature conservationists widened. It was no longer simply a conflict about whether a few protected species should be sacrificed for a field sport. It had turned into a debate about whether the underlying management necessary for driven grouse shooting was harming the health and functioning of the uplands as a whole.
- The evidence for grouse-moor management having wider harm to other wildlife and to upland ecology in general grew and grew. Illegal persecution of birds of prey continued, heather burning was intersified, and the grouse-shooting industry adopted an ever more entrenched position.

CHAPTER FIVE

The beginning of the end – 2014

As Gandhi said: 'First they ignore you. Then they laugh at you. Then they fight you. And then you win.' We will win!

> Chris Packham, addressing the Hen Harrier Day
> rally on 10 August 2014

No year in the short history of driven grouse shooting has been remotely like 2014. This was the year in which things got a lot tougher for the men in tweed.

What follows is a personal account of the passage of 2014 as it relates to the future of grouse shooting, the conservation of Hen Harriers and the wider environmental impacts of grouse management. By the end of the year, the debate had shifted considerably.

1 January

In my first blog of the New Year I often set out a few things I intend to do over the coming 12 months. They tend to include 'See my first UK Duke of Burgundy butterfly', because that's something that always seems to pass me by, but this year, looking ahead to August, I write 'Help organise a peaceful protest over grouse shooting's role in the demise of Hen Harriers in England, attend Bird Fair, attend daughter's wedding.'

I'm sure that others will organise the Bird Fair and the wedding, but I have no idea of where, what or when will be the peaceful protest over Hen Harrier persecution. And I have no idea whether I will be able to make a difference in this way. But it's my way of committing myself to action – I've written it down and published it, and even if no one notices then I need to do it.

It feels a bit like jumping off a cliff and hoping to land safely. I can already feel the air whistling past my ears, but it's a long way down yet – plenty of time to build a parachute!

14 February

A new Twitter account, @birdersagainst, has appeared and the website of Birders Against Wildlife Crime (BAWC) is soon to follow. This is a bunch of birders, many of whom I know, who want to put wildlife crime, not just raptor persecution and not just birds, into sharper focus.

16 February

We are in north Norfolk on our wedding anniversary, and what could be more romantic than waiting, at dusk, to see whether we can see our 66th species of the day – a Hen Harrier.

Roydon Common is the largest remaining area of heather heathland and valley mire in Norfolk, and on a warm summer day it is a place to look for the rare Black Darter dragonfly and to listen at dusk for the churring song of Nightjars. But at dusk in February you have the chance to see Hen Harriers coming in to roost on the flat valley floor. We reckon the three blokes with binoculars are probably looking for Hen Harriers too, so we go and stand by them. We nod and smile but, because we are all British, no conversation breaks out. We have a warming cup of coffee from a thermos and nibble chocolate as we peer out into the gloom.

We have seen Hen Harriers here before but the three blokes give the impression of being locals, so it comes as no surprise that they spot a distant harrier first. It's a long way away but the long wings and tail, the light flight and the sharp white rump give no room for doubt. We have several sightings of what might be a single bird, or might be up to three. They arrive quite high, at around tree-top height, and then fly around over the broad valley bottom and its rushy vegetation for several minutes, presumably looking for safe places to settle on the ground.

19 February

John Armitage's e-petition calling for the licensing of sporting estates has passed 10,000 signatures a matter of a week before it is due to close. This means that the government will have to write a response to it, as it clearly has a degree of public support.

27 February

John Armitage's e-petition closes at 10,429 signatures. It is only the tenth of more than 1,000 e-petitions launched on the No. 10 website, and aimed at the work of Defra, to pass the 10,000-signature mark. John has worked hard, with help from a few friends, to get this e-petition over that line, and he ought to be proud of what he has done. We will have to wait and see the Defra response to the idea of licensing of grouse moors.

7 March

Today the RSPB issues a statement saying that 'burning, drainage and other forms of intensive land management in England's iconic peat-covered hills are threatening to create a series of environmental catastrophes.' Natural England's own figures show, according to information received by the RSPB, that:

> only around 10 per cent of our finest wildlife upland peatland sites are in good condition. An RSPB assessment of the scale of burning on England's upland peatlands has revealed at least 127 separate historic agreements or consents allowing burning of blanket bog on sites internationally important for birds and deep peatland habitats. The UK Government has confirmed all of those agreements are on areas managed for grouse shooting.

Mike Clarke, RSPB's chief executive, comments:

> England's uplands are some of our most iconic, extensive and important landscapes. Our assessment shows they could be among our most damaged too. For the benefit of wildlife, the environment and wider society there is an urgent need to restore these landscapes by blocking drains, re-vegetating bare peat and bringing an end to burning.

This represents the latest aftershock from the ever-rumbling-on Walshaw Moor case. The RSPB says it is

> not sure whether Walshaw represents a particularly intensive example or if it is typical of the historic agreements and consents

from Natural England for burning of blanket bog habitat that appear to be routine on grouse moors in English blanket bog SACs. Despite a presumption against burning on these sensitive habitats in the Government's own Code of Practice, it appears to have become the norm on grouse moors in England.

In other words, the Walshaw case might be the worst-case scenario, or it might not be, but it is only one of 127 cases where burning appears to be breaking the code agreed by government (admittedly a previous government), the Moorland Association and the National Gamekeepers' Organisation. That agreement seems to have gone up in smoke.

24 March

John Armitage's well-supported e-petition has received the following response from Defra:

> The Government is aware of incidences of illegal killing of birds of prey and Ministers take the issue very seriously. To address this, senior Government and enforcement officers in the UK identified raptor persecution as a national wildlife crime priority. Raptor persecution is subject to a prevention, intelligence, enforcement and reassurance plan led by a senior police officer through the Raptor Persecution Delivery group. The National Wildlife Crime Unit, which is funded by the Government, monitors and gathers intelligence on illegal activities affecting birds of prey and provides assistance to police forces when required.
>
> Shooting makes an important contribution to wildlife control and conservation, biodiversity and to the social, economic and environmental well-being of rural areas, where it can provide a supplement to incomes and jobs. The overall environmental and economic impact of gamebird shooting is therefore a positive one and it has been estimated by the industry that £250 million per year is spent on management activities that provide benefits for conservation.
>
> When carried out in accordance with the law, shooting for sport is a legitimate activity and our position is that people should be free to undertake lawful activities. There are no current plans to restrict sport shooting in England. This Government encourages

all shoot managers and owners to ensure they and their staff are following recommended guidelines and best practice to reduce the chances of a conflict of interest with birds of prey.

We acknowledge that crimes against birds of prey are abhorrent but it should be noted though that, despite instances of poisoning and killing of birds of prey, populations of many species, such as the peregrine falcon, red kite and buzzard have increased. While a small minority is prepared to kill birds of prey, and where possible these people are brought to justice, this demonstrates that the policies in place to conserve these species are working.

This is a response so lacking in logic and relevance to the original e-petition that it can only be seen as a brush-off rather than a thoughtful answer. It looks as though this government response was dictated by a group of arrogant grouse-moor owners. On what basis do Defra assert that 'the overall environmental and economic impact of gamebird shooting is therefore a positive one'? How can they ignore the plight of the Hen Harrier, which failed to breed successfully at all in England last summer, and instead state that 'this demonstrates that the policies in place to conserve these species are working'? That sentence could, with more honesty, have ended:

> ... but we recognise that the fact that around 300 pairs of Hen Harriers are missing from the English uplands, and that this is due to illegal persecution, shows that the policies in place for this species are not working. Furthermore, the low densities and breeding success of Peregrine Falcons nesting in areas dominated by driven grouse shooting also demonstrate that the policies in place to conserve this species are not working well enough. In fact, let's be honest, sites designated partly for their populations of birds of prey in upland England are drastically under-performing in acting as conservation measures. In fact, we the government are doing an awful job for nature.

2–3 April

I walk around Stanwick Lakes, near my home in Northamptonshire, first thing this morning and hear my first Willow Warbler of the year – it is rather late but nonetheless appreciated. Later the same day I hear my second Willow Warbler of the year at the RSPB nature reserve at Conwy in north Wales. I have a cup of tea with the site manager, Julian Hughes, who once worked with me at the RSPB headquarters, and then seek out two other former RSPB staff members, Alan Davies (Julian's predecessor at Conwy) and Ruth Miller.

Alan and Ruth are world record holders. What do you think the world record was? Ballroom dancing? Mixed doubles tennis? No, Alan and Ruth have seen more species of birds in a calendar year than anyone else on Earth – a story they tell in their book *The Biggest Twitch*. When they gave up their RSPB jobs they sold their house and spent the money on a round-the-world trip. Now they are settled back in the UK writing, talking, leading birding holidays and, sometimes, wishing they were in far-off lands seeing even more birds. But on this dull evening in north Wales, with rain forecast for the morrow, we drink wine and chat about birds and birders. It is really nice to meet up, but the point of my visit is to get some help from Alan and Ruth in locating a couple of Hen Harrier territories that I will be able to revisit through the year.

Given how difficult it is to predict how many Hen Harriers there might be in northern England, and where they might be, north Wales seems a better bet for a place to try to spend time with the birds. And in any case, much of the discussion about harriers and grouse-shooting centres on northern England and Scotland – Wales, as so often, tends to get ignored. I want to understand the Welsh situation better, as much as I want to see Hen Harriers in Wales.

We expected to wake to rain, but it is fine, if a little dull, when Alan and I set off into Snowdonia. We are going to visit two sites where Hen Harriers are regular, and I will call them the Lake Site and the Valley Site (which doesn't give much away in a land of lakes and valleys). En route we talk, and I realise that Alan belongs to the small group of people who are even more passionate about raptor persecution than I am. Fittingly, as we near the Lake Site, passing through a few small villages with very Welsh names, a Sparrowhawk and a Goshawk are in the air above us.

We park and walk up the track to the lake. It still isn't raining and there is plenty of bird song. We are high in the hills on unfenced moorland with heather all around us. The main songs we can hear are those of Skylarks and Meadow Pipits – Hen Harrier food – and there seem to be plenty of them.

Alan points out the hillside where Hen Harriers have nested in some recent years, and I wonder if I will be lucky enough to see food passes and visits to the nest on my subsequent visits. As we sit a Golden Plover sings, unseen, in the distance. It is the first that Alan has heard near here for years, as it is a species that has declined in numbers in Wales.

A Stonechat chats, adding its voice to all the Meadow Pipits. The birdsong is good to hear, and it feels as though spring is arriving even up here in the hills in early April. A Redshank is yelping by the lake shore and occasionally breaks into song. This is indeed spring, although on this visit it is a spring without any Hen Harriers.

As we sit on a small mound to get an all-round view an Otter surfaces close to us. We watch it dive and surface for a minute or so. A fantastic view. On each dive we can see its breath bubbling to the surface, and on its last dive we follow the bubbles as the Otter swims underwater for over 50 metres before surfacing and then disappearing. Back at the car, we eat Welsh cakes and drink coffee, look for early Wheatears but see Pied Wagtails instead, and congratulate ourselves on our Otter.

Heading to the Valley Site, we follow the oldest and slowest driver in Wales up the steep and winding road into the hills. We pass oak woods which will soon have Pied Flycatchers, Tree Pipits and Redstarts, and then enter a wide valley surrounded by impressive hills. At the end of the road we park, and Alan tells me that a pair of Hen Harriers has often nested close to here.

There are more Meadow Pipits and more Skylarks here, and more Stonechats – but fewer Otters, and the same number of Hen Harriers. At times like these, my mind starts to wander. I start thinking about other things and paying less attention to looking hard for birds. I am brought back to the reason we are here when Alan, who is made of much sterner birding material, says he has spotted an interesting raptor high above the distant hills. It takes a few seconds to get onto it as it is high and it is distant – but it is a high and distant Hen Harrier.

I keep the bird in sight as Alan tries to find it in the 'scope. I almost lose it as my first Swallow of the year flies past, distracting me, but I find it again and it drifts along the ridge; it seems to be heading out of our valley into whatever valley is on the other side of the hill (which might even qualify as a mountain). You always hope that if you keep watching the bird it will slam on the brakes, turn around and come and impress you with its aerial feats, so close that you don't need binoculars to enjoy the scene. But they rarely do, and this one doesn't – it just keeps going and disappears. But still, we have seen a Hen Harrier in the distance (and an Otter up close) and I now have two potential Hen Harrier sites to visit through the year.

5–7 May

This morning my blog, and that of Birders Against Wildlife Crime, announce that events are being planned for Hen Harrier Day, 10 August, in Derbyshire, Lancashire, Yorkshire, Cumbria and Northumberland. The North West Raptor Protection Group are organising the event in the Forest of Bowland and I will take on Derbyshire, with BAWC members setting up the other events. This gets a good reception, and now we have to get on with it. I'd better go to Derbyshire and have a look!

Later the same day, though, I set off for north Wales after 22:00. The plan is to arrive at about 02:00, sleep in the car at the Lake Site and then be awake bright and early for a Hen Harrier-filled dawn.

The journey is long and rather tiring, and there are more road works than are good for a fast journey, but I arrive on site, having seen a Barn Owl down in the valley, at around 02:30. Getting some sleep is easy, and I wake around 05:50 to see a Wheatear perched on the stone wall near the car. As I walk up the track there seem to be fewer Meadow Pipits and Skylarks singing, although there are plenty flying around the heather, but I hear several Red Grouse calling, which were not in evidence on my first visit with Alan.

At the Lake itself the Redshank are either gone or are quiet, but they have been replaced by noisy Common Sandpipers displaying and calling. I guess they haven't been here very long and they are making the most of a still sunny day while the

Redshanks are settled on their nests. There are Teal on the lake and Cuckoos singing in the distance. This seems to be a good year for Cuckoos – I am hearing them everywhere I go.

I lean against a stone building by the lake shore and scan the landscape for Hen Harriers. I give it a couple of hours and then decide it might be time for breakfast. As I walk back to the car I mull over what I know about the status of the Hen Harrier in Wales.

I remember years ago that grouse-moor managers used to say, 'What about Wales?' as a challenge to our view that Hen Harriers were rare because of persecution on grouse moors. The grouse moors in Wales were few and far between, and there hadn't been any driven grouse shooting in Wales for several decades, but Hen Harrier numbers weren't that high either. Our answer was that high persecution levels in England meant that few recruits got through to Wales, which limited the population size and acted as a brake on its increase. 'Wait and see,' we used to say, and having waited, we now saw an increasing Hen Harrier population. Numbers in Wales increased 33% between the last two Hen Harrier surveys (2004 and 2010) to 57 territorial pairs – around 15 times the number found in the whole of the (much larger) apparently suitable habitat in the north of England where grouse moor management is a much larger part of the upland scene. You couldn't get a much clearer demonstration of the malign impact on Hen Harriers of a landscape dominated by grouse shooting. In Wales, Hen Harriers are benefitting from the lack (or light levels) of keepering. Far from being an awkward counter-example, Wales shows exactly what would happen to Hen Harrier numbers if grouse shooting disappeared from the uplands of England.

Betws-y-Coed looks like the place to get breakfast, but a café near the railway station turns out to be not particularly cheap, not particularly friendly, and serving food that is not particularly warm. If only I had the local knowledge of Alan and Ruth to fall back on – but they are showing people birds on Anglesey today.

Before heading to the Valley Site I search a few roadside woods for oak wood birds. There are Redstarts everywhere. I am pleased to recognise their Robin-like song, as it isn't one that I hear often.

A Wood Warbler's song tumbles down through an oak wood that itself tumbles down the steep slopes of a valley side. This small trans-Saharan migrant, declining more than most other declining woodland species, fills the wood with beauty as it pours out its song, saying 'Come get me' to females and 'Stay away' to males. To me, it is the essence of Welshness on a spring day.

But welcome though they are, these birding bonuses are just that. I am hoping to see a Hen Harrier at the Valley Site – otherwise this visit is going to be a blank. The road up to the valley is noticeably different from the way it looked a month ago – more lambs, more leaves on the trees, more Redstarts on the fences and more Cuckoos in the valley itself. But fewer Hen Harriers. Not one, in the full three hours I spend there. Admittedly, I do spend about an hour of that time asleep in the car – it was a short night, after all – but I am disappointed by the blank. I wonder whether Alan would be spotting distant Hen Harriers every few minutes. Or perhaps, more embarrassingly, nearby Hen Harriers. It's difficult to know what you've missed, because you missed it.

But it is time to go. I need to be in the Peak District tonight in order to chat to some locals tomorrow about Hen Harrier Day and what we are going to do. I drive out of Wales and eventually through some back roads of the Peak District to Buxton.

The next day, I call in to Buxton police station and have a chat with the officer on the desk about what one has to do if planning to hold a public event. She gives me a form.

Later, I meet some people I hardly know in a pub near the A6 in Buxton for lunch. We talk about what we should do for Hen Harrier Day here in the Peak District. Should we hold an event in the national park itself, perhaps on or near a grouse moor, or should we go for something in the town of Buxton to reach out to far more normal people? We were all impressed by a rally held in Inverness town centre earlier in the year to protest at a mass-poisoning of Red Kites. Would an urban or rural event get more engagement, be easier to organise, have more impact, attract more publicity? The meeting is useful in terms of the options that are explored, but for me the most important thing is getting some moral support locally for the idea.

In the afternoon I head off to the Goyt Valley just outside Buxton to have a look at a former Hen Harrier site. When a pair of Hen Harriers was located on a grouse moor here in 1997, a round-the-clock watch was instigated to protect them. Three wardens were employed, and the birds raised three or four young from their five-egg clutch. Because of the nest location it was possible to set up a public viewing scheme and thousands saw the birds – the first Hen Harriers to nest successfully in Derbyshire since 1870. This was one of only eight successful nests in the whole of England that year, so the thousands who saw the birds, and enjoyed watching food passes between the busy parents, were seeing something quite special.

In 1998 a pair of Hen Harriers returned to the Goyt Valley, but there was no nesting. Local observers think that the returning birds were certainly disturbed, but they may also have been killed. In 2003 Hen Harriers returned again to the Goyt Valley but failed and, again, local observers felt that there was a strong possibility of human interference. As is apparent, it's often difficult to know why a pair of Hen Harriers has failed – and perhaps raptor workers are sometimes too eager to lay the blame on persecution in every case. However, it is clear that where a nest is found and guarded around the clock then it's very likely to do well unless the adults 'disappear' – which makes you wonder how many nests are found by others and dealt with.

The Goyt Valley is a potential site for an event on Hen Harrier Day, and that is another reason for looking at it. It has car parks, it has a history of Hen Harriers and it is close to Buxton. It is also rather pretty. It is on the list.

9 May

BBC Wildlife magazine has included an article about Hen Harriers and grouse shooting. This magazine is extremely nervous about saying anything controversial at all, but even so they have explored the issues surrounding raptor killing – after all, what can be controversial about asking people to stick to the law? I was asked for a 100-word quote, and I am a bit miffed to discover that it has been halved in length without me seeing it. If they had asked for 50 words I would have given them 50 words (just not the 50 words they have extracted from my 100 words). But these things happen.

These are the 100 words I submitted:

Without grouse-moor management our uplands would be different – and better. They would be more like Scandinavia with fewer Red Grouse but more Black Grouse. The blanket bogs would be in better condition and store more water (reducing flooding downstream) and carbon as peat. Too much of northern Britain is an industrially managed grouse-shooting factory where one economically important species is given priority over everything else, including protected raptors such as Hen Harriers. Funnily enough, elsewhere in the range of the Red (or Willow) Grouse, the Swedes, Russians and Canadians aren't planning to introduce grouse shooting to save their wildlife!

But the article has superb photographs of Hen Harriers, by Laurie Campbell. The Countryside Alliance's Tim Baynes is quoted along the lines of 'Grouse shooting is good for waders and good for the economy.' That seems to be the line that the grouse shooters are taking.

13–15 May

I have been invited to speak about Hen Harriers at an upland conference at Newton Rigg College near Penrith, Cumbria. The theme of the conference is balance in the uplands. Hen Harriers get a few mentions even before my talk, the last of the conference – and I certainly mention them.

In his talk, the chief executive of The British Association for Shooting and Conservation, Richard Ali, absolutely condemns illegal killing of birds of prey, including Hen Harriers. I ask Richard how many Hen Harriers BASC would like to see in the English uplands, given that scientific estimates suggest that there could be more than 250 and yet there were only two pairs last year. His answer: 250 pairs.

Richard also says that 47,000 people participate in shooting Red Grouse each year. That's quite a lot – enough to get Old Trafford about two-thirds full. That only leaves about 63,953,000 of us who don't participate in grouse shooting, then.

Another fact picked up from the conference is that there are 147 grouse moors in England. Since every grouse-moor owner I have ever met has said that his grouse moor could cope with a pair of Hen Harriers (but no more than one), then if only someone weren't bumping them off we would be halfway to Richard Ali's aim of having 250 pairs of Hen Harriers.

The director general of the National Trust (and former top mandarin at Defra) Dame Helen Ghosh gives a talk about the National Trust's High Peak vision. It is a polished performance. She sets out what the National Trust is planning to do in the context of its overall work in the uplands. She makes the point, and reiterates it in response to questions, that the NT exists to deliver its charitable objectives, not to be nice to its tenants (even though the NT obviously wouldn't want to be nasty to its tenants). NT exists to deliver a public benefit, and it is in that context that they will deliver their High Peak Vision.

The subject of 'rewilding' comes up – because the NT vision for the High Peak is a nod in that direction. I will touch on this subject too, the next day, in my talk. There is something to be said for 'rewilding' – certainly in contrast to the 'dewilding' of the uplands that goes on across grouse moors.

A more natural, less intensive land management may well have its place in the uplands of Britain. The argument would be that a more natural landscape might well deliver more public benefit than an intensively managed one. Will less grazing, less drainage and less predator control deliver a landscape with more carbon sequestration, better water quality, less flooding and a more diverse wildlife community? The answer might well be 'yes'. It's certainly worth investigating on a large scale in upland areas.

Landowners should expect to be paid for delivering these public benefits, instead of following more traditional economic activities in the uplands – like sheep farming. And we also hear from a sheep farmer, Neil Heseltine, who is a very good speaker.

Neil tells us that he is a sheep farmer from Malham in Yorkshire. He obviously loves his sheep. We see images of his sheep as lambs and as ewes, shorn and shaggy. We see them winning prizes at the local show. We get to know his sheep. Neil is a sheep farmer.

But when Neil tells us about the economics of his farm, things look a little different. The gross margin (to simplify – profit) on Neil's sheep enterprise is less than £500 a year. That's for all of his sheep – not per sheep. All that work, and all the love that goes into sheep produces only £500 income for Neil and his family.

Neil has some cattle, too. He obviously isn't quite as enraptured by cattle as he is by sheep. He tells us that the cattle mooch around the hills a bit, need a bit of help sometimes when calving, but basically just get on with it. The gross margin from the cattle mooching around is £11,500. But Neil is a sheep farmer. That's how he, cleverly, portrays himself in this talk, and that's where his heart is. Neil also mentions that grants and subsidies are a bigger earner for him than either sheep or cattle – and to me that means that upland farmers like Neil, and other upland landowners receiving similar important payments, are working for the taxpayer. They are working for you and me.

Another of the speakers, Robert Sullivan from estate agents Strutt and Parker, tells a similar tale for upland farming overall. His point, or at least the point I take away, is that profits on upland farming are low. It's not surprising, is it? Trying to grow anything at the top of a hill on poor soils is difficult. Robert also points out that there is a lot of variability in gross margins, which must partly be due to different circumstances of farm size, topography and location but is also due to a wide variety of skills and varying efficiency amongst farmers. The 'best' farmers are much better than the 'worst' farmers in turning a profit. That is, if they make any profit at all on farming.

For the truth is that many upland farms don't actually make any profit from farming. How do they survive, then? They survive because they receive income support from you and me through the Common Agricultural Policy and, if they choose, they get money by signing up to environmental schemes and are paid for trying to produce a better environment. Most of the income of a typical upland farm comes from payments from the taxpayer, not from producing food.

I'm totally happy with that. I like the idea of my taxes, and those of your taxes and those of everyone else, going to Neil and others to produce the type of upland that we want. I am struck by the amount of tweed in the room in Newton Rigg. Those of us who live in towns are paying for the activities that happen in the uplands through our purchases, and through being tourists, but to a very large extent through direct income support and environmental grants. Upland landowners, whether sheep farmers or grouse shooters, need to recognise that everyone has an interest in how the uplands look and what goes on in them, because everyone is paying for those activities.

In my talk I discuss some of these issues, arguing that we do indeed need balance (the theme of the conference) but that it is basically a balance that should take account of the fact that *everyone* is paying for the upland way of life, and so everyone should have a say in it. But when it comes to wildlife crime then it isn't a question of balance – it's a question of sticking to the law.

I pause once or twice to let this message sink in, and I survey the room, with its sprinkling of staff from BASC and the Moorland Association, and some trainee gamekeepers at the back of the room too. Some meet my gaze and others look away.

After my talk a BASC employee states that disturbance of Hen Harriers by birders is a problem, and a representative of the Moorland Association says that there has to be a compromise on the problem of Hen Harriers. Before I leave, an acquaintance tells me that my talk was 'brave', saying 'They won't have liked hearing that at all.' For a few days afterwards I receive emails from attendees saying that they couldn't give me more support on the day because they were scared to fall out with the large upland landowners represented in the room.

I head away from Newton Rigg with a feeling of some relief. It's a sunny day and I'm happy to be on my own again, but I am thinking of what needs to be done. I have been reminded of the intransigence of the shooting industry.

The Forest of Bowland has few trees – it's not that type of forest. As I enter the area I pause to look at one of the finest views in England: over Morecambe Bay, with the Lake District in the distance. It feels good to be alive on a sunny evening like this. I stop at the attractive bridge over the River Wyre and listen to a Redstart singing from the Alders, and I am surprised at the lack of a Dipper on what looks like a perfect stretch of river.

I stand on the bridge and think back over the last couple of days. There was not a hint of remorse from the grouse shooters, and no hint of contrition, nor suggestion that they would give an inch. It is an interestingly arrogant position to take.

Is it time for the nuclear option? Is it time for someone to launch a third e-petition on the subject of grouse shooting, and this time to go for a full-blown ban rather than better regulation? And should that person be me? We have learned from the e-petitions of Chrissie Harper and John Armitage that the subject is likely to attract quite a lot of support – enough to make people in the grouse industry and their friends in Defra sit up and take a little notice. But I think, successful though they were, we also learned that Chrissie's and John's e-petitions were a bit too complicated and didn't grab the attention. 'Ban driven grouse shooting' has a much catchier feel to it – but is it what I want to do?

This area, for many years, was the stronghold of the Hen Harrier on English moorland. Between 2002 and 2008 two-thirds of all the nesting attempts in the English uplands (83 out of 125, with two lowland nests in that period) were within a few miles of where I am now. Part of Bowland is owned by the utility company United Utilities, and they have managed the land with conservation rather than grouse shooting as a prominent consideration; much of the rest is owned by three shooting estates including that of the Duke of Westminster. Most (65 out of 83) of the nests were on the United Utilities land, although the birds also did well on the adjacent grouse moor. This year, as I cross the moor wondering whether to launch an e-petition to ban driven grouse shooting, two of England's four pairs of Hen Harriers are nesting on this great heathery expanse – although at the time I do not yet know that the survey results will show that there are two here, nor that there are just four in the whole of England.

I press on through a sunny spring evening, happy to be on my own with my thoughts. I drive over the imposing ridge of Pendle Hill and down into the area around Burnley. I am heading from Lancashire into Yorkshire, and Hebden Bridge is my intended target.

At Hebden Bridge I search for the Crown Inn in Crown Street, as it has a place in this story. The young man behind the bar checks me in to a room and takes my order for a steak and a pint of beer. The room is perfectly OK and the steak and beer are delicious. I look around the bar as I sup my second pint, and it is all in very good order and rather smarter and shinier than many pubs. That is because it has been completely refurbished after summer floods of a couple of years ago. On 22 June 2012 the beer cellars beneath my feet were filled with 3 metres of water and the room in which I sit was filled to a depth of 30 centimetres with dirty water that had poured off the hills above the town. Three weeks later, on 9 July, Hebden Bridge was flooded again. I hope to hear more about this tomorrow morning.

When I come down to breakfast other guests are helping themselves to cereals and fruit juice. Mostly they seem to be a group who are here for a business conference; they are dressed to impress and are talking about the presentations to come. Two northern ladies bustle about bringing food and drinks and spreading friendliness through the room. I ask if the landlady, Lesley Wood, is around and I'm told that she cooked my break-fast, and that she'll be available to spend a few moments chatting to me after breakfast.

I heard Lesley on the radio last year, talking about the impact on her business of the Hebden Bridge floods. At the time of the first flood Lesley had been away as her mother was ill, and she died on 23 June. I sympathised with how she must have felt, returning to her business after the death of her mother and finding it in chaos. A few weeks later Prince Charles visited the town; then the heavens opened again and the second flood occurred. This time Lesley was here. She tells me that she stood in the square just up the road and saw the water streaming down from the hills. The water was less than half a metre deep but was flowing fast through the streets, and people had to hold on to lampposts to keep their feet.

Lesley hadn't cried for a month after the death of her mother and the flooding of her business. There had been so much to do and she kept telling herself, 'At least I am insured', but it wasn't that simple.

The hotel was closed for six months and everything had to be stripped, a new floor laid and new walls built. Through this time Lesley was fighting with the insurance company, who made her feel as though the floods were her fault. In the end, she reckoned she got about 50% of what she should have received, and it took a long time to build up the business again. When she reopened in time for Christmas on 22 December 2012 business was slow. It took well over a year for it to get back to anything like it had been – Hebden Bridge had the label of a 'flood town', and people were nervous about staying there. Soon after the opening, it rained hard around New Year's Eve and Lesley had driven in to Halifax to buy sandbags just in case. Now the hotel was fitted with flood doors which could hold the water back for a while, but Lesley worried every time it rained – and it rains quite a lot in Yorkshire.

The Crown Inn was just one of hundreds of local businesses affected by the floods. Lesley had spent more than £100,000 on refurbishment and repairs; her business had been closed for six months and then had taken another 15 months to return to anything like normal levels. That's quite an economic impact for one small business, and Lesley's was a story replicated hundreds of times. Over 500 homes and businesses were affected, and on the night of 22 June alone West Yorkshire firefighters took 120 calls for help from the public. The total cost must have been at least £50 million.

On 22 June around a month's worth of rain fell in one day, and towns up and down the Calder Valley were affected. If it hadn't rained so much there would have been no flooding, but the more interesting question is – what led to the scale of flooding that happened? Clearly, if such floods were common-place, then no one would have built a town on the site of Hebden Bridge.

Some local people think they know the answer, and it is the increased intensity of the management of nearby grouse moors. The 'Ban the Burn' campaigners believe that the intensive burning of the grouse moor above the town, the Walshaw Moor estate, has led to faster run-off and lower water storage in the hills. Whatever rain falls stays for less time on the hills and gets into rivers and drainage systems much faster.

On Sunday 12 August 2012, less than two months after the floods, and on the traditional start of the grouse-shooting season (although, it being a Sunday, that would have to wait until the Monday), residents of Hebden Bridge and campaigners from across the country marched from the town centre on a Ban the Burn protest walk to the Walshaw Moor grouse-shooting estate. Dongria Kondh, one of the walkers, says:

> Here in Hebden Bridge we know the real hardship of flooding – shops and businesses in our town are still shut, and many of our friends and neighbours have suffered irreplaceable loss. In order to reduce our town's vulnerability to flooding, we need the upland catchment to be managed to promote healthy blanket bog, with sphagnum moss to act as a sponge in heavy rainfall events.
>
> It seems grotesque that the taxpayer is paying for the exact opposite – £2.5 million is about five times as much as is in the Calder Valley flood recovery fund! If Walshaw Moor wants public subsidies, it must use them for the public good and completely restore the blanket bogs on its estate.

Some don't agree with this. *Modern Gamekeeping* magazine referred to the Ban the Burn campaign as 'a rag-tag collection of around 50 campaigners' who claimed that traditional moorland management for grouse shooting results in 'very significant carbon emissions', 'adverse impacts on water quality' and 'the destruction of a globally significant habitat type'. *Modern Gamekeeping* quotes Simon Thorp, the director of the Heather Trust, thus:

> The tenuous link is made between grouse shooting, burning and flooding and this appears to be at the root of the campaign ... I have every sympathy with the residents of Hebden Bridge who have been flooded out, but I do not think that grouse shooting is the problem. The analogy of the uplands being a sponge is now seen as old hat; when the uplands are saturated with water, as happens in summers like this one, they will behave like saturated sponges and water will run off them. Fast.

Well, there are plenty of academics who seem to think that there is quite a lot of ecological common sense in that 'old hat', but we'll have to wait and see what the evidence shows.

Being so close, I have to go and have a look at the famous Walshaw Moor which sits high above Hebden Bridge in Bronte country – this is where *Wuthering Heights* was played out in the mind of Emily Bronte. I stop at the summit of the Keighley road out of Hebden Bridge, before it drops down to Oxenhope and Haworth and then carries on to Keighley itself, to survey the moorland. There are certainly plenty of Red Grouse, and the wind is chill. Or indeed, wuthering.

21 May

In the days after my trip north I was still wrestling with whether calling for an outright ban on driven grouse shooting was the right thing to do or not. My problem is that I am a wishy-washy liberal, and therefore I don't like banning things. I am always looking for a compromise that moves things to a better place. But in this case there seemed plenty of people on my side of the argument who might compromise, and nobody on the other side of the argument who was giving an inch. It felt to me that the grouse shooters knew this only too well. Hen Harrier numbers had been reduced almost to zero, and some of them behaved as though any increase on that number would be a great concession by their side – the criminal side – of the argument. This position combined immense arrogance with what I saw as a shameless version of moral blackmail – agree with us or the Hen Harrier gets it! Even though the Hen Harrier has *already* been getting it.

From the tactical point of view, calling for the banning of driven grouse shooting would be a good idea. It would create a more extreme position, as the Countryside Alliance had often done (but in the other direction), so that the compromise position would suddenly be shifted – and it would shift to somewhere close to where the RSPB had always been.

But the trouble with being a wishy-washy liberal is that I have this great desire to be fair. I keep vacillating. I drafted an e-petition on banning driven grouse shooting and showed it to a few people. And then I put it away and thought about it. Was it simply over the top to go for a total ban? Was it fair? Could I live with it, as my name would always be associated with that move afterwards, whatever happened?

And I worried a bit about whether it might fall flat on its face, in which case it would be a complete waste of time.

After a while I wrote this conversation to persuade myself that even a wishy-washy liberal should want to ban driven grouse shooting, and a version of this appeared on my blog later in the year, to help other wishy-washy liberals get things straight in their heads.

A: I don't like banning things.

B: Well, you say that, but it isn't really true, is it? Are you campaigning to relax the banning of murder in our society and instead try to persuade murderers not to be nasty to their victims? I doubt it. Are you wondering whether the abolition of slavery was a bad thing and hankering after a time when you could chat up slave-owners and show them the error of their ways instead of forcibly banning their practices? I doubt it. You see – you do like banning things, it's just that you're not sure about banning this thing. Have another look at the case against driven grouse shooting and then stop being wishy-washy and be decisive.

A: I don't mind banning things. It's just that grouse shooting doesn't seem important enough to ban.

B: How strange of you! It's partly because grouse shooting is a minor event in terms of the number of people involved, and because of its economically trivial value, that banning it is a no-brainer. All these things are a question of balance, and if grouse shooting really were important to lots of people, or economically, then we should pause much longer for thought, but a niche field sport that involves killing animals for pleasure is hardly in that category, is it?

A: OK, I don't mind banning things, and grouse shooting isn't very important, but it can't be that big a deal can it?

B: Well, at least you are getting to grips with the issue now! Thank you. I can't think of another industry which is so trivial in importance but whose impacts on wildlife are so huge – can you? Many species of protected birds of prey are either absent or at low densities on grouse moors, and nesting success is very low too. This is a countryside industry that harms the countryside. And then there is all the heather burning, access closures, water problems and so on to take into account. Look again at the issues involved and think about them, please.

A: OK, so I don't really mind banning things, and grouse shooting is hardly a human right, and it does cause a lot of harm, but can't we improve it and make it OK?

B: You really are wishy-washy, aren't you? There are several answers to this. First, there is a form of grouse shooting, walked-up grouse shooting, that doesn't have all the faults of driven grouse shooting, and those it does have it has in smaller quantities. This e-petition is explicitly aimed at driven grouse shooting because of its unacceptable impacts on soils, water, landscape, wildlife, etc. Second, the ills of driven grouse shooting are systemic – it's difficult to remove them without just getting rid of the land management system as a whole. That's a fault with the current Defra-'led' discussions on Hen Harriers – they are only seeking to address part of a bigger problem (and they aren't getting very far with that anyway).

A: OK, isn't there something a bit less draconian we could do?

B: I guess we could. We could introduce vicarious liability for wildlife crimes, but that would be a partial solution to one of the many problems, so it's hardly the answer – and anyway, government has ruled it out. Or we could argue for grouse-moor licensing, which might be a more embracing solution (though not by any means a complete one) – but government has ruled that out too. And in any case, we might find that banning driven grouse shooting has more public support than either of those wishy-washy measures did.

A: OK, so maybe I am up for banning grouse shooting because it is damaging, and maybe there isn't another way to do it, but shouldn't we talk to grouse shooters and see whether they have some ideas?

B: We've done that. We've done that in good faith but with increasing exasperation, for many, many years, in fact many decades, and it has got us nowhere. In fact, because we are wishy-washy liberals we have talked for far too long and been taken for a ride by the grouse-shooting industry. While we have talked, the plight of the Hen Harrier has worsened considerably, the amount of damaging burning of blanket bogs has increased and so has the environmental damage as a whole. The grouse-shooting industry has shown no sign of wanting to get its own house in order. Grouse shooting has known exactly how to deal with wishy-washy liberals like you and me – they kept us talking while they kept doing exactly what they wanted to do. There is no sign of good faith from them, and that persuades me that although talking was important and could have led to some sort of unsatisfactory compromise, further talking is useless. If we could find the answers by talking then we would have done so by now because we wishy-washy liberals are always keen to meet the other side halfway – but there has been no movement.

A: OK, but just a little bit more talking, perhaps? Actually, no. I know what you will say, Mark, and you are right. There comes a time when even the wishiest and washiest liberal has to make up their mind and take a stand. More talking won't help, other solutions have been explored, it isn't a big deal – let's ban it. After all, we aren't talking about a fundamental human right – other countries get by without having this strange British field sport. And the problems caused by grouse shooting are absolutely, firmly identifiable and can be attributed to that activity and no other. You are right, Mark. It's difficult to get out of the habit of being a wishy-washy liberal. But I'll sign your e-petition happily now.

B: Thank you! Can you please do it straight away, as I know you will wishily-washily change your mind again once you leave this place. I know – I vacillated for years over this subject.

25 May

I am travelling south from seeing my son in Edinburgh to my home in Northamptonshire. The A68 through Jedburgh and Otterburn really is one of my favourite roads in Britain. One travels through a variety of ground – forestry plantations, rather overgrazed sheepwalk, a lot of in-bye land and some moors that are burned for driven grouse shooting.

These land uses dominate the landscape of much of northern England and the patterns they form on our hills are a result of shifting economics, government policy, the decisions of individual landowners and chance. Each is an intensive land use with its adherents and proponents. None is the guardian of the 'natural' uplands of Britain. Each has made massive mistakes, and each has its list of good points and bad points. When you look out over the uplands of England you see an intensively managed landscape almost everywhere you look. Although we go to the hills to get away from it all, to flee the cities with their houses and traffic, to feel the wind on our faces and to commune with nature, we are not heading to the wilderness. There is no wilderness in England; everywhere is managed, and in the uplands much of it is mismanaged, even now.

I stand in the sun by the side of the road on the moors above Weardale. There is heather moorland all around and the landscape is scarred by the geometric patterns of years of heather burning for grouse. Now, the aesthetics of landscape are a funny matter – some will look out on these moors and see a glorious natural scene that is far in advance of the sheepwalk or forestry plantations but others will look at the patterns of burning and cutting of the heather and see a scene that is just as heavily touched by humankind.

What cannot be denied, though, is that this scene is rich in ground-nesting birds. Golden Plovers are singing in the distance and a Lapwing looks as though it probably has chicks nearby. Curlews bubble in the medium distance. This feels like a place where some wildlife is doing very well. I have seen the heads of Red Grouse poking out of the heather all the way across to this point, and as I step a little way off the road an adult Red Grouse flies up near my feet, followed by a brood of small chicks exploding in every direction and flying a short distance and then tumbling and running off to seek more cover.

This place is a hot-spot for ground-nesting birds today – and this, for a birdwatcher who has set his face against driven grouse shooting because of the toll of illegal killing, is one of the inconvenient truths. These moors are rich in ground-nesting birds in a way that is hardly matched on the British mainland; only on a few nature reserves in southern England – such as the Elmley Marshes nature reserve managed by Philip Merricks and the RSPB reserves at the Ouse Washes and the Nene Washes – can I recall such densities of waders. But those nature reserves are places where nature is given priority, rather than where a land-use system enables ground-nesting birds to flourish, and so the comparison is a little unfair.

Standing here in sunny Weardale, with the sounds and sights of waders, is a challenge for someone who is pondering whether the land use that allows these species to be present should be opposed. Is the lack of Hen Harriers a price we should pay for the presence of breeding waders? It's a fair question, because these are two sides of the same coin. They are both

consequences of the same land-use system, which removes predators, legally and illegally, in order to provide shooting days to
enthusiasts and paying clients. The proponents of driven grouse
shooting push the wader numbers for all they are worth, as they
know that this is a telling argument for many of us. I don't blame
them – for it is a telling argument, and it is one of the few at their
disposal.

However, I remember reading an article about the grouse
moors of Michael Stone in Weardale (I might be looking at his
land at this very moment) and nearby Eggleston, in which he
said that his gamekeepers killed 600 Stoats a year on those two
moors. That's a huge toll year after year. If there were a pile of
the 600 Stoats killed at Weardale by the side of the road where I
stood then I think I would feel very differently about the
bubbling sound of the Curlew I can hear. What would a pile of
600 dead Stoats look like? And then there are the Red Foxes and
the Weasels and the Carrion Crows too, all of them killed legally
(provided that legal methods are used). Whilst there is no
suggestion that illegal methods are used on Michael Stone's
grouse moors, it is clear that on some shooting estates there is
considerable illegal killing as well, not just of birds of prey but
of Badgers, Hedgehogs and who knows what else.

This aspect of the necessary management for driven grouse
shooting is not promoted by the shooting lobby – they prefer to
talk about the natural aspects of wild game – but uncompromising and determined predator control is needed to bump up
numbers of Red Grouse to levels where bags are high and profits
are generated to match.

28 May

Today my e-petition is published, worded as follows:

Ban driven grouse shooting

Responsible department: Department for Environment, Food and
Rural Affairs

Intensive management of upland areas for the 'sport' of
grouse shooting has led to the near-extinction of the protected
Hen Harrier in England, as well as increased risk of flooding,
discoloration of drinking water, degradation of peatbogs and
impacts on other wildlife.

Grouse shooting interests have persecuted the Hen Harrier to such an extent that, despite full legal protection for the last 60 years, it is almost extinct as a breeding species in England (2 pairs nested in 2013) despite there being habitat available for 300+ pairs. The investigation of wildlife crimes against such protected species is time-consuming, difficult to prosecute, and ties up valuable police resources.

Grouse shooters have failed to put their own house in order, despite decades of discussion, and government has proved incapable of influencing this powerful lobby group.

The time has now come for the public to call 'Enough!' and require the next government to ban driven grouse shooting in England.

3–5 June

Another 'drive overnight and sleep in the car' visit to Wales. I wake around 5 a.m. and walk up to the Lake Site. It is a very clear day this time – the distant mountains are more obvious than I have seen them before. I am only beginning to get to know these two areas of north Wales, but their charm is winning me over. I like having an excuse for visiting these sites, but it does occur to me that my strike-rate of Hen Harrier sightings isn't very high – one sighting (which I wouldn't have made if Alan hadn't been with me) on two visits to the two sites. I'll start thinking it's a bit of a waste of effort if I don't see anything this time either.

It is very obvious that although most of us would call the first week of June still a part of spring, as far as moorland birds are concerned the breeding season is coming to an end. As I reach the lake I notice that its surface is covered with mist. There are no waders singing or calling, and the Meadow Pipits and Skylarks are rather quiet, too. A pair of Swallows is taking food into the building against which I leant last time and my presence would disturb them, so I find another vantage point on a ledge of stone near the lake shore and settle down to look for Hen Harriers.

The hill in the far distance is a little misty. I see a pattern of light rocks on the hill that I haven't spotted before, and I try to turn them into an image in my mind – and can't manage it.

There are several drake Teal on the lake, which suggests that there might be quite a few females sitting on clutches of eggs nearby. I hope for Otters, but a watched lake never otters – as they say.

The mist is fading as the sun grows stronger. I look at the pattern of rocks again and it seems slightly different but I still can't make it turn into an image of any note. I can just about see the stone wall near where the Hen Harriers have nested in the past but I don't hold out much hope that they are there this year, as the previous visits have been blank ones. Still, it is a lovely spot to sit and think and watch the natural world go by.

I rather wish I had some chocolate to eat but I don't, and my mind turns to the Kit-Kat advert of the 1980s where a photographer is waiting at a zoo to photograph Giant Pandas: when he turns his back to eat some chocolate the Pandas emerge, dance around very photogenically and then head back into their refuge just as he finishes his break and starts looking again. In this frame of mind I might not be at my sharpest to see a Hen Harrier if one appears.

And I get to thinking whether there might be a male Hen Harrier skydancing behind me right now while I am looking the wrong way. What a silly idea! But one that grows on me. I resist the impulse to stand up and look round behind me because it's just silly. But nobody would know, would they?

So I stand up, look round and see a grey shape in the distance. There was the occasional Common Gull over there earlier in the morning, but as I raise my binoculars to my eyes, and although the bird is very distant, I know it will be a male Hen Harrier – and it is.

It is a brief view, but a wonderful bird. It flies from left to right low over the hillside; for a second it almost stalls as though looking for something amongst the heather and then it continues across the track up which I had walked and disappears into dead ground. I guess it is going to hunt over a small wet flush just around the corner of the track so I walk back to see, but the Hen Harrier has gone. Barely ten seconds in view but it has made all the waiting and watching worthwhile. Every day I see a Hen Harrier is a good day.

I head back to the lake in case the male is just about to drop off some food at a nest on the far hillside, but there is no sign of him for the next hour. The mist clears and the constellation of stones resolves itself into a small flock of sheep.

I drive to a roadside café on the A5 and have a celebratory fry-up for breakfast. It is 4 June 2014. On 4 June 1954 the Churchill government had enacted the Protection of Birds Act, which gave full legal protection to almost all wild birds, their nests and eggs. *Almost* all, because 'game' were excluded from the all-round protection and because some species of 'vermin' (although the Act does not use that term) were exempted, too.

The Protection of Birds Act was a rare example of a private member's bill becoming an Act of Parliament. Each parliament, there is a ballot of all backbench MPs, and those at the top of the ballot can introduce a bill that stands a chance of becoming law. Very few such bills ever do make it that far, but even so they can be a very useful way for an individual MP to raise an issue, potentially to get government support, and for the bill to become an Act of Parliament. In 1954 it was Lady Tweedsmuir, the Conservative MP for Aberdeen South, who guided the passage of what became the Protection of Birds Act, which received royal assent exactly 60 years before I saw 'my' Hen Harrier in north Wales and settled down to a celebratory breakfast.

It is well worth reading the debates in Hansard that led up to the Protection of Birds Act – it is like travelling back in time to a different age, with a much higher standard of politeness and knowledge than I would expect in a similar debate in parliament these days. MPs of all parties discussed the pros and cons of protecting all birds' eggs from collection, and the government was initially determined that making all egg-collecting illegal would reduce the chance that young people (mostly boys) would gain an interest in birds and natural history. They had a point, and who knows, maybe I would have thought the same if I had been involved back then, but nowadays you would get short shrift if proposing the re-legalisation of egg-collecting as a way of providing kids with an appropriate entry point into natural history. It's a good example of how changes that are opposed but eventually come to pass are rarely reversed in the future. We don't have a campaign to remove the vote from women, to reintroduce slavery or to resume sticking kids up chimneys to clean them, and – I mention this just in passing – once driven grouse shooting is banned there will be no reversing that radical shift, because future generations will regard its absence as the norm. We British are a very conservative bunch. We don't like change, but when we get it, we rarely opt to switch things back again.

There are probably only one or two more pairs of Hen Harrier in England now than when that Act of Parliament protected them. Is that really progress? I don't think so.

I visit the Valley Site a bit later in the day, but with no luck there (or maybe it is lack of skill, not luck), and since Alan and Ruth are now in Finland watching Steller's Eiders (and Julian is unavailable for tea) I post a few postcards of Welsh sheep to friends and drive along the north Wales coast. I am heading back to the Peak District, but I have an invitation to tea in Cheshire first.

I can't actually remember how I first came across Findlay Wilde, but I first met him and his family at the Bird Fair at Rutland Water in 2013. Findlay writes a blog, is a bird ringer and is a highly articulate advocate for nature. He has written a couple of guest blogs on my site. Oh yes, and he's 12 years of age (or he was on this day when I invited myself to his house for tea with the family). We eat pizza and chat about birds and the plans for Hen Harrier Day. As I keep telling people, nothing is planned yet – there are two months to go!

Findlay tells me he is planning to build a scarecrow for a village competition – and his is going to be a giant Hen Harrier. I wish him well but wonder what is going to come of this as I head back to Buxton for another night.

The next morning, before meeting some more locals for lunch in another pub near the A6, I visit the Derwent Valley, in the Dark Peak, part of the scene described in the RSPB 'Peak Malpractice' reports. The Derwent Valley is definitely a potential site for a rally for Hen Harrier Day. Standing in the large car park of the Fairholmes Visitor Centre, with its snack bar and toilets, it seems a good bet. I walk around and come to the open grassy space at the foot of the Derwent Dam. There are a few people walking across it, and I imagine that on a weekend in August with the sun beating down there might be quite a few people. How many people will turn up for a rally in support of a bird of prey that they hardly ever see?

And it's not a bird that is seen very often in this valley, the scene of too much raptor persecution. In 2006, a pair of Hen Harriers settled to nest in Stainery Clough, just in South Yorkshire but above this valley, and another pair nested in Barrow Clough on the Derbyshire side of the border. Full-time wardens and scores of volunteers were drafted in to guard the nests, just as had happened in the Goyt Valley in 1997. The nests were fine but both the males disappeared. The volunteers swung into action and provisioned both nests, each of which fledged five young from a clutch of six. One of these young was tagged and followed to the Yorkshire Dales, where it bred in 2007. In 2008, in Upper Derwentdale, a pair of Hen Harriers was present and the female went missing. Then another female appeared and paired up with the male, and then she went missing. Adult Hen Harriers rarely disappear from their nests away from grouse moors, and yet that is often their fate near grouse moors in Derbyshire. So this site seemed fitting, nestling as it did in the Peak District National Park and in an area where dark deeds had been done to Hen Harriers and other raptors.

That's what I was thinking, and that's what my two local friends confirmed at lunch time. The Derwent Valley had always been a prime contender for the site of the rally, and that's how things seemed to be moving, too.

10 June

I have received a helpful email from the chief executive of the Peak District National Park, Jim Dixon, who used to work for me in the RSPB, and whose letter sets out potential sites that we should consider for our protest rally and some contact details in the police, Severn Trent Water, the National Trust and the national park itself. Top of the list is the Fairholmes Visitor Centre, so we all seem to be thinking along the same lines. This is a great help.

Jim has also helpfully set out the national park's own policy on its own land within the national park:

Peak District National Park Management Plan 2012

There are a variety of sports based on wildlife, traditionally called 'field sports' or 'country sports'. These include shooting, hunting and fishing as well as falconry. Well managed field sports are an important part of land based economy, as they retain traditional land management skills, provide important employment and have the potential to manage land in ways sympathetic to national park purposes. A particular focus should be on encouraging more sustainable forms of game and land management, for example, on moorlands, grouse habitat management practices which sustain a broad spectrum of birdlife, and pheasant shoots which do not adversely impact on native woodland. Encouragement should be given to fisheries where river habitats are managed for self-sustaining populations of native fish such as brown trout, and where artificial stocking is avoided.

I reply to Jim, thanking him, and saying that the Fairholmes Visitor Centre seems the best option and that I will be in touch with Severn Water about the arrangements.

13 June

Another email from Jim Dixon tells me that he thinks Severn Trent have some misgivings about the event and I should hold off announcing where the rally might be held. So I do. Conversations with Severn Trent are slightly tense – I don't feel that they are that welcoming of the idea that lots of nature conservationists are going to visit their visitor centre, but I'm sure they'll come round in the end.

23 June

My blog announces that (provisionally, as discussions are still under way) the site and time of our Hen Harrier rally will be the patch of grass in front of the Derwent Dam at 10 a.m. on 10 August. The exciting additional piece of news is that Chris Packham will be attending to show his disgust at the plight of the Hen Harrier.

I was in touch with Chris weeks ago on the off-chance that he was in the country and free on the day, and that he might

give his support to a rally. He and I have talked about Hen
Harriers many times, and most recently at a Hampshire
Ornithological Society meeting at which we were both
speaking. But I hadn't heard anything from Chris until recently,
and he had explained that he was clearing his involvement with
the BBC, who employ him now and again to present TV
nature programmes. But I have just had a very enthusiastic
email from Chris – he is on board. I know that this will give the
day a huge boost, but it also increases the pressure on me to
fix things with Severn Trent Water, who are still playing hard to get.

And it is beginning to look as though the plans for Hen
Harrier Day events in Yorkshire and Cumbria might not come
to fruition – so the pressure is mounting on the three remaining
events in Derbyshire, Lancashire and Northumberland to
deliver.

25 June

My blog breaks the news that Simon Barnes is leaving *The Times*
newspaper. Simon is the paper's chief sports writer and also
writes two columns a week on natural history. He has been
outspoken about the plight of Hen Harriers many times in his
column, but then he has been outspoken about other things too,
and that has been one of the reasons why many of us would
glance at *The Times* now and again.

I do wonder if Simon's stand against illegal persecution of
raptors over the years might have upset some people, and I
notice on Twitter, and elsewhere, that others wonder the same.
If you are a criminal (if you instruct your gamekeepers to kill
protected wildlife on your grouse moor) then the last thing you
want is to read about your crimes in your favourite newspaper
over breakfast. If you are rich and powerful and have contacts,
you might be inclined to 'have a word'. Far-fetched? I decide to
contact Simon and ask him what he thinks.

This is his email reply (probably sent from Wimbledon!):

> I wondered about that myself, but I have no idea how these things
> are decided. Their line to me was that they were selling their
> top striker because they could no longer afford his wages. I was

pretty shocked, though I was aware that a decent salary makes you vulnerable. I've been writing for *The Times* since 1982, and I'm sorry it had to end like this. I've been able to work on some great stories – elephant corridors in India and London 2012, the Peak District and Wimbledon 2013. I'm making rather a point of not looking backwards right now, so I'm trying not to speculate on why I left.

So there you go – it was bad news for sports lovers and nature lovers, and not great news for a great writer either. My contacts in the press were very surprised that it had happened. None of us, including Simon, was sure why he had lost his job.

26 June

The RSPB calls for licensing of driven grouse shooting. On Martin Harper's blog the case is set out as follows:

Driven grouse moors are the most intensive form of game management and the trend from some has been to increase the shootable surplus of birds: burning on peat or non-peat soils, medicated grit, and both legal and, still, some illegal predator control. Hen Harriers are for some grouse-moor owners their least-loved bird.

Given the near-eradication of the species as a breeding bird in England and the intensity of the management of our uplands we cannot accept the status quo.

The RSPB is 125 years old this year. It spent much of its first fifty years campaigning for law reform to prevent the wanton destruction of wild birds. Today, we think more reform is urgently needed.

We need and expect the grouse shooting community to change: the industry must demonstrate they can operate in harmony with birds of prey and help to restore the environmental quality of our hills.

So, today, we have written to the organisation representing the moorland owners of England explaining why we believe it is time to regulate the industry. A copy of the letter is shown below.

We shall also be writing to the major political parties to urge them to introduce a robust licensing system to govern driven grouse moor management after the election.

... and ...

No other country in Europe has such lax laws governing hunting with no control on quotas or intensity of management. Illegal killing of birds of prey, including Peregrine Falcons and Goshawks, continues and our upland environment remains in a parlous state: just 10% of the 162,000 hectares of blanket bog designated as SSSI are in favourable condition, and inappropriate management leads to water contamination and increase in greenhouse gas emissions. This was the context for our formal complaint to the European Commission to protect Walshaw Moor, part of the South Pennines Moor SAC, SPA and SSSI. We took this unprecedented step to stop inappropriate burning on degraded blanket bog, which is preventing it from being restored, as required under EU law. We wouldn't have to take this action if our uplands were being managed properly.

If birds of prey populations were flourishing and if our uplands were in better condition, perhaps there would be no need for a licensing system to guarantee standards. But that is not the case in England, which is why we need a licensing system to govern grouse-moor management to deliver environmental outcomes. This would complement other proposals such as the introduction of an offence of vicarious liability for illegal killing of birds of prey (to match the system in place in Scotland), and greater efforts to restore our peatlands.

The growing concern about Hen Harriers in England has also seen birdwatchers unite to dedicate 10 August as Hen Harrier Day with a series of rallies being organised across northern England. We will be supporting the day offering ways for people to get involved and we will be emailing our supporters with more information about how they can support Hen Harrier Day during July. We want people to unite to call for the end of persecution of this extraordinary bird.

This represents a ratcheting up of the pressure on grouse shooting in the run-up to the general election.

27 June

Ethical Consumer magazine features a campaign 'against greed and intensification on England's grouse-shooting estates', calling for a consumer boycott of businesses connected to grouse shooting:

> From pubs and hotels promoting themselves to the industry, to shops and restaurants selling grouse, there are a wide range of businesses to be potentially avoided. Don't forget to write/email the companies involved to let them know what you are doing and why. And share your knowledge of company connections with others via our TurnYourBackOnGrouse forum and other social media channels.

4 July

I publish an open letter on my blog to the chief executive of Marks and Spencer:

> Dear Marc Bolland,
>
> Last year you came under some pressure because of the stance of M&S on selling Red Grouse meat in your London stores. We are approaching the Inglorious Twelfth again – how time flies! – and I am writing to ask you to be more open and informative to your customers this year. I would ask you not to sell Red Grouse as it comes from an industry that reeks of criminality.
>
> With a couple of accidental lapses, I have boycotted your stores for the last year. This is more of a pain for me than it is for you as I am just one customer but I am just the type of person who likes M&S, who wants to spend their money with M&S and who would choose M&S in preference to other stores where I now shop.
>
> However, I think others may join me this year as *Ethical Consumer* magazine's very recent report on the problems with grouse shooting suggests a boycott of companies associated with grouse shooting. Because of your high-profile stance on this issue last year you are in the firing line.
>
> I should let you know that as well as the *Ethical Consumer* report this year there will be events across the north of England where people protest against the criminal killing of protected wildlife

by too many of those associated with grouse shooting. These are organised for 10 August. Why don't you come to the event on 10 August in the Peak District and talk to some of your customers, and to Chris Packham, who is supporting the event?

Also, feelings are so high that recently an e-petition was launched on the government website calling for grouse shooting to be banned in England. It is already in the top 2% of such e-petitions and has only been up and running for a matter of five weeks.

Selling grouse meat is a trivial part of your business. You will need scores of people to buy grouse from you to replace just the lost profits from my purchases with you through the year. If you persist with selling grouse meat, it sends a clear signal that you actively want to support this industry and are siding with an industry that causes environmental damage and is intimately associated with wildlife crime.

Please let me know what you intend to do on this matter.

I wonder whether this letter will have any effect, as I drive between the Peak District and north Wales. I've spent some time in the Peak District meeting a few locals, who are now becoming good friends, and I have had another look at the Fairholmes site where we plan to hold our Hen Harrier Day rally in little over a month's time.

On my way to meeting Alan and Ruth I have a quick look at the Valley Site, but by now it is raining heavily and there is little chance of Hen Harriers being very active. Later, we chat about being freelance, put the RSPB to rights, gossip, catch up on birds seen since we last met (lots by them, few by me), enthuse about Hen Harriers and eat a very good curry. Early the next morning I slip out of the house and drive to the Lake Site for one last look. I'm lucky, as the forecast is for rain and yet it is quite a sunny early morning.

This is my fourth visit to this site and I've grown to like it a lot. This time the Meadow Pipits keep a low profile and I think back to their songs in April and May. There's not a Stonechat to be seen and no waders are calling. It's a short season up in the hills and we are coming to the end of it. The nearest Hen Harrier nest is likely still to have chicks and so I still have a chance of seeing a bird. I keep an eye on the far hillside, as that is where I imagine I might see them, and I throw an occasional glance down the track to the area where I saw the grey male a month ago. But I am enjoying the fine early morning and being in the hills.

There are several drake Teal on the lake, and a Cormorant and a solitary Great Black-backed Gull. Every ripple on the water surface makes me wonder whether an Otter is about to appear but none does. Instead, a ringtail Hen Harrier flies past, down the eastern side of the lake, over the heather and behind a hummock. She emerges again further away and I watch her hunt for a few moments before she disappears from view. Another short sighting, but another treat. And I think again of the fact that there are more than 50 pairs of Hen Harrier in these Welsh hills and fewer than a tenth of that number in the whole of England.

11 July

Tim Birch, the conservation manager of the Derbyshire Wildlife Trust, writes a guest blog for my website. Here are a few quotes:

> It's clear to me now why, as a teenager in the Peak District, I was never lucky enough to spot Hen Harriers skydancing on the moors – because they were and continue to be relentlessly persecuted by people who won't tolerate these magnificent birds on their grouse moors.
>
> Indeed, as I've discovered, the situation is actually far worse and extends far beyond the Derbyshire moors. It's not just Hen Harriers that have been relentlessly pursued but other birds of prey including Peregrines and Goshawks.
>
> Let's not forget that these birds are legally protected and all this is happening within a National Park in a highly developed country – the UK – not the lawless Amazon frontier but right here, right now in one of our most spectacular landscapes in the heart of England.

… and …

> I've met with many members of the public recently in the uplands of the Peak District National Park in the course of my work and when you explain that protected birds of prey aren't able to breed in a national park due to persecution every response is one of incredulity. How can that be happening in a national park

they say? Aren't national parks supposed to protect our precious wildlife?

… and …

I now sense a growing movement of people who want to strengthen our links with the natural world and restore it – not destroy it. This is why I and the Derbyshire Wildlife Trust will be supporting the Hen Harrier Day on August 10th in the Peak District.

   We gained the right to access our uplands with the mass trespasses of the early twentieth century in the Peak District – we led the way in this part of the UK. Now we need a mass movement of people to show the way again and reclaim our natural heritage on these uplands. Our Hen Harriers and other upland wildlife desperately need our help. I hope to see many of you there.

This is great local support for a national event.

12 July

Findlay Wilde's Hen Harrier scarecrow, named Harry, wins the local competition. I'm not surprised – Harry is quite a beast, and Findlay is quite a boy! He is donating the £85 prize to the Skydancer project and the thought is that Harry will be attending Hen Harrier Day in a month's time.

19–20 July

The Game Fair is a fascinating event. Each year it is held in the grounds of a major country house, and it covers a huge area with tents and marquees spread across the land like the encampment of an enormous army. The sound of gunfire is actually present as experts and amateurs compete in clay-pigeon shoots. Silently, fly fishermen present their flies to fish with experts miked up to commentate on the action. You can come away having eaten well, bought a hunting safari in Africa, seen a cookery demonstration, watched well-trained dogs perform and badly trained dogs embarrass their owners, and have encountered a wide choice of locations from which to buy a bacon sandwich.

You will see a lot of tweed, from that encasing red-faced gamekeepers sweltering in the sun, to mini-skirted young ladies working for expensive land agents or shooting agent firms, to the country set meeting their mates.

All the shooting- and fishing-related organisations are present for the three days and it's a good place to meet people by design and by accident. The RSPB has long had a stand at the event, and I have attended scores of Game Fair days over the years. For the RSPB it was an opportunity to show one's face, recruit new members and put one's point across. There was always something to talk about. Generally the reception of the RSPB, not an anti-shooting organisation (though sometimes perceived as the enemy), was positive. There were some lively discussions and very few nasty moments over the years. Borderline was one case when a young female RSPB staff member was told that she was a 'hard-faced bitch' by an irate 'gentleman', but she has worn that insult with pride ever since. Over the line was the year when a man pointed a shotgun directly at the face of a rather mild-mannered RSPB staff member and told him that this was what he'd like to do to 'you all'. Generally, the days were pleasant and the weather, sometimes torrential rain, sometimes baking sun, was a greater determinant of staff morale than the reception by other Game Fair attendees.

This year the Game Fair is being held in the grounds of Blenheim Palace, in the prime minister's constituency. I can't make the first day, the Friday, but I spend Saturday and Sunday looking around and having a few chats.

One of the things being discussed is an e-petition just launched by the Game and Wildlife Conservation Trust's director of fundraising, Andrew Gilruth, which calls on Defra to publish the report of the Hen Harrier Sub-group of the Uplands Forum. This e-petition suggests that there is a plan already written that should be published because it will help the conservation of Hen Harriers. Here is what it says:

Hen Harrier Joint Recovery Plan – publish it

Responsible department: Department for Environment, Food and Rural Affairs

There are thousands of square miles of suitable habitat, but very few breeding pairs of Hen Harriers in England. If the remaining chicks die, the Hen Harrier will effectively be extinct as a breeding species in England. Defra said it would stop extinctions like this.

In August 2012 Defra asked moor owners, gamekeepers and conservation groups, including the RSPB, to work together and write a single plan to restore England's precious Hen Harrier. They reviewed the evidence and scientific literature to prepare their joint plan. Since January 2014 Defra could have published the plan; but has not.

For the sake of the Hen Harrier, Defra must resist external pressure to meddle with the plan. England's Hen Harrier population is too fragile to wait any longer.

You have it in your gift to save the English Hen Harrier and return it across our skies. Do it.

Be brave and publish the Hen Harrier recovery plan today – the clock is ticking.

It is written as though there is nothing that the GWCT wants more in the world than to see lots of Hen Harriers flying over their members' grouse moors. The real position is that there is a big fight going on behind the scenes in the working group. The grouse shooters want to be able to manipulate the nests of any Hen Harriers nesting on their grouse moors. Having been in this game for many years I see this as no more than the current manifestation of a series of calls to be able to kill Hen Harriers, limit their breeding success or ship them away altogether and release them somewhere far away from grouse moors. All of these proposals are for the benefit of grouse shooters and not for Hen Harriers.

The current version of these ideas is a 'brood management' project (which is labelled as 'brood meddling' by some witty opponents on Twitter) in which the young of any Hen Harrier nests on grouse moors are removed, reared in captivity and then released. This has the same impact for the grouse-moor owner as killing the Hen Harrier chicks, because they do not need to be fed on his grouse, but it is done with an air of respectability under the pretence of a conservation project and therefore will be hyped up by shooting interests as a great compromise. It doesn't do very much for the Hen Harrier.

As I understand it from the snippets of information that leak out of the sub-group from all of the organisations involved, including Defra, the RSPB isn't totally against this idea but would only support it when there are lots more Hen Harriers nesting on grouse moors. The figure of 50 pairs seems to be around the level that the RSPB would favour. This seems reasonable to me, as it recognises the truth of the Langholm project, that Hen Harriers can be a pest for driven grouse shooters, but requires the level of wildlife crime to be reduced before the criminals are rewarded. There is also the question of whether such action would even be legal while the population of a protected bird is at such a low level. It seems to me that the RSPB has offered a massive compromise, and I think they are right to offer it, but the grouse shooters are too intransigent to take it up.

The Gilruth e-petition is born out of frustration that the RSPB won't cave in on this issue and that therefore the chance of agreement is stalled. The grouse shooters are trying to paint the RSPB as the unreasonable ones, but that isn't going to wash, and in my opinion it's just a somewhat tawdry public relations move rather than a serious attempt to find a compromise. It's as though two opposing football teams, before the match, have their team huddles at their own ends of the pitch and then have to shake hands before the game can start. The players on the RSPB team have walked to the halfway line and are holding out their hands while the grouse shooters are still on their own goal line. No doubt if the RSPB walked down to the edge of the penalty area the grouse shooters would simply be encouraged and would remain on the goal line. Only if the RSPB crossed the whole pitch would the grouse shooters regard this as a good 'compromise'.

I think the grouse shooters have been banking on the fact that the referee of this game is potentially the Secretary of State for the Environment, Owen Paterson. If so their scheme has come unstuck this week because Paterson has lost his Defra post, and has left the Cabinet. He has been replaced by Liz Truss, who instead of attending the Game Fair is stuck in London and is said to be in Cabinet discussions over events in Ukraine.

But still, we now have the Gilruth e-petition, backed by the shooting community, in a kind of opposition to my own on banning driven grouse shooting. With the serried ranks of GWCT, BASC, the Countryside Alliance and the National Gamekeepers' Organisation promoting the Gilruth e-petition I'm rather concerned that it might overtake mine in the next month before Hen Harrier Day. It feels like David (that's me) against a whole bunch of Goliaths – but, of course, David did win. We'll see.

I have a go at clay shooting before I leave – they call it Pay and Clay. Ten shots and four hits – pretty rubbish really! Although, to be fair to me, I missed the first five and then got four out of the last five, so there were signs of improvement. I think it probably helps to close one eye and look straight down the barrel (maybe I should have started doing that earlier). So I have now contributed to the economic benefit of shooting to the UK economy – to the tune of a tenner.

25 July

The cover of the monthly magazine *Birdwatch*, for which I write the 'political birder' column, is a beautiful male Hen Harrier accompanied by the words 'Stop killing our harriers' and the exhortation to join the campaign for change. This will sit in thousands of newsagents shops across the country for a few weeks and land in the homes of thousands of birders. It is a striking way to publicise the campaign, and inside the magazine the editor, Dominic Mitchell, rams home the messages of my four-page piece (lots of nice pictures of live Hen Harriers and dead grouse) about the e-petition, the up-and-coming Hen Harrier Day and a range of other things that birders can do to help this amazing bird.

On the same day, Marks and Spencer bow to public pressure and are quoted in *The Times* as having decided not to sell grouse meat, as they had planned, in two London stores. The head of agriculture at M&S says that 15 estates in North Yorkshire and the Scottish borders had agreed to comply with a code of prac-tice (drawn up with the help of the RSPB and Game and Wildlife Conservation Trust), but that M&S has decided not to take grouse from the estates because it lacks independent confir-mation that they are complying with the code.

Amanda Anderson, director of the Moorland Association, is quoted as saying:

> All game shooting is predicated on a very strong conservation principle of you eat what you shoot. Grouse is a wonderful premium product unique to this country. M&S wanted to roll

it out. To try to stop that route from the moor to plate is wholly irresponsible.

The decision by M&S is a significant blow to grouse shooting. Not because it has removed a lucrative outlet for grouse meat sales but because of its symbolic significance and the publicity it has received. A major retailer has been persuaded not to sell a meat product because it cannot confirm the practices of its suppliers, and this has been achieved through consumer pressure alone. It is quite a fillip to the friends of the Hen Harrier.

31 July

The e-petition to ban driven grouse shooting passes the 10,000 signature milestone in just over two months and thus will trigger a response from Defra as to what it thinks of the idea.

8 August

This week, in the run-up to Hen Harrier Day and the Inglorious Twelfth, Hen Harriers have come to the high street thanks to Lush cosmetics. All Lush shops have posters of Hen Harriers in the window, the staff are briefed and customers will be asked to show their support for Hen Harriers by signing a postcard to HM The Queen asking for her support.

I stroll into the Northampton branch of Lush and ask about this 'Hen Harrier campaign thing'.

Martyn is able to tell me loads – and all of it is right. He really knows his stuff although he clearly isn't a 'birder'. When we get to the e-petition to ban driven grouse shooting I admit that I know a bit about this already and then I stay and we chat, and I answer a few questions from the guys.

Joe is impressive, too. When I comment that grouse shooters say that grouse shooting brings money into upland communities he says 'So does tourism', quick as a flash, and when I say that grouse shooters tell us that other species benefit from manage-ment for Red Grouse he says 'But they can't need it, can they? What did they do before grouse shooting?' Sometimes, we make things seem more complicated than we need.

It seems that two blokes selling soap and toiletries in the middle of Northampton can see through the main arguments of the grouse-shooting lobby without much help from anyone else – let's just remember that. Or, more importantly, maybe grouse shooting should remember that.

I sign my postcard to the Queen and leave with a shopping bag full of smelly things (nice smells, of course) and a big grin on my face. If Lush staff are all as good as Martyn and Joe then the message about Hen Harriers will be spread far and wide among the shoppers of the UK over the next few days.

9–10 August

I head up the M1 towards the Peak District for Hen Harrier Day. Stopping at a service station I check, as has become a habit, the state of play of the e-petition and find that it has passed 13,000 signatures. The latest 1,000 have poured in over a couple of days. I also read an email from Jim Dixon, telling me about the fourth pair of Hen Harriers that a few weeks earlier was discovered by Geoff Eyre on his grouse moor (actually owned by the National Trust), nesting above the very site to which we are heading for Hen Harrier Day. I already know about this pair, as news always leaks out about these things – in fact I have been told about the pair by half a dozen people, all of whom told me not to tell anyone.

I meet up with Ruth Peacey, Jez Toogood, Adam Clarke and Nick Wilcox-Brown to scout out the location for tomorrow's gathering. We look at the area of grass in front of the dam of the Derwent Reservoir and plan exactly where we should get people to assemble. It is a lovely mild sunny August day. As we stand on the grass trying to imagine it full of Hen Harrier Day protesters we notice a couple of Buzzards on the grouse moor above us, and a Sparrowhawk flies over the trees. But there is no sign of England's fourth pair of Hen Harriers, nesting up on the hills above the car park.

The car park and visitor centre are quite busy. How busy, I wonder, will it be tomorrow? Will anyone turn up? Will it just be me and Chris Packham looking like a couple of prats on our own? Will the media show up, as they have promised, or will there be no coverage of the event? And will the forecast storms arrive tomorrow just on time to dampen everything – the last knock-ings of Hurricane Bertha are being tracked across the Atlantic and the weathermen say that it is set to dump half of the Atlantic Ocean on Britain some time tomorrow morning. It is difficult to tell, but we only have about 19 hours to wait to see.

Even if it *is* only Chris and me, we know that a social media 'thunderclap' will send out a message to 'Save the Hen Harrier' to more than two million social media accounts on Twitter, Facebook and Tumblr tomorrow morning at the time the event here begins.

I also show my face at the office in the visitor centre to intro-duce myself to the Severn Trent staff there. They seem quite relaxed about the event now that it is happening, and they are very helpful. We talk some more about the prospects of rain, lots of rain, lots and lots of rain.

There's not much else I can do to prepare for tomorrow, so I head off to Buxton to check in to my hotel, where a group of us are meeting in the evening. There are a dozen of us for dinner, including several local friends who have been helpful in advising and in more practical ways on the run-up to tomorrow, Chris Packham and the shadow Defra minister (and former Defra minister in the last Labour government) Barry Gardiner MP. We spend a jolly evening together, and we get to talking about what Hen Harrier Day might look like next year! Hang on, I think – can we get this one under our belts first, please? The dinner is my way of thanking people for coming to the event and for helping to set it up. Everybody there is a volunteer – no one has been paid to attend, no one is doing any of this for any reason other than that they believe in the cause. I find myself being thanked by everyone rather too much for organising things, which seems rather premature since we don't even know whether anyone will turn up tomorrow. And that is particularly true because the weather forecast has got steadily worse as time has passed, and presumably more and more certain with the passing of time. It seems that we are in for an absolute soaking, and that might put people off. After all, they aren't getting anything except a few words of thanks from me and Chris Packham – would you drive a long way to stand in a downpour for that? We will see.

I wake early the next morning – I always do. I throw open the curtains and look out on a fine, almost bright day. From my hotel room in Buxton I can see the tops of the hills towards the Goyt Valley and it looks as if it is going to be a nice day. Maybe it won't rain after all. But will anyone turn up?

I drive to the Derwent Valley the pretty way, to Sparrowpit and then down the mini-gorge at Winnats into the Hope Valley to Castleton, Bamford, across the Ladybower Reservoir and up to the visitor centre. I arrive before 8 a.m. and the day still looks fine. I put on my Hen Harrier Day T-shirt and wait to see what will happen.

We drink coffee and eat cake as we sit in the car park. The odd car drifts in, we aren't going to be completely alone after all. The skies are beginning to darken but my hopes are rising as time passes. The kiosk at the visitor centre is doing a good trade in bacon baps and cups of tea as more and more people arrive. People I know come up and say hello to me, and people I don't know do too. There are ex-RSPB colleagues, a few of whom are here 'officially' (both local staff and from the headquarters at The Lodge) but many more are present as 'themselves'. The Wildlife Trusts are well represented, including their England director, Stephen Trotter, and many staff, trustees and members from the Derbyshire and Sheffield Wildlife Trusts. Local birders come and say hello. There is a small group of people from the Forest of Bowland who have come across from Lancashire. Alan and Ruth have driven over from north Wales. The Hawk and Owl Trust has brought a car-load of staff up from the south, including their relatively new chairman, Philip Merricks.

The Wilde family arrive in two vehicles. One is a van carrying the enormous model of Harry the Hen Harrier in all his glory. It is a spectacular sight, and Findlay's Dad takes Harry off to set him up on the grass where we are to gather.

I feel the first drop of rain, and now the cars that are arriving have their windscreen wipers going. Chris Packham has got here too, and I first see him, standing in the rain, toe to toe with the director of the Moorland Association, Amanda Anderson (who has clearly come along to keep an eye on us all). TV cameras arrive, and Chris is interviewed. Ruth, Jez, Adam and Nick are doing a great job filming the crowds and doing short interviews with attendees. By now it is bucketing down with rain, everyone is soaked, but there are hundreds and hundreds of people present.

At close to the appointed time, we set off with our placards and banners to the grassy patch and I say a few words before handing the megaphone over to Chris Packham.

Chris is just fantastic. He speaks with passion and wit. I am listening to what he is saying but I am also looking out over the crowd of people gathered in the rain in front of us. There is a sea – appropriately enough, considering the weather – of colourful cagoules and waterproofs, there are banners and plac-ards, there are Wildlife Trust logos dotted around (I've noticed the Wildlife Trusts are very good at that) and there are many upturned smiling faces. As Chris ends his speech with the words 'We will win!' a big cheer rings out, and there are more photo-graphs and then a lot of milling around smiling.

Harry the Harrier becomes a focal point for photographs. I have my photo taken dozens of times in front of him. If we hadn't had him there we would have missed him enormously – that Findlay Wilde can teach us all a thing or two about campaigning.

I am surprised at the distance that some people have travelled, just to be part of this event, just to stand on a patch of grass and listen to a couple of short speeches! There are people here from Essex, several from London, from Hampshire, and of course many from the local area. They are here, they tell me, because they want to speak out and to be counted, and they want the plight of the Hen Harrier to be better known and better under-stood by politicians and decision makers. And they want the criminals who are killing these birds to know that the public are watching them.

As people left they were counted by a former professor of genetics, so it must be true that there were about 570 attendees on the day. I think of them as the 'Sodden 570' and they were all fantastic. Well, maybe almost all. I heard a report of a very unsympathetic landowner being present – in fact I think our eyes met during Chris's speech – and also that a gamekeeper who had been convicted of a wildlife crime was there. But for the most part we were a band of like-thinking nature conserva-tionists incensed that a protected bird was at such a low ebb in England, and that it didn't nest (except for the one that we had to keep secret!) in this national park.

Chris Packham was just fantastic on the day. He stayed right until the end and talked to everyone who wanted to talk to him, had his photograph taken with everyone who wanted their photograph taken and had an argument, and a proper argument, with anyone (there were only a couple) who wanted to have an argument with him.

12 August

On the opening day of the Red Grouse shooting season, the e-petition to ban driven grouse shooting passes 14,000 signatures. The media coverage of the day this year is very different from any in its past. Usually this day is marked by a few pieces in the *Daily Telegraph* and *The Times* stating that grouse shooting is a traditional British sport that is of great value to the economy and where wild game is shot. This year the coverage contains many references to the turn-out on Hen Harrier Day, and to the fact that many are calling for controls or a total ban of the practice.

15–17 August

The Bird Fair is an annual event in the birder's calendar where thousands mass at the Leicestershire and Rutland Wildlife Trust's reserve at Rutland Water and socialise.

I have a recently published book to plug. It's called *A Message from Martha*, and it's about the extinction of the Passenger Pigeon, which happened a century ago, in 1914. So I am busy giving talks, signing books and chatting to people about Passenger Pigeons, Hen Harriers and birding times and people.

Lots of people are wearing Hen Harrier Day T-shirts. Many of the 'Sodden 570' are present and exchanging smiles as they pass each other. Many, many people are talking about Hen Harrier Day and how pleased they are that it happened. I bump into three of the guys from Birders Against Wildlife Crime and we decide we'll have to talk properly about 'what next?'

The Wildes are about – both Findlay and family and the two-and-a-half-metre tall Harry the Harrier, who is perched at the wildlife crime display. I have my photograph taken with Findlay in front of Harry again, and this time it isn't in a downpour.

Chris Packham is busy doing various events and I hardly see him over the three days. Alan and Ruth are around too, but we only snatch short chats through the event.

One reason I enjoy the Bird Fair more this year is that it seems that there is more debate about issues – and I like that. The slaughter of spring migrants in Malta and the slaughter of Hen Harriers in the UK seem to be two big issues about which people are talking – in talks and in private.

1 September

My e-petition to ban driven grouse shooting passed the 10,000-signature mark on 31 July, and today it receives a response, after nearly five weeks of brow-wrinkling thought on behalf of Defra:

> It has been estimated that £250 million per year is spent on management activities that provide significant benefits for con-servation. Shooting makes an important contribution to the rural economy. When carried out in accordance with the law, shooting for sport is a legitimate activity, and our position is that people should be free to undertake lawful activities should they wish to do so.
>
> Landowners are free to manage wildlife on their land, provided it is carried out appropriately and legally, in accordance with any the relevant wildlife legislation.
>
> **Hen Harriers**
> It is encouraging to learn that there are four hen harrier nests this year which have chicks, given that in 2013 there were no known Hen Harrier fledglings in England. Some of these fledglings will be tracked with satellite tags we have funded.
>
> The Uplands Stakeholder Forum Hen Harrier Sub-group was set up in 2012 with senior representatives from organisations best placed to take action to address the decline in Hen Harriers. These include Natural England, the Moorland Association, the National Gamekeepers' Organisation, the Game and Wildlife Conservation Trust, the National Parks Authority and the RSPB. Defra welcomes the involvement of all parties.
>
> The Sub-group has developed a draft Joint Action Plan containing a suite of complementary actions intended to contribute

to the recovery of the Hen Harrier population in England. We are working with Sub-group members to finalise the Plan.

Illegal killing of birds of prey

The killing of birds of prey is illegal, all wild birds being protected under the Wildlife and Countryside Act 1981. Anyone who kills or injures a wild bird is committing an offence and could face jail if convicted.

Bird of prey persecution is one of the six UK wildlife crime priorities. The England and Wales Raptor Persecution Priority Delivery Group leads on action to address these crimes through prevention, intelligence and enforcement activity.

The National Wildlife Crime Unit gathers intelligence on illegal activities affecting birds of prey, providing assistance to police forces when required. Earlier this year the Government confirmed that the Home Office and Defra would together provide funding until 2016, demonstrating the Government's commitment to tackling wildlife crime.

Alongside this, there have been successful conservation measures which have led to increases in Buzzard, Peregrine and Red Kite populations over the last two decades.

Peatland

In February 2013 we, along with the devolved administrations, made a statement of intent to protect and enhance the natural capital provided by peatlands in the UK. In September 2013 the Pilot Peatland Code was launched with the aim of promoting the restoration of UK peatland through business investment. It is intended that the Code will assure restoration delivers tangible benefits for climate change alongside other benefits such as restoring habitats for protected species and improving water quality.

The last decade has seen increasing numbers of conservation initiatives (such as Nature Improvement Areas and Sites of Special Scientific Interest) many of which are focused on peatland restoration in the UK. We are working with a wide range of partners on peatland restoration, including landowners and environmental NGOs.

Rural Development Programme

We are committed to helping create a more sustainable future for the English uplands, which are endowed with natural assets that are important for delivering a range of valuable 'ecosystem services', including food and fibre, water regulation, carbon storage, biodiversity, and recreational opportunities for health and wellbeing.

We will be investing over £3 billion in agri-environment schemes (Environmental Stewardship and its successor) in the next Rural Development Programme 2015–2020. Addressing loss of biodiversity will be a priority for the new Programme. In addition funding will look to maximise opportunities to deliver biodiversity, water quality and flooding benefits together. Defra is working with a wide range of interests to finalise scheme details in good time for 2015.

That's quite a long response, but not a very good one. It doesn't really address the issue of banning grouse shooting except by saying that it is currently legal – yes, I know that, that's why I am seeking for it to be banned! I would much rather, in a way, that the response had laid out a long list of reasons why banning grouse shooting wasn't right, couldn't work or would be a financial disaster. That would give us all something to think about and argue over and might move the debate onwards. But it is interesting that banning grouse shooting is not ruled out by the government response.

2 September

On this Tuesday evening the World Land Trust has organised a 'Controversial Conservation' evening at the Royal Society in London. It involves Chris Packham, Bill Oddie, Andrew Gilruth (from the Game and Wildlife Conservation Trust), John Burton (CEO of the World Land Trust), Garry Marvin and me. Andrew is a bit outnumbered but he does really well – considering the sticky wicket on which he has to face some hostile bowling.

My points are the usual ones:

- Hen Harriers are killed illegally and this is wrong.
- They are killed by grouse-shooting interests, not by anybody else.
- There are some good things and bad things about management for driven grouse shooting but in my view, and you must make up your own mind, the 'bads' outweigh the 'goods' by a considerable margin.
- We have talked a lot and the time for talking is past.

- Grouse shooting has failed to clean up its act. It has had its chance, and it is now time for it to cease as we don't need it socially, economically or certainly ecologically.
- Let's ban it – sign here.

24 September

Sky and Hope, female Hen Harriers fledged from United Utilities land in the Forest of Bowland in Lancashire, have gone missing.

Scientists tracking the movements of the young Hen Harriers became concerned when their tags stopped transmitting. Sky's satellite signal stopped suddenly on the evening of Wednesday 10 September, with the data suggesting she was roosting at her last known location, while Hope's last known location was sent on the morning of Saturday 13 September.

Both of the birds had left their nest sites on the United Utilities estate several weeks earlier, but had remained in the Bowland area since fledging. Searches have been made, but neither Sky nor Hope has been recovered.

Experts think it is improbable that the loss of satellite transmission is due to technical failure. Only a tiny percentage of Hen Harriers fitted with satellite tags since 2007 have stopped transmitting when it was known the tracked bird was alive.

Bob Elliot, RSPB head of investigations, says:

In our experience, this satellite technology is normally very reliable and it is rare for them to fail for technological reasons. Losing two birds in such a short time frame and in the same geographical area is strange.

Based on the last known data and our understanding of the technology, Sky appears to have suffered a catastrophic tag failure at roost suggesting either natural predation or human intervention as the likely causes for her sudden failure to transmit. However, we would not expect natural predation to stop the tag transmitting data so suddenly. Hope's tag was transmitting reliably, with no evidence of any technical problems.

Chris Packham is quoted as saying:

It's incredibly disheartening to discover that two of this year's chicks have already apparently failed to survive. It shows how vulnerable Hen Harriers are and that four nests are nowhere near enough. Without satellite tagging, these disappearances might never have come to our attention but technology is on our side and we will keep watching.

The satellite technology is really pinning down where birds are dying, and when. We'll have to see what, if any, information comes out about these latest mysterious disappearances.

1 October

Two reports have been published that hit at the heart of the arguments for driven grouse shooting – one on wider environmental impacts, and the other on the economics of grouse shooting.

The EMBER (Effects of Moorland Burning on the Ecohydrology of River basins) study by the University of Leeds (funded by the Natural Environment Research Council and Yorkshire Water) has been a five-year study of ten river catchments – five that have lots of heather burning for driven grouse shooting, and five that do not. The study area was the north Pennines. The results of this major study indicate, in just about every respect, that burning of heather imposes a cost on the taxpayer and society.

The report shows that heather burning puts particulate matter into your rivers, makes rivers more acidic, reduces the numbers of many invertebrates (some of which are replaced by ones characteristic of knackered rivers), reduces the soil quality and organic matter of the peat, lowers the water table and makes carbon loss to the atmosphere more likely.

Farmers simply wouldn't be allowed to behave in this way.

'Altering the hydrology of peatlands so they become drier is known to cause significant losses of carbon from storage in the soil,' said co-researcher Professor Joseph Holden, continuing, 'This is of great concern, as peatlands are the largest natural store for carbon on the land surface of the UK and play a crucial role in climate change. They are the Amazon of the UK.'

This study has shown that there is a tendency (not proven) for burned catchments to be 'flashier' and more prone to high flows after heavy rain, and this supports the arguments of the Hebden Bridge 'Ban the Burn' campaigners who claim that intensified moorland management upstream of their town was a factor in disastrous and highly costly floods. The EMBER study supports their views but doesn't prove them – it could have weakened them, but it certainly hasn't done that.

Peat particles washed into rivers lead to discoloration of water, which is largely a cosmetic problem, but increases water bills when water is treated. Acidification of water supplies is a more serious treatment problem.

The 'traditional' moorland burning season runs from today until 15 April (which is much too late in the year anyway, particularly with climate change – many nesting birds must have to flee their nests as the flames engulf them). Some of the press coverage includes:

- The *Independent* newspaper: 'Commercial grouse shooting is ruining the countryside of northern England and warming the planet as swathes of upland peatlands rich in wildlife are burned to provide the best conditions for red grouse.'
- Chris Packham (quoted in the *Independent*): 'The old adage that shooting is good for the countryside is no longer holding water in front of an increasingly sophisticated audience.' Indeed, Chris, and according to this study the land they manage isn't holding water either!
- The *Scotsman*: 'Heather burning on Scotland's grouse moors may be causing serious damage to peatlands, rivers and wildlife.'
- Lead researcher Dr Lee Brown (quoted in the *Scotsman*): 'Until now there was little evidence of the environmental impacts of moorland burning. Unsurprisingly, a push away from moorland burning without solid scientific evidence to back up the need for change has created a lot of tension. The findings from the EMBER project now provide the necessary evidence to inform policy.'
- *The Times*: 'The owners of grouse moors who set fire to heather to promote green shoots for young birds to eat are polluting rivers and contributing to climate change.'
- Adrian Blackmore, Countryside Alliance's director of shooting (quoted in the *Independent*): 'Burning has been a vital management tool in our uplands for more than a century and one that has provided significant benefits to wildlife, creating as it does a mosaic of different-aged

heather which provides protection for many species of threatened ground nesting birds.' – which is not a response to this detailed, long-term scientific report, merely an admission that the problems have been in existence for more than a century. Might be time for a change, then?

Ecosystem impacts have always been the smoking shotgun for driven grouse shooting. This study shows that there are measurable impacts of burning on wider environmental health. All the impacts in this report are deleterious impacts. All are ones that scientists have suspected for a long time. Many sound a bit complicated, and perhaps trivial, but it all adds up to a clear message that as well as affecting wildlife through directly killing it, driven grouse shooting affects the environment through altering it in ways that are generally harmful – and all for a few days blasting away at Red Grouse!

The grouse-shooting community, if they have cared at all about what the rest of us think, has generally fallen back on the argument that grouse shooting is of economic importance. This has always seemed to me to be very weak ground and only of concern if you have an unhealthy interest in dosh. It reminds me of the story of the Kray twins being the largest donors to an appeal for the victims of the Aberfan disaster – to what extent does money exculpate other sins?

But the other report published today shoots holes in the economic importance of shooting. Today's report (published by the League Against Cruel Sports, based on an analysis carried out by economists from Sheffield Hallam University and Cormack Economics) analyses in some detail the findings of a study that was commissioned by the shooting community and published a couple of months ago by Public and Corporate Economic Consultants (PACEC).

The PACEC report claims that shooting contributes £2 billion to the UK economy. That's £2,000,000,000, and it is a big number – but the size of the UK economy is £2,000,000,000,000, so the whole of shooting is a drop in the economic ocean.

I'm not against the whole of shooting, I'm against that species-killing, habitat-damaging, environment-polluting, atmosphere-carbonising part of it that is driven grouse shooting. How big a

share does that kind of shooting have? Well, considering that
the PACEC report includes clay-pigeon shooting, which is a
pastime involving 150,000 folk, and all that wildfowling on the
coast, and all those pheasant shoots and partridge shoots, then
I'd guess it might be generous to allow grouse shooting one-fifth
of the putative total of £2 billion – let's say £400 million then
(it's a guess, it doesn't matter much, really).

First, I'd pay £6 a year for driven grouse shooting to stop –
and if you would too then we may have a solution already!

But now we have to bring in today's analysis of the shooting
industry's report. It's a bit heavy-going, as economics usually is,
but I've read it and it is rational and fairly convincing. It suggests
that the PACEC report overestimated the value of shooting to
the economy many times over. They think that an estimate of
nearer to £500 million would be closer to the mark – a four-fold
reduction (so getting rid of grouse shooting would cost each of
us only £1.50 a year. I'll pay a few other people's share too at that
price).

Other problems arise with the PACEC report. It includes the
money, our taxpayers' money (through agri-environment
spending), that goes to grouse shooters. Clearly, stopping driven
grouse shooting would not lose that money from the economy,
it would just go to other, perhaps more deserving, land managers.
Perhaps we could give sheep farmer Neil Heseltine a bit more
money. I'd probably vote for that.

But let's not get bogged down in the figures, because they
aren't worth much at all. For one thing, the environmental costs
of driven grouse shooting ought to be removed from the overall
figure, but aren't. How much is each Hen Harrier worth? What
is the cost of carbon emissions? How much higher are water bills
because of the need to remove particulates from water supplies?
None of these things was costed in the PACEC report – and
they should have been. If they had been, then I'm pretty sure
that grouse shooting is running at an economic loss for society
as a whole.

There is no way that you can make grouse shooting look like
a big earner – it's a tiny thing economically. It's a tiny thing that
is underpinned by wildlife crime and which causes environmental damage.

Today, the evidence piles up that grouse-moor management damages the wider environment and isn't worth much, if anything, to the economy.

10 October

20,132 postcards for the Queen!

This morning, Paul and Hilary from Lush, accompanied by me, delivered a couple of boxes of postcards (the rest will follow later) to the Queen. Well, not directly to Her Majesty herself, but to her house. And no, not to the front door, wherever that is, but by the side entrance.

After a long period of negotiation with the palace the actual handover took less time than I believe it took me to shave this morning! Our identities were checked and then we were escorted, by a nice police inspector, into the building where a man in livery, with braid, took our boxes of cards. I can't say he looked thrilled, but there you go! And then we were escorted back to the real world of the busy London pavement.

We were told that Her Majesty might get to see a postcard or two, but she would certainly see mention of them on a list of correspondence received. The importance of this handover is that the views of more than 20,000 people from the high streets and shopping centres of the UK have been delivered to the head of state and the centre of the Establishment.

I think Lush did a fantastic job in their shops, in just one week last August, to enthuse people to speak out for nature. Those shoppers for bath bombs often came into the shops never having heard of a Hen Harrier and went out feeling angry that these birds are being killed illegally by grouse-shooting interests.

As we stand on the pavement outside Buckingham Palace I wonder how many of the people passing by would know of Hen Harriers – not very many, I guess. Many are tourists, and the Americans would know the bird as the Northern Harrier anyway (but they would be more likely never to have heard of it); the Scandinavians might know it quite well if they were interested in birds, and Russians, Chinese and Koreans all stand a chance of knowing the Hen Harrier from their countries. But none would know much about driven grouse shooting, that peculiarly British pastime.

One would be much more likely to find some grouse shooters inside Buckingham Palace than outside, I guess. I do hope that Earl Peel, Lord Chamberlain of the Royal Household, former owner of Gunnerside grouse moor and vice-president of the Game and Wildlife Conservation Trust, gets a chance to flick through the postcards signed by Lush customers.

10 October

The e-petition launched three months ago by the GWCT's Andrew Gilruth did not overtake my own by Hen Harrier Day. In fact, despite support from GWCT, the Moorland Association, the Countryside Alliance, gamekeepers and BASC it did not reach 10,000 signatures until mid-September.

This e-petition said that a plan to aid the recovery of the Hen Harrier had been developed by a group of stakeholders (as I believe we are supposed to call them – I loathe that term), and it urged Defra to publish that plan, but right from the start it appeared to be a poorly judged publicity stunt rather than a serious contribution to the debate. I have called it the non-joint non-plan, and Defra's response does much the same. Because it isn't agreed it isn't a plan for action, and until it's agreed it won't be joint.

The Defra response to the GWCT's e-petition reads as follows:

> The Government is concerned about the Hen Harrier population in England and acknowledges the need to take urgent action.
>
> The latest survey undertaken in 2010 found only 12 pairs in England. In 2013 no young fledged for the first time in over 50 years and although we are encouraged that there are four nests this year with good numbers of young, Hen Harrier populations are so low that recovery across their former range is unlikely to occur unaided.
>
> In its document 'Biodiversity 2020: A strategy for England's wildlife and ecosystem services', the Government set out priority actions. One of these is to 'Take targeted action for the recovery of priority species, whose conservation is not delivered through wider habitat-based and ecosystem measures'. The Government

considers that Hen Harriers merit additional action to reverse the decline in their population numbers.

In 2012 Defra established the Uplands Stakeholder Forum Hen Harrier Sub-Group to seek shared solutions for Hen Harrier recovery. The Sub-Group comprises senior representatives from Natural England, the RSPB, the Game and Wildlife Conservation Trust, the National Gamekeepers' Organisation, National Parks UK and the Moorland Association.

Since the establishment of the Sub-Group, the members have developed a draft Joint Action Plan which contains a suite of complementary actions intended to contribute to the recovery of the Hen Harrier population in England. The e-petition suggests that the Joint Action Plan could have been published in January 2014, but final agreement is still being negotiated. Since the Sub-Group members all have a role to play in delivering the suite of actions, it is important to secure as much agreement as possible before publication so that it can be implemented in the cooperative and pragmatic way needed to help the recovery of the Hen Harrier in England.

That is a rather perfunctory response. However, it does, for once, actually answer the question posed rather than ramble around it in an unconvincing manner. It also reminds us that as recently as 2010 there were a dozen pairs of Hen Harriers in England – and even that is a poor show when there is enough available habitat for 330+ pairs (although Defra do not mention the 330+ figure: they never do – it's too embarrassing). Under this government the Hen Harrier population has fallen in just four years from twelve to four pairs, and there is just a hint in the Defra response that they are waking up to the fact that they need to do something about this.

The ill-judged plea to publish the non-joint non-plan was an attempt by the grouse shooters to railroad Defra, the RSPB and the public into agreeing that we want lots of grouse shooting and will live with few Hen Harriers. That, quite palpably, isn't the case.

The non-joint non-plan would have allowed, it seems, chicks to be moved from one of the Hen Harrier nests in the Forest of Bowland this year because it was too close to the other nest, despite there only being four pairs in England.

Even this government wouldn't be foolish enough to position itself on the side of the grouse shooter instead of the Hen Harrier this close to a general election. Maybe afterwards ...

23 October

My copy of the RSPB membership magazine has arrived – and what a fine cover it has! A ringtail Hen Harrier.

Inside there are pages and pages on Hen Harriers: there is a long, excellent article by Stuart Winter, a mention of them by Martin Harper, another mention in Mike Clarke's opening piece and also mention of satellite tagging of Montagu's Harriers and the excellent Simon Barnes railing at raptor persecution – didn't he use to do that in *The Times*?

The RSPB gives a few words on page 53 to three options for making things better. One is the Moorland Association's 'There, there, it's alright really – don't you worry your pretty little heads about it' approach (although maybe you'd better read it for yourself), and in the centre is the RSPB's pitch for licensing of grouse shooting, and taking another view is my 'Ban it!' suggestion.

The RSPB and I are in complete agreement about the problem and the cause of the problem, but we have a difference of opinion, a friendly difference of opinion, about the solution.

The RSPB states that self-regulation has failed and that sites are being destroyed and damaged by poor grouse-moor management, and that birds of prey are persecuted. Yes, self-regulation has failed, but so has actual regulation in this case. It isn't legal to damage important wildlife sites or to kill birds of prey – and yet it happens. It happens because it is difficult to catch the miscreants, and because the grouse-moor owners are rich and powerful. Neither of those reasons is removed by a 'stronger' form of regulation. Regulation will fail in future as it has failed in the past, and for the same reasons.

That's why the only workable solution on the table, and on page 53 of *Nature's Home* magazine, is to ban driven grouse shooting. I'm grateful to the RSPB for the space they have given to this matter, and I'll be even more grateful to RSPB members who read the articles, think about it and then sign up for a ban on driven grouse shooting.

23 October

Today I went to Margate. I went to other places too, but I went to Margate first and foremost. It has been a funny day in a way – it has had elements of looking backwards as well as living in the moment, and a bit of looking forward.

I woke early, and that made the rest of the day easier. I drove to Sandy, which I used to do often but now do very rarely, and parked at Sandy station in time to get the 06:20 to King's Cross. Most of my fellow-passengers were dressed for work, wearing suits and looking at their phones. I was dressed for play, in jeans and a scruffy fleece, and reading a book. But I'm used to being the odd one out. From King's Cross it was a short stroll to St Pancras, where the Margate train had just arrived at its platform.

I had travelled to Margate to see the Jeremy Deller English Magic exhibition, which includes a rather large mural of a Hen Harrier. One good thing about the Turner Contemporary is that there is free admission. Another is that there is an enormous Hen Harrier, clutching a Range Rover in its talons, on the wall.

Now, as I looked at a Hen Harrier that would strike fear into any gamekeeper or grouse-moor owner, and that was large enough to tackle livestock, never mind fluffy grouse chicks, I was becoming a little puzzled. It was a mural – but apparently this same mural was in Venice last year – and how do you move a mural? And the catalogue said it was painted by Sarah Tynan – so who is Jeremy Deller? I had assumed he was the artist. But the notes on the wall also made clear reference to the events at Dersingham Bog all those years ago. This image was a protest about the impact of shooting on nature, and a very large protest at that.

I turned to the attendant, whose badge named her as Mandy, and asked sheepishly whether photography was allowed (expecting the answer no) and was told it was, so I took some photos and got talking to Mandy, who explained that Jeremy

Deller was the moving force behind the exhibition and had brought everything together, and dreamed it all up, but that a variety of folk had done the artwork. Sarah Tynan had led on the Hen Harrier image, especially on the central part of the bird, but that a variety of people had painted the rest of it, including Mandy herself. Wow! Mandy had painted some of the bird's right wing.

Margate is the third place that this Hen Harrier has landed – being repainted from a projected image each time, I was told. And when the exhibition is over it just gets painted over and disappears. Wow again! But there will always be a Hen Harrier on that wall, under other paint. What a nice thought.

Mandy knew lots about Hen Harriers, including the recent disappearance of Sky and Hope in the forest of Bowland – I was impressed. I went downstairs after thanking her, and was pleased to see that the Deller/Tynan/Mandy Hen Harrier was on sale as a postcard. I bought all that were on display (74 of them). The lady and gentleman who sold them to me also knew about Hen Harriers – and Sky and Hope. I was impressed again.

I left the gallery and headed back to the station. On the train I wrote lots of postcards to friends of the Hen Harrier such as the GWCT, the Moorland Association and BASC, as well as Defra and Natural England, and a few rather closer friends too. This type of cultural exposure of the Hen Harrier's plight is very valuable – it will help to spread the word further and to different groups of people. I wonder how many grouse shooters have seen the mural I saw today.

This date is a significant one – it is seven years since whatever happened at Dersingham Bog happened at Dersingham Bog. The actual anniversary is tomorrow, but the weather forecast for tomorrow is horrid, so I made the trip today (and I wanted to be able to blog about it on the anniversary – so that made today's journey necessary too). So that is where I headed, from Sandy station, after my return train journey.

I drove past and around Sandringham and posted my postcards at Dersingham Post Office. Some will arrive tomorrow on the actual anniversary and others next week. It seemed the right place to post them.

I sat for a while overlooking Dersingham Bog in what I took to be the place where, seven years ago, the Natural England warden and others had heard the shots and reported seeing the birds fall from the sky. I could picture the scene and was rather relieved that I didn't see any Hen Harriers – that would have seemed rather spooky, I think. When I left, a little before 18:00 (which was when the alleged events were said to have occurred), there was still plenty of daylight and, if anything, it seemed a bit early for Hen Harriers to be coming in to roost. I hope all the friends of the Hen Harrier enjoy their postcards and note the date on which they arrive, and the location from which they were sent.

27 October

Caroline Allen is a practising vet and the Green Party spokesperson on animals, as well as co-chair of the London Green Party. She has written a guest blog for my website, which includes the following:

> Shooting birds such as grouse and pheasants is portrayed by its supporters as a wholesome country activity, in tune with nature. The dead birds are then sold to a growing market as ethical, free-range and healthy. In reality this couldn't be further from the truth.
>
> From environmental degradation and a devastating impact on local wildlife, including protected birds of prey, to severe welfare issues, this is an industry based on lies and misinformation.
>
> The issue of shooting grouse has gained a high profile recently with the launch of a petition to ban driven shooting, which has already gained more than 18,000 signatures. The government's response thus far has been very weak, which is no surprise given the millionaire landowners in their ranks and amongst their supporters.
>
> The Green Party is clear on this subject: we support a complete ban on grouse shooting. Our policy states that we oppose the killing of, and the infliction of pain and suffering on, animals in the name of sport or leisure and will work to end all such practices. On a recent visit to Ilkley, Green Party leader Natalie Bennett offered her support to the Ban Bloodsports on Ilkley Moor campaign, which has also had strong support from local Green Party campaigners. In addition we value and work to

protect our precious natural environment and wildlife. It is clear that this industry is in complete opposition to these aims.

Wildlife is in great danger anywhere near a commercial shoot. The legally protected Hen Harrier has been driven to the brink of extinction by grouse-shooting interests, with only two pairs nesting in 2013. This government has shown scant regard for the legal protection afforded to birds of prey: last year the government agency Natural England issued licences to allow the destruction of the eggs and nests of Buzzards to protect a pheasant shoot. This is also a government that chose a millionaire landowner, whose family estate runs shoots, as wildlife minister, the same minister who in 2012 refused to ban carbofuran, a deadly poison used to kill raptors, which prompted the Green Party MP, Caroline Lucas, to state: 'The minister's shocking refusal to outlaw the possession of a poison used only by rogue gamekeepers to kill birds of prey illegally would be inexplicable were it not for his own cosy links to the shooting lobby.' Benyon refused, saying that poisoning was an offence anyway, and that outlawing the chemical 'may not be a proportionate course of action.'

And it is not just birds of prey that are targeted: any wildlife seen as predators are fair game, with gamekeepers using snares, traps and poisons to kill tens of thousands of animals each week, including protected species such as badgers and otters. Even domestic pets have been caught up in the carnage. Snares are heavily used by gamekeepers; they are horribly indiscriminate and cause significant suffering. The Green Party is calling for an immediate ban on the use of snares.

The local ecosystem is also damaged, rather than protected, by the presence of shoots. In the case of grouse shooting, gamekeepers burn the heather on these important moorland habitats in order to promote new growth for the chicks [sic] to feed on. The EMBER Report (Effects of Moorland Burning on the Ecohydrology of River basins) showed that burning heather is much more damaging than previously thought.

The report showed how burning heather dries out and warms up the peat it grows in, causing it to disintegrate and release large amounts of carbon dioxide. Peat is a vital carbon sink and the release of carbon dioxide has a significant impact on climate change.

The burning also has profound effects on the water table, including an increase in the release of pollutants such as toxic heavy metals into rivers, a reduction in the number and diversity of insects in rivers draining from burned areas and an increased risk of flooding.

It is clear that this industry is not only damaging the environment, harming wildlife and millions of birds, it is also conning people. Only the Green Party will stand up to the landowners who are causing this damage while falsely claiming to be protecting our vital natural heritage.

This is an interesting and powerful official statement from a political party that has recently done well in the European elections and which looks poised to grow in support in the 2015 general election. Will we see any similar statements from other political parties over the coming months?

10 November

Adam Watson, a famous ecologist and co-author of the New Naturalist book on grouse, is quoted in Scotland's *Sunday Herald* as having found 'massive declines' in Mountain Hare numbers over the last 10–20 years on grouse moors around Deeside. 'I would say that spring abundance of adults has been reduced by at least five-fold to 100-fold on most of these moors,' he said. The account in the *Herald* reads, in part, as follows:

Mountain Hares are facing extinction in large parts of the Scottish Highlands because landowners are killing thousands of them every year in order to protect the grouse-shooting industry, wildlife experts have warned … The distinctive mammals are being shot and snared by gamekeepers on grouse moors due to fears that ticks carried by hares spread a viral disease, which can be fatal to grouse.

'A preventable catastrophe has befallen the Mountain Hare,' said Dr Adam Watson, a veteran mountain ecologist. 'This is a national scandal.'

This follows an earlier revelation that some 1,500 Mountain Hares were killed this spring on shooting estates in the Lammermuir Hills, south of Edinburgh.

13 November

The RSPB today urged Defra to publish the workable elements of the Hen Harrier Action Plan and put the contentious element on brood management out to public consultation. The RSPB rejects the brood management element of the unpublished plan on the grounds that it is unacceptable and legally ambiguous. Martin Harper wrote in his blog:

> The Hen Harrier is one of our most iconic birds of prey, but it is currently in danger of being lost from England and it needs urgent action to save it. Defra has worked hard with the shooting industry and conservation groups to produce a Hen Harrier Action Plan, and we believe that the workable parts of this plan must be published and implemented now to help save this bird of prey. We think the more contentious elements, for which there is a plethora of unanswered questions, should go for public consultation, while the rest of the plan fulfils its purpose of protecting harriers.
>
> We believe that brood management is a distraction, taking emphasis and resources away from tackling illegal killing. Brood management is worth considering once the Hen Harrier has returned to the hills and moors of England. But to do it early could see young birds released to their deaths.
>
> The Society has no confidence that released birds will be allowed to fly free from harm. It is a sad reality that illegal killing of birds of prey continues, often linked by [sic] those with an interest in shooting. The evidence is real and compelling – gamekeepers continue to be convicted for the illegal persecution of birds of prey and there is a strong association between raptor persecution and grouse moor management. We will have no part of a project that could put a species at risk.
>
> We recognise that brood management has become a totemic issue for the shooting community, and that some have chosen to use strong-arm tactics against the RSPB. We reject the industry's claim that only by removing chicks from nests will gamekeepers and shooting estates accept the plan. Aggressive and intransigent campaigning by the shooting sector is threatening to derail the plan, consign Hen Harriers to further years of persecution and ride roughshod across attempts to work with progressive voices in the industry.

Ministers are accountable for preventing the human-induced extinction of species, and the illegal persecution of the Hen Harrier is the main reason for this bird's desperate plight. It surely makes sense to publish elements of the plan which have agreement. We're urging Government to recognise the urgency of this situation and implement a plan to save the harrier, so that Hen Harriers can once again be a regular feature of the skies above our moors.

That's quite a tough statement, and it comes after the RSPB has faced weeks of attacks in the media from the pro-shooting lobby. Clearly the shooters are not compromising at all, and want brood management to kick in straight away. I'm glad to see my former colleagues showing quite a bit of mettle.

14 November

Allen, Frank and I meet at Rules restaurant for a boys' lunch. Rules is one of a number of restaurants in London that specialises in wild-shot game. I want to have a look at it, so that's why I am treating my two friends to a meal here. Rules, in Maiden Lane, Covent Garden, is said to be London's oldest restaurant, established by Thomas Rule in 1798. At that time it was supposed to be frequented by 'rakes, dandies and superior intelligences', but today they had the three of us.

As you enter through the front door it is like entering a lost age, probably an Edwardian age, with the waiters in their livery and the dining rooms decorated with ancient horseshoes from winning horses of the Edwardian age, drawings of Edwardian politicians, portraits of Winston Churchill (who certainly enjoyed dining here) and an amazing portrayal of Margaret Thatcher dressed as a cross between St George, Henry V and Britannia. Framed theatre bills and drawings of gamebirds are hung on the wall, and the white tablecloths set off the dark wood of the furniture, the red leather, the dark wood panels and the brown and yellow lampshades. A few stuffed birds inhabit the rooms – we are overlooked by a Ptarmigan and a Jay. I'm almost sure the Jay was cheeky enough to wink at me.

Rules started as an oyster bar, and I start with oysters accompanied by a tankard of Guinness – very good they both are too. Grouse is on the menu but as I have spent the summer encouraging the banning of driven grouse shooting I opt for the rump steak, which is also excellent. My companions go for fish and partridge.

This was just a reconnaissance visit, really. I was curious to know what Rules looked like. Maybe next year a greater focus should be on the food chain that profits from the grouse industry. Rules is interesting in that it has its own grouse moor, and it therefore ought to be able to answer questions about its management – but other restaurants, like M&S as a retailer, may struggle to reassure their customers that the grouse they sell are not tinged with a taste of illegal activity. And then of course there is also the whole issue of lead in game meat. Which restaurant without its own grouse moor (as Rules has) would happily serve game meat with so much lead in it that it would be banned from sale if it were pork, chicken, beef or lamb?

23 November

I was talking at the North West Bird Fair at the Wildfowl and Wetlands Trust centre at Martin Mere yesterday, and I stayed overnight in Preston. This morning I am up early and travelling into the Forest of Bowland again. Shortly after dawn, I stop and stand on the bridge over the River Wyre. It still looks perfect for Dippers and there still isn't one there. The Redstart that sang from the riverside Alder in mid-May has been replaced by a plaintive Robin.

The last time I leant on this bridge, six months ago, I was on my way south from Newton Rigg and heading to Hebden Bridge. It was here that I paused and wondered whether to launch my e-petition.

My main concern, as a wishy-washy liberal, was whether calling for a ban on this activity was really 'fair', or whether it was a bit over the top. I had struggled with that in my wishy-washy liberal way, but I'm glad I came out where I did because there has been nothing from the grouse shooters in the last six months that has made me regret it at all. When wishy-washy liberal meets complete intransigence (especially when it is dressed up as being reasonable), then even the wishy-washiest get a harder edge to their opinions.

Turning to the merits of the counter-arguments, there has been nothing that has surprised me. The three main ones deployed by the grouse shooters concern impacts on other wildlife, impacts on the rural economy and impacts on land use.

As far as other wildlife is concerned, we are mostly talking about wading birds. But more waders on the ground, despite the fact that I love them to bits, is actually the side effect of a completely mangled ecology, with most predators being taken out of the system altogether. Add in the other environmental impacts on flooding, carbon emissions and water quality, wildlife crime and damage to peat bogs, and those arguments will work with a few birders but not with those who take a broader view of the ecological costs and benefits.

The financial arguments are footling, really. The sums claimed by the grouse shooters sound large but are small, and they haven't stood up to closer scrutiny. We can be quite certain that, if we cost carbon and water quality and flood risk properly, then the management of the moors for driven grouse shooting is costing us money – even if a few people are making lots of money from it.

There is one last argument which often makes an appearance, and I have been thinking about it as I travel through Bowland on this sunny Sunday morning. It goes something like this: 'Be careful what you wish for. If we don't have grouse shooting then we'll have many more sheep, and many more conifer plantations and many more wind turbines and, as a result, far less wildlife than we do now.' It's not convincing. Here in Bowland, I have been driving through an Area of Natural Beauty (with its Hen Harrier logo!), an SPA and an SSSI. It's just not possible, in the planning system, to wreck such protected landscapes. Many grouse moors are, ironically, in national parks. No one is going to allow some disgruntled grouse-moor owner to put wind turbines across the North York Moors once he is stopped from shooting Red Grouse – it just won't happen. It is a scare story that gets its veneer of plausibility from the past, because in the past, before the designation of so much of the uplands for its environmental value, grouse-moor owners were sometimes a bulwark against forestry and sometimes against overgrazing – although not always, and not everywhere.

The last time I leant on this bridge I was also worried that if I launched an e-petition it might fall flat on its face. There are no regrets on that score – it now stands at well over 19,000 signatures and looks set to reach 20,000 by Christmas. And back then, Hen Harrier Day was a dream and a worry, but now it has been successfully achieved and rated as a success. Jumping off the cliff was the right thing to do, and there was a soft landing.

I have a last look for Dippers, and still can't see any, and then spend some time, on a sunny day, driving around the beautiful Forest of Bowland. I explore small roads and look over the area where Sky and Hope were both lost earlier in the autumn. Perhaps, on my travels, I pass the house of someone who shot them.

Later in the day I drive alongside the famous Wemmergill Moor and later I look again at Weardale. I am enjoying the hills, the sunshine and the opportunity to think about things.

As I turn south for the long drive home I stop in the Yorkshire Dales and see a quarry where Peregrines used to nest successfully but have failed every year for ages. On the adjacent grouse moor is an area where a burn has got out of control and has removed all the vegetation from a steep slope. Further on, I walk through the heather to see a pile of grit marked with a small plastic flag, and I count another 200 of them on the hillside in front of me. This is grouse country, pretty to look at on the surface, but a damaged landscape, dominated by the financial incentive of big money.

Today is Sunday and there is no grouse shooting, and the season has less than three weeks still to run, but there are plans afoot to mark that end with another event. And this time, it might not rain.

9 December

I'd spent the previous evening, in fact until half past midnight, in a St James's club, eating and drinking with a grouse-moor owner. We enjoyed each other's company and talked a lot about Hen Harriers and raptor persecution, but we knew that we'd talked it over so many times before that the chances of a revelation or a solution arising from our conversation was remote. As the number of brandies we consumed increased, the conversation moved more to gossip, teasing and general bonhomie. We were pretty much talked out over Hen Harriers and Red Grouse – we were happy to agree to differ, with smiles on our faces.

As I walked back to my bed, I wondered whether the self-inflicted wounds of high alcohol consumption might have been encouraged by my host as his way of sabotaging my performance for the morrow (or actually later today). Tuesday 9 December was the date of a hastily organised Rally for Nature, convened by the RSPB, the Wildlife Trusts and the League Against Cruel Sports to provide nature lovers with an outlet for their fears and desires, and an opportunity to express them to their politicians at a critical time ahead of the next Westminster general election in May.

The date of this rally had not only been chosen to coincide with the time when the political parties would have their heads wrapped in towels thinking about what to put into their election manifestos, but it was in the last few days before the parliamentary recess. And also, and this was in no way a coincidence, it was the penultimate day of the Red Grouse shooting season for 2014.

I had suggested to a range of organisations and individuals that some sort of event at the end of the grouse-shooting season would provide a fitting book-end, after Hen Harrier Day on 10 August two days before the killing started. And this time we would meet in London, in suits, and enter parliament. And this time – I hoped – the weather would be fine.

The RSPB seemed pretty keen on the idea, as were the Wildlife Trusts, but these two organisations wanted to widen the scope of the day to include wider conservation issues, of which wildlife crime was just one element. That seemed fair enough to me – if I had been in their position I would have done the same – and so the Rally for Nature was general, slightly lacking in focus, but an event that could attract quite a lot of support.

There was a certain amount of to-ing and fro-ing as the League Against Cruel Sports (LACS) came on board. The RSPB and the Wildlife Trusts haven't worked closely with LACS in the past – they have hardly worked together at all – so the inevitable discussions over wording, and details of the event, and who to invite, and how much it would cost, and how much each organisation would pay, were a little more cautious and a little more

elongated than they would have been between organisations
with a long track record of working together. I was glad that
I was able to help things along a few times, but the RSPB's
Martin Harper did the main task of bringing people together to
a common place. And the RSPB's parliamentary team were the
main practical organisers of the day and the run-up to it – they
did a good job.

And so, on the day, as we assembled in Dean's Yard near to
Westminster Abbey, everybody was in a jolly mood. The sun
was shining, we were in our suits (at least those speaking from
the platform were), the room was set, the placards were piled up,
the venue was just about booked out for a morning and afternoon 'sitting' of constituents seeking to see their MPs, and the
speakers were all in place or on their way.

In the morning there were five short speeches, from Mike
Clarke (the RSPB's chief executive), myself, Stephen Trotter
(for the Wildlife Trusts), Caroline Lucas MP (Green, Brighton
Pavilion) and Kerry McCarthy MP (Labour, Bristol East). The
chief executive of LACS, Joe Duckworth, chaired the session.
In the afternoon I was in the chair, Joe did the bit on wildlife
crime, and the MPs were Julian Huppert (Liberal Democrat,
Cambridge) and Sir John Randall (Conservative, Uxbridge
and South Ruislip).

The capacity of the room was around 200 people for each
sitting but there were some no-shows, so there were a few empty
seats. However, the atmosphere was very good. Lots of passionate
nature conservationists.

We walked, twice, the short distance around the block to the
Palace of Westminster, where many of us met our MPs. I saw
mine, Andy Sawford (Labour, Corby), in Portcullis House on
the other side of the road from the tower housing Big Ben.

The day was a success because it was put together at quite
short notice. It was a success because just about every MP in
parliament received a communication from a constituent on this
matter. And it was a success because it brought three major
organisations together in a new coalition: RSPB, the Wildlife
Trusts and the League Against Cruel Sports. On the day, it was
a success too – there were lots of smiles, people got on well,
nobody fell off the stage, the parliamentarians made excellent
speeches and it felt like a good event.

It was also a success because Charles Moore, former editor of the *Daily Telegraph* (and grouse shooter; not to be confused with Charlie Moores, leading light in BAWC) felt moved to criticise those hundreds of people who were exercising their democratic right to protest – although he did call me an 'expert campaigner'.

17 December

The e-petition reaches 20,000 signatures whilst I am asleep on Tuesday night. It has achieved this inside seven months and without the active support of any wildlife conservation organisation. It just shows what can be done by a small group of people with determination and a Twitter account!

By contrast, Andrew Gilruth's e-petition, having reached 10,000 in September, languishes at below 11,000 today. David has beaten a bunch of Goliaths, at least as far as e-petition signatures are concerned.

29 December

I've been reading the seven-year report of the Langholm 2 project, prompted by the very different interpretations of two of the partners of the study, the GWCT and the RSPB, both of whom have blogged about it. You can hardly believe that they are talking about the same piece of research.

This study is the 'let's throw everything at the problem' demonstration study, which is attempting to get the Langholm estate into a state where lots of Red Grouse can be shot there again, even if there are plenty of Hen Harriers and other raptors.

Seven years into the ten-year study there are suddenly lots of Hen Harriers – 12 females who produced 47 fledged young. This population increase is probably due to the large numbers of voles this year – far more than in any year of the Joint Raptor Study, I'm told. And, of course, the Hen Harriers now receive diversionary food rather than having to go out and catch their own Meadow Pipits or Skylarks or Red Grouse, so they aren't having much impact on Red Grouse populations at all. Already the Red Grouse population has passed the level at which shooting was feasible and profitable in the early days of Langholm 1, but the grouse shooters are trying to portray this great success as a failure – it's all rather odd.

The GWCT is suggesting that restoring the Red Grouse July counts (on which decisions on the amount of shooting that should follow are based) to levels not seen since 1992, when grouse shooting took place, is a 'fail' rather than a 'pass' even though the project has three more years to run. It's very strange that the RSPB is saying 'Let's get some grouse shot at Langholm' and the GWCT is saying 'Not enough grouse to shoot yet'. I see this as another bizarre attempt to spin the information, and the reputation of the GWCT has dropped a bit further, as far as I am concerned.

We'll have to see what happens in the final three years of the study but, to some extent, Langholm is likely to be side-lined by then. If grouse shooting can't find a way to live with Hen Harriers and other aspects of nature then it is surely doomed. The tide of public opinion is moving too quickly against this 'sport'.

31 December

So where does that leave us all? 2014 was the year of the Hen Harrier. It had seen the first public protests against illegal killing of Hen Harriers on Hen Harrier Day at a range of sites across the country, which received much publicity and changed the whole tenor of media coverage of the opening of the grouse-shooting season. My e-petition to ban driven grouse shooting had gained considerable support through taking a more radical line than that of the major wildlife organisations, and despite not being promoted by them. Birders Against Wildlife Crime had come into being. The RSPB, the Wildlife Trusts and LACS had started working more closely together on wildlife crime issues than ever before. A major retailer had decided not to put grouse meat on its shelves in response to public pressure. The RSPB had hardened its stance and called for the licensing of driven grouse shooting, and had rejected a brood-management scheme for Hen Harriers. On the English uplands, Hen Harrier populations remained very low, and satellite-tagged birds had disappeared in circumstances that suggested that they had been killed. The economic case for grouse shooting had been taken apart, and the ecosystem services case that grouse-moor management was unsustainable had been firmed up by a major scientific study.

No longer was the discussion about whether Hen Harriers and grouse shooting could co-exist; it was increasingly about whether grouse shooting had any legitimacy as a land use.

The grouse shooters were rattled. Their case for continuing the sport was being challenged in public and with determination. The next general election was approaching fast and this government, a government more friendly to grouse shooting than could necessarily be expected of the next and future governments, had done nothing concrete to please the grouse shooters. They were desperate for a scheme to manage Hen Harriers and were looking more and more desperate, more and more frantic and more and more unreasonable.

This was also a significant year for grouse shooting because ordinary people began to make their voices heard, through rallies, through e-petitions and through social media. It was no longer the case that everyone waited for the RSPB response on an issue – they could speak up themselves. The people found their voice. The many began to realise that they could influence the few.

And it had been great fun, too. I had spent time with lots of great people, and made lots of new friends.

I wish I had had a few more stunning views of Hen Harriers through the year. They had been quite elusive, considering I was on their side. But I thought back to my last trip to north Wales, in early December. It was a dull afternoon on Anglesey when Alan Davies and I stood looking over the Malltraeth estuary and its flocks of Shelduck, Oystercatchers and Curlew. Ravens were continually overhead with their deep calls drawing my eye upwards. A pair of Stonechats perched on the barbed wire fence by our side. Little Egrets stalked the mud and occasionally flew over the trees. In front of us stretched a wide flat saltmarsh, and in the distance we could see the estuary mouth to the southwest. The saltmarsh was bordered by forest, birch trees, still with some golden leaves, at the base of the woodland and much taller conifers filling the slopes behind.

This time I saw it first, and I said 'What's that?' as it disappeared into a creek or a dip in the land. But when it emerged in a second or two Alan said, 'Male Hen Harrier' – and so it was. We watched it for a few seconds as it flew quickly along the saltmarsh looking down for signs of a vole or a bird to flush and then catch. It kept flying left and disappeared behind some trees, and we congratulated ourselves on a pretty good view – but then it was back, giving us much better and extended views.

This was an adult male, with no sign of brown in its plumage. The grey male Hen Harrier, a grey ghost, with its very pale underwings, particularly noticeable when the bird pauses in the air or almost stalls to look harder at a patch of ground, its white rump and its black wingtips – this is such a classy-looking bird. It was visible on and off for about 20 minutes, at first around a kilometre away, and then occasionally coming closer, to within 300 metres. Each time he disappeared we thought that was it for the evening, but he kept coming back. During his absences we would scan the saltmarsh up and down from where we were for other harriers, perhaps a ringtail or two coming to roost with 'our' male – but none appeared.

Where had this bird come from? Was it the male I had seen up at the Lake Site in June? Maybe, although the chances were slim, and it might not even have been a Welsh bird. It could have come from England (although that was unlikely since there are so few), from Scotland, from the Isle of Man or maybe even from Ireland. We'll never know, and we were both sure that it was not a bird carrying a satellite or any other sort of tag – we could see it so well through Alan's excellent telescope.

Why do Hen Harriers roost together? Why don't they just sit in a tree at night rather than roost on the ground and have to look and listen for Red Foxes and other ground predators until dawn? What determines their wide wanderings, which can take them into so much danger? There is much still to understand about this raptor, but each time the male returned we watched it, enjoying the great view of a marvellous bird.

At one point a Sparrowhawk emerged from the forest and started mobbing our bird. Neither of us had seen this before. The Sparrowhawk was quite persistent – it went on for about 30 seconds or more. The Hen Harrier wasn't much bothered by it, it seemed, although its hunting was interrupted and it had to show the Sparrowhawk its long legs, and the claws at their ends, a few times. What was in the Sparrowhawk's mind? I have no idea.

As the light faded no more birds turned up and we found it more and more difficult to follow our male. Almost our last view was of him flying with the estuary mouth far behind him and the sun setting behind that. The male Hen Harrier flew through the thin strip of orange sky as though flying down a tunnel of light – its characteristic shape, black, against the bright sunset. I've never seen the like before and I guess I never will again.

It was a treat that we both enjoyed. It was only fair – it was Alan's birthday. But we might have seen nothing and it still would have been worth trying. Or we might have seen a ring-tail, and that would have been good, but the adult males are just superb birds. And we could have seen it just briefly, or just the once. But we had a feast of multiple views. We were both buoyed up by our success and by what we had seen. As we walked back to the car, Alan voiced one of the thoughts that had kept entering my head: 'How could anyone kill that?'

Perhaps 2014 will pale into insignificance compared with 2015 or 2016, but today it seems that the ground shifted this year. One year, there will come a time when driven grouse shooting is a thing of the past. What, I wonder, might that look like?

*

What I would like you to take away from this chapter:

- The major change in 2014 was not that the evidence increased for the environmental and wildlife harm caused by driven grouse shooting, although it certainly did, but that more people became involved in the issue. No longer was this a subject discussed by interested parties in private – thanks to Birders Against Wildlife Crime, the Northwest Raptor Protection Group, the Raptor Persecution Scotland website, *Ethical Consumer* magazine, *Birdwatch* magazine, Chris Packham and myself, aided and abetted by many others, the future of grouse shooting was now a talking point amongst birders, nature conservationists and environmental-ists alike. And the discussion was not limited to tinkering with the existing system, but it went so far as to include the idea that we should just dump grouse shooting altogether as a harmful activity beyond redemption.

- A few blokes (for they were, mostly, blokes) had raised the issue sufficiently through social media, a provocative e-petition, use of the traditional media, an old-fashioned public rally and every other means they could think of to bring the issues increasingly to the public's attention. And the public had responded by turning out in their hundreds, by signing the e-petition in their thousands and by sending messages through social media in their millions. And all organisations involved in the private debate had had to raise their game to respond to the outpouring of public anger through the year, which included hundreds of people on Hen Harrier Day.

- The events of 2014 raised the hope that popular protest could play a part in saving the Hen Harrier and improving the management of our uplands.

CHAPTER SIX

The sunlit uplands

Yesterday is not ours to recover, but tomorrow is ours to win or lose.

Lyndon B. Johnson

The year is 2046. Terry used to work as a gamekeeper in the uplands. Let's hear what he has to say, in his own words:

You know, it's funny looking back. I'm not sure why we fought it so long. The writing was on the wall after the first Langholm project. It was either grouse shooting or protected wildlife – you couldn't have both, and how were we ever going to persuade a predominantly urban population that a bunch of toffs in tweed should be able to tell their gamekeepers to shoot a beautiful bird just so that they could shoot more of another bird, largely for sport (in other words, largely for the fun of it) a few weeks later? It was a hopeless case. The only way we could win was if no one noticed what we were doing.

Some of the landowners argued that the Hen Harrier should lose its protected status – but that was never going to happen, was it? Blimey! And these people are running the country in the House of Lords! I hope they show more judgement there. Some say the weakness of leadership on our side, although I don't really think of it as our side anymore, was due to problems in the IQ department, caused by eating too much lead-poisoned game meat, but I wouldn't know about that.

The raptor killing was really the nail in the coffin of driven grouse shooting. Once the RSPB got stuck in to this issue they were never going to give up – they don't, you know. Over the years it came and went in profile but wildlife crime is not an easy thing to live with if you're trying to market a countryside pursuit that involves killing things as a way to appreciate the countryside. Many people think that argument is strange enough, but when you add in the legal killing of huge numbers of crows and Foxes and Stoats, and then people keep going on about all the other stuff that is killed illegally too, then this love of the countryside seems to include an awful lot of killing of wildlife. It was a mess, all right.

All those hundreds of Stoats I've taken out of Fenn traps were OK because the public generally never saw them. What the eye didn't see, and all that! Even Foxes – nobody really knows how many Foxes there are or should be in the hills, and the farmers were happy to see them go, so the legal killing of mammals didn't cause us any problems, really. No one saw the bodies, no one saw the actual deaths and no one noticed they were gone – except those who were keen that they were gone. Not a problem.

But the birds of prey – we went far too far there. It was easy enough to kill them – there aren't lots of coppers up in the hills – but it was so easy, and we were so incentivised and pressurised to kill them, that we wiped them out from large areas of the country. Whole counties which should have had scores of Peregrines and Hen Harriers had none, basically – and if a couple got through one year then the keeper got it in the neck from his boss, too.

We actually used to have a laugh in the early days when I was a keeper and the RSPB published its *Birdcrime* reports – they didn't know the half of it. They would have a list of a hundred suspected or confirmed incidents involving birds of prey (I can't remember what they were really), but the fact was we knew that wasn't just the tip of the iceberg, it was the tip of the tip of the iceberg.

There was a group of us keepers once and we reckoned we could name 20 large estates that were killing every year the same number of birds of prey as the RSPB had got wind of for the whole of the country. It was part of the job, and it wasn't a hard part. In fact it was easy.

We gamekeepers called ourselves a profession. Obviously it wasn't a profession like being a doctor or a lawyer but we had a range of skills and we were proud of what we could do. Probably like most professions, there were some practices that we all thought we could improve – snaring was always a tricky issue, but better and kinder snares were brought in over the years.

Although there would always be some idiot who would still be using old ones – and of course it was those snares that some walker would come across and photograph a Fox with the snare biting into its leg and blood everywhere. Or some other idiot would leave his snares unchecked for too long and someone would find a long-dead animal.

But, generally speaking, keepering became a bit more scientific and a bit less based on prejudice as time went on. The old Game Conservancy Trust did a lot to increase our knowledge and to help keepers do a better job. I had a lot of time for them in the old days, but they became addicted to spin as time went on. I guess what some of us were doing was so difficult to justify it was easier to pretend it wasn't happening. In the end they folded – there wasn't much call for science when no amount of science could justify what was happening.

In the end, with all that satellite-tag stuff, you could hardly point your shotgun at a bird of prey without fearing it might be a tagged bird that was being monitored in real time by some 20-year-old working for Natural England or the RSPB who would be picking up the phone, in her nice warm office, and phoning the police as soon as the bird stopped transmitting. I know of a few keepers who've said they missed their shot because they had that picture in their heads.

But plenty of tagged raptors bit the dust, or the peat anyway. There was that year in the late 2010s when all those harriers died in the summer and then those eagles in the autumn – it was carnage!

I don't know how much money was poured into satellite-tagging Hen Harriers but it was money well spent from their point of view. For a while, our side could shrug off the missing birds and keep muttering, 'Tag malfunction, probably tag malfunction' – but once there were so many tagged in different parts of the country then the pattern was clear for all to see. Birds tagged in Wales did fine, their tags didn't pack up, unless they travelled to grouse moors in the north of England, and then their lifespan was quite short. Same with the birds on the Isle of Man – safe as houses there, but travel across to Lancashire, or get as far as Yorkshire, and the tags had a high 'failure rate'. And so many birds were 'failing' on grouse-moor areas that even though no one could tell who'd killed them (apart from that prat who was filmed doing it, of course), then there was no ducking the fact.

There had been no ducking the fact anyway, it's just that it was so much more newsworthy if a known bird, with a known life history of travelling around the country, died in suspicious circumstances. And the RSPB and others weren't fools – they made sure all the birds were named by the local primary schools – my daughter was at one of them! – for maximum tear-jerking effect. The birds that survived became interesting characters with their life histories well known, and the ones that disappeared became victims that everyone cared about. Very clever stuff.

And then, and then, there was the autumn of dead eagles in Scotland, wasn't there? Obviously, the one that people remember best is the one found at Balmoral, because that was a media frenzy, even though everyone knew it had been poisoned else-where. It was a few months after the old Queen had abdicated in favour of King Charles and that had been a fair old media storm, of course. Then King Charles made a speech, quite a political speech, in favour of the environment and with quite a lot about nature in it, using Balmoral as an example of sound habitat management. And then Prince William, clearly with his dad's blessing, talked about how upset he was that rhinos and tigers were killed abroad – and then a poisoned eagle turns up at Balmoral!

For a while the story was out there that it had actually been poisoned on the royal estate, but it wasn't that bad – the RSPB and others were quick to say that the eagle had been behaving strangely for a few days, had visited several estates and had simply died at Balmoral. But there was all that film of the RSPB and a bunch of coppers driving through the Balmoral estate, locating the poisoned eagle and taking it off for analysis. That image of it being held with its wings outstretched looking so forlorn, a mighty bird brought low by poison, and then taken away in a plastic bag, with Balmoral in the background, will stick in a lot of people's minds.

Of course, the estate had to make a very firm statement about its opposition to breaking the law, and the prince's condemna-tion of wildlife crime seemed to everyone to come from the heart. It wasn't a great day for shooting estates. And then as luck would have it, a bit like buses, along came another couple of dead eagles in other parts of eastern Scotland, both dying on grouse moors, and there wasn't such a rush to say that it couldn't possibly have been the owners who did it this time. No prosecutions ensued, but nobody would forget the summer of dead Hen Harriers and the autumn of dead Golden Eagles.

There was a time when the gamekeeper was a highly respected figure on the estates, especially upland estates. The head keeper had a lot of power. It was partly because he commanded a bunch of fit young men who were probably handy with their fists and wouldn't take no for an answer, but it was also because we were respected for the work we did – hard work, sometimes unpleasant work, skilful work and tough work. With the rise of the media, especially social media, and the increasing technology that showed that birds were going missing, it became much more difficult to hold your head up high when you went into the village to pick up a pint of milk or post a letter.

I remember that happening once. I'd been up early in the morning, driven up onto the moors to check some traps and snares and I decided to check a pair of Goshawks in a nearby wood. The wood wasn't on our estate but the owner did a bit of shooting, and he wanted to keep in with my owner, and so we had access to bits of his land. I went into the wood and flushed a Gos off a kill, it was on a Pheasant too, and as it flew off I got off two shots and brought it down. Feathers everywhere.

I picked up the body, checked that it didn't have any sort of transmitter on it, and then buried it in the wood a little way off the path. The chances of anyone finding it were tiny. As I drove back for breakfast I listened to the end of the *Today* programme on the radio and the last item was some smart-Alec from the RSPB talking about keepers killing birds of prey. It did make me feel a bit odd, and later that morning I was almost sure Mavis in the post office gave me a funny look. Had she heard the programme too? Did I look a bit guilty?

There wasn't much that you could do if you were the newest, youngest keeper on a moor, you had to fit in. If the estate was a killing estate, and so many of them were, then you had to kill raptors or you were out on your ear and labelled as a trouble-maker. One of the ways that some managers ensured they had their staff under their thumb was that they would secretly video a keeper breaking the law and use it to put the pressure on if ever they had to do so. A young keeper might be taken to a quarry up on the moors in a Land Rover with several other keepers and dropped off with the words, 'This is a Peregrine site – you know what to do.' And all the other keepers would stare the lad down if he looked at all doubtful. When he shot the adult Peregrine off the nest he was filmed by another man hiding in the heather, but he'd never know his crime was on film unless it became necessary. The lad would be picked up a few hours later and all the other keepers would be especially friendly to him. If he had any doubts he'd soon get over them, and then killing became a habit.

We had a variety of ways to get rid of Hen Harriers, not that we saw them that often on our moor, but shooting at roosts was a favoured activity on many moors. Harriers use pretty much the same areas to roost in each night and each year, they must remember them from year to year as they travel around the country (it's quite clever of them, really). A walk across the area that they used for roosting near dusk, just a line of two or three men, would flush the birds, and we would usually get a few of them. The most I've seen killed on a roost visit was three, but I've heard of much larger numbers at other roosts. It was pretty easy, pretty effective, and we'd all go to the pub afterwards and those who hadn't shot a bird would have to buy the drinks for those that had.

I remember one keeper telling me he'd seen another man finish off a Hen Harrier nest by releasing a tame ferret down-wind of the nest and letting it eat the eggs. When the guy from the RSPB came along to check, some townie I'm sure, he'd have thought it was a case of natural predation. Gone were the days of deliberately leaving bootprints by the nest just to make the point to the raptor workers that it was our work.

Ice, or sometimes dry ice, was another weapon in the armoury. Pour it on the eggs and they'd chill and fail, but the bird would keep incubating for ages after the eggs should have hatched. The eggs were killed, there were fewer mouths to be fed with grouse chicks, and the evidence literally evaporated.

On some moors they would leave a single pair of Hen Harriers through the season, but often only one egg would hatch and one chick would fledge (if any!). This was done simply by visiting the nest when the female was incubating and giving all but one of the eggs a good shaking to kill off the embryos. The one chick that hatched would get all the parents' attention, but with only one mouth to feed they weren't too much of a problem. Some of the large moors used to pull this trick so that they could say that they'd had a successful nest and look good when the RSPB or Natural England came round checking on nesting numbers and their success. Of course they'd tend to leave the nest with the single chick at the edge of the moor, so that the neighbouring estate would share the problem anyway.

And that was a problem sometimes; if the keeper on the neighbouring moor was lazy or had an overactive sense of legality, then you might get a Hen Harrier nest close to your moor but on your neighbour's land. Usually a phone call, or better a face-to-face chat, would resolve the issue and you'd find that the nest had failed soon afterwards – it's good to be neighbourly. But if the keeper were frit then he'd often tell you to do the deed yourself and that would be almost as good. Although once when I did do that it almost came unstuck as the other keeper ended up in court and my boss felt he had to pay the legal expenses for the other estate.

But if a neighbouring estate was very reluctant to sort out birds of prey then they'd soon realise that they weren't part of the community – they'd be ostracised. There were plenty of jobs on a moor where an extra pair of hands came in useful, and keepers often helped each other out with burning, beating and a host of repair jobs. A keeper whose beat had too many birds of prey might well find that his fellow keepers weren't so keen to give him a hand when he needed it – the message got through pretty quickly.

If a keeper found himself working for a killing estate and wasn't up for the level of killing that was expected, then his contract would be terminated. Some of these moor managers really played hard ball – they used to say that nothing would stop them delivering a good day's shooting. If the sacked keeper went to an employment tribunal, then he might find that dead sheep kept being dumped on his garden path in the middle of the night – that's pretty scary for a family man with young kids. Not many of them could stand that type of pressure – remember they were living, most of them, out in the wilds and we all know that the law doesn't reach right up into the hills.

Imagine the impact on a keeper's wife of a car load of men wearing balaclavas parking their Land Rover in your driveway, facing your kitchen window, and just sitting there staring at your house for half an hour. They don't say anything, they don't do anything, but they are on your property and the warning is clear. It's not the type of intimidation that most people have to face, but it happened in my world.

The keepers all knew that they were vulnerable – most of them were in tied accommodation and so were dependent on the estate for somewhere to live through retirement, too. The stories got around the keepering community quickly, as you can imagine. One old keeper, on a big estate, was coming up to retirement and the estate came and inspected his house and outbuildings – well they weren't his, they were theirs. They found a rusty tin of alphachloralose in the barn and sacked him on the spot because it was illegal to possess it as a poison that had no possible legal use in the uplands. That way, they got him out of his cottage and brought in a real hard-nosed, no-compromise keeper from Scotland who really went to town on birds of prey in a way that the old keeper never had.

We killed everything in those days. We even killed off the Merlins on some moors even though they were harmless little falcons (although I have seen a couple of Red Grouse chicks in Merlin nests in my time). Those raptor workers were a funny lot – they were dead keen! And they wanted to ring everything. We'd rather they weren't on the moors at some times of year, there was too much going on, and so we'd just get rid of anything they wanted to ring so that there wasn't any reason to ask for permission to come onto the moors late in the year. We'd have left the Merlins alone if the raptor workers had left us alone.

But there were some raptor workers that were so keen on their Merlins that they would turn a blind eye to us killing Peregrines and Hen Harriers just so long as we let them come and ring the Merlins. These guys were worth their weight in gold – we looked good because the birds were being ringed and monitored and so we could restrict access to just that one guy and tell all the awkward ones to sling their hooks!

There were some stand-offs between raptor workers and keepers over the years. Some of the raptor workers were a bit mouthy and they'd sometimes find their cars scratched or in severe cases all their tyres slashed. There's nothing better to make you think about what you are up to than to get back to your car after hours walking the hills in the wind and the rain, and find that all your tyres are down, you have no phone reception and it's a Sunday. Quite a few of the more prying guys were encouraged to find another hobby in that way.

I didn't feel guilty about killing birds of prey in those days, I'd killed so many Carrion Crows, Foxes and Stoats over the years, hundreds and hundreds of them, that the occasional bird of prey really didn't seem to make much difference. I don't think a Hen Harrier suffers any more than a Carrion Crow, does it? But I did wonder whether people were talking about me behind my back and wondering whether our estate was 'at it' with birds of prey. And of course we were – it's just that we could keep on denying it because nobody could pin it on us personally.

The fact that raptor workers and the RSPB, and that lot called Birders Against Wildlife Crime, kept talking about 'illegal persecution', 'wildlife crime' and 'criminals' really got under the skin of the owners. It made some of them angry, and it made others think.

There was that ridiculous incident with members of the pro-hunting lobby, fronting up an attack on the RSPB for everything from … actually I can't remember what they were supposed to have done but it was so transparently an attack from shooting interests, and so ill-targeted, that nobody paid it any attention. In fact, if anything, it mobilised the RSPB membership and got them to put pressure on the RSPB to do more and make more of a stand.

No, the news spread through social media – do you remember Twitter – pretty old-fashioned-looking now, isn't it? – and there was no way of keeping a lid on it. In the old days the rumours of raptor killing, or even the proven cases, were a one-day wonder, but with social media any old dear with a computer could help spread the word and there was nothing that our side, even the dukes and earls, could do about it. The scale of illegal killing had to be kept a secret, and there came a time when it couldn't be any more.

For years it was possible for grouse shooting to shrug off its crimes, but growing public awareness put paid to that. Whole websites grew up that publicised wildlife crime. Raptor Persecution Scotland was one of the first of them, and one of the best, we all used to read it to see what other keepers had been up to, and to read about the sentences that were handed down. So did our bosses, and just as we wondered, so did they, whether we would end up being featured there one unlucky day.

When the snob value of grouse shooting diminished and those lads from the City went back and people asked them whether they'd seen any birds of prey when they were out shooting, then the whole thing rather lost its shine. It was public opinion that closed down grouse shooting. It was when the crimes couldn't be denied and the knowledge of them spread widely that it became more and more difficult for people to brazen it out and talk about 'just a few bad apples'.

*

What am I doing now? I'm working as a land manager in the Peak District. I've been sent to college and on loads of courses and I now have a pretty good job, but I'm still out in the open air a lot, which suits me fine. My life has changed beyond recognition and I am so much happier now although I am coming up to retirement soon. I've had two jobs really, 25 years as a gamekeeper and almost as long working for the National Trust. We are now stewards of the land, and I feel proud of what I do in a way that I never was when I was keepering.

Instead of a single-focus land use which was simply designed to produce as many Red Grouse to be shot as possible, I am involved in all aspects of the life and ecology of the hills.

I guess I'm part of the development of the National Trust High Peak Vision that they started back in the 2010s. It's worked well – people have come from all over the world to see what we've done, and of course we led the way amongst national parks in England and Wales. The National Trust's new chief executive is always going on about how the Kinder Scout mass trespass led to the concept of national parks in the UK and eventually to the right to roam, and how the Hen Harrier Day rallies over the years in the Peak District had led to the banning of driven grouse shooting. You'd almost think the National Trust started the whole thing off! What a hoot! To be fair, it was the focus on wildlife crime and the poor condition of the peat bogs in this national park that helped deliver change right across the uplands of England, and a shift to a less intensive type of management that conserved wildlife and also, very importantly, delivered carbon storage, clean water and a much reduced flood risk. A great deal of the moorland rehabilitation was done here – and many of the scientific studies that demonstrated its value to society as a whole, too.

There was a big campaign in the late 2010s to change the whole focus of English national parks. Although they'd been set up to protect natural beauty they were clearly falling far short of this goal. When there are precious few birds of prey living in national parks whose aim is to conserve natural beauty, then it's a pretty glaring elephant in the room. Wildlife crimes were committed in national parks just as often as outside them, and the 'Peak Malpractice' reports had made that clear for the Peak District in particular. Nobody was doing much about it except wringing their hands and saying how much they disapproved of people killing birds of prey, but then they sat in the same room as the wildlife criminals and treated them like fine upstanding leaders of the community. Eventually, through changes in personnel over time, and changes in political climate, and a continuing campaign through the media, publicising wildlife crime, this position became untenable.

Obviously, in these parts we are very proud of being the first national park to ban grouse shooting within our boundaries – it was the Labour/Green coalition that made that possible. We were the first national park to put the proposition to local people and it was carried overwhelmingly. Rather surprisingly, the Yorkshire Dales was the next in line. I wouldn't have predicted that, but then we keepers didn't get out much and talk to normal people. Clearly, the no-compromise, no-tolerance line that many moorland owners had taken wasn't so popular after all, and in a secret ballot, where the landowners couldn't tell how people were voting, there was a big majority for ending driven grouse shooting. It wasn't really that anybody locally bothered about grouse shooting, they just didn't like grouse shooters much.

Anyway, once there were two national parks where driven grouse shooting wasn't allowed, then people could see what impact it had. Pretty quickly the Red Grouse numbers went down but nobody locally really noticed that – it's not as though Red Grouse came into people's gardens or anything. Fewer Red Grouse made no difference at all to most people. But the Hen Harriers came back quite quickly. With two national parks without grouse shooting there was a critical mass of land where they were safe. It was a bit like Langholm – in the first major vole year Hen Harriers reached double figures in each national park and that made their absence from the North Pennines, the North York Moors, Northumberland and most of Cumbria all the more noticeable. It was almost as good as an experiment.

The campaigns run by the Wildlife Trusts and the RSPB (that was before they merged, of course) to encourage tourism in the national parks where raptors were left alone made a big difference to the local economies of the Peak District and the Yorkshire Dales – people flocked in (pun intended!) to see Short-eared Owls, Merlins, Ring Ouzels and all the other birds, as well as Foxes and Badgers. People voted with their feet (in their walking boots) and with their wallets. It became a matter of pride for all those Hen Harrier Day protesters to come back and spend a weekend to show their support. Many B&Bs gave 10% off to members of the Wildlife Trusts, the National Trust, the RSPB and BAWC – who'd have thought it? The grouse-moor owners didn't realise that townies would pay good money to see a few Foxes up close. We'd been bumping these things off for years and years and now I have a team of people who spend scores of evenings taking people's money and showing them Fox cubs! Talk about killing the goose that lays the golden egg.

What we did here, and what happened in the Yorkshire Dales, led the way. Now people write about how the national parks found their purpose in life again in the late 2010s. By the mid-2020s grouse shooting was in steep decline because the public knew it depended on wildlife crime, and the politicians and policy makers were following the 'Nature's Gifts' (what used to be called 'ecosystem services') agenda. And local communities were supporting the changes they saw on the ground. Money poured into the Peak District from central government, the EU, local government, business and NGOs, and that money benefitted those who were trying to make a living here. The national parks that were slow to realise what the future would look like, the North York Moors is the obvious example, lost public support – some even talked about withdrawing national park status. And then, on the other hand, once grouse shooting was on the wane in the North Pennines Area of Outstanding Natural Beauty, that's what really clinched it when they applied to become a national park. By the time parliament finally banned driven grouse shooting in England in 2030, it was fizzling out anyway. The national politicians were catching up with local decisions rather than leading the way.

If you look at the hills where Red Grouse were once driven towards the guns in late August, you'll see that the chequer-board of burned patches has gone. We still burn the heather now and again, partly for old times' sake but also in a few cases to reduce fire risk. We don't have to do it very much, as the cattle that graze the hills keep the heather under control but allow woodland to spread up the cloughs and valleys, establish on the cliffs and ledges, and form patches across the hills. Some of the old grouse butts are still standing – in fact they are a favourite picnic place for walkers on some of the trails that cross the moors – but today's kids don't have any recollection of grouse shooting, and they don't miss it. They appreciate the Peak District National Park for its natural beauty and as a resource right on the doorstep of Sheffield and Manchester. As far as they're concerned it's a great place to visit, with lots of wildlife, and they have a vague appreciation of the ecosystem services it delivers.

The tops of the hills are still blanket bogs, but they are in so much better condition now that they are not burned. And the ravages of air pollution have been removed. Peatland restoration has gathered momentum apace now that peat is valued as a carbon store.

Last week the prime minister made a speech about climate change and she was boasting about the fact that England and Wales had increased our carbon storage through land management more than any other EU country (although now that the EU is down to a manageable dozen countries again, that isn't saying quite as much as it used to). Some muttered under their breaths that it was only because we had such knackered uplands, after a couple of centuries of mismanagement, that we were able to do so well, and there is some truth in that, but it's not the whole truth. As the Country Land and Business Association pointed out, upland landowners have responded readily and with enthusiasm to the incentives for carbon storage. Now the landowners round here are making a fortune out of the peat payments they receive, and they're all boasting about the quality and growth of their *Sphagnum* instead of their heather.

The old grouse shooters weren't sold on the idea of climate change, but there is no doubt about it these days – although, to be fair, there wasn't much doubt about it then either. But the weather has changed and with it the vegetation of the uplands a bit. Certainly the birds are a bit different. I'd never seen a Dartford Warbler before a few years ago – I'd heard they lived down south on heathery places in Dorset and Hampshire, but now they are up here in the hills living alongside the Meadow Pipits and Skylarks and being eaten by Merlins and Hen Harriers.

Talking of Hen Harriers, there are more of them here now, they're quite a common sight, but not so many as everyone thought there would be. I guess it's the change in land use, with all these birch and Aspens spreading over the moorland slopes. But it might be the local Golden Eagles that keep the Hen Harrier numbers low. In fact, nobody really pays that much attention to Hen Harriers now, nor to the Red Grouse that used to be the commonest birds on these hills. How things change.

No, it's the eagles that the visitors want to see, and many of them do. They are eating the occasional grouse, Black as well as Red, and deer and plenty of hares and Rabbits. Who'd have thought that Golden Eagles would be nesting in the Snake Pass in an area where not a single raptor was left alive a few decades ago? Those eagles are worth hundreds of thousands of pounds, maybe millions actually, to the local economy each year – they are a real bonus on top of the government payments for low grazing and little burning, which are rewards for land management that stores carbon and manages water resources so much better too. And it's nice that we don't have to go abroad – to Scotland or Norway, for example – to see eagles any more.

There is a lot more woodland here these days, too. People like that. It's a good idea for a busy national park because it brings in the visitors, and on busy days the crowds aren't so obvious if they're spread through a woodland rather than lines of people in red cagoules strung out over the moorlands. Of course there are now Red Squirrels in our woods and they are very popular. Some really rare butterflies, both Pearl-bordered and Small Pearl-bordered Fritillary, have come back, too. And now you hear lots of warblers singing in the woods. One of my favourite spots is where the forest has spread over one of the lowest grouse butts in the Park – lots of birdsong where once there was lots of gunfire.

Here in the High Peak we were a bit hacked off that we missed out on being chosen as the site for the first Lynx reintro-duction programme in England. We reckoned that we were wild enough for them, but the money and the project went to the Lake District instead, lucky buggers! That would have been an enormous money earner. Still, we are doing pretty well now compared with the bad old days. There is more money and, of course, a lot more of it stays in the local community compared with the previous regime. In those days, the money from grouse shooting was all spent by the owners in London clubs and at Royal Ascot.

The work of us gamekeepers was hard in the old days, and it's quite a change to be paid for doing rather little, just not doing a bunch of bad things like heather burning. Some criticise it for being money for old rope – and in a way it is. But my new boss is keen to point out that he is providing a public good, through reducing carbon emissions, which benefits everyone in the world, and that must surely be better than earning money from blasting birds out of the air. He's got a point, although the way he puts it doesn't go down well with some of the old keepers, who still hanker after what they call the 'good old days'.

We also get money from the water companies, as our land use now sends cleaner, less acidic water downstream. The operating costs for treatment plants have come right down – they are only used a few times a year after exceptional rains, whereas they used to be operating all the time. Water bills have come down slightly as a result, although I don't think anyone will have noticed that in these days of summer drought. The people who have noticed, though, are fishermen. I'd love a quid (sorry, I mean a euro, it's hard to shake off old habits) for all the times I've been told that the rivers around here have come alive again in the last decade. There are people yanking trout, and big trout, out of rivers in northern England that were hardly worth fishing in the shooting and burning days. Less acidic water, less particulate pollution, and a bit less of the sudden massive floods have sorted all that out. You don't have to be a fisherman; I'm not one myself, but you can see the insect life in and flying above the becks and rivers round here and really see the difference. There are more Dippers and Common Sandpipers and Grey Wagtails as a result, too.

And home insurance bills have decreased a bit for an awful lot of people living downstream of many upland areas because of the reduced incidence of flooding. It's actually very rare now that a lowland town is flooded by flash floods of water coming off the hills. You've got to think that land management is a big part of that change. Well, we get paid for it anyway, so what do I care?

Of course, we're lucky that we're in a national park here. Here in the Peak District there's money available for loads of stuff connected to tourism. It is an amazing turnaround – these days you can tell whether you are in or out of the national park just by looking around you – the landscape is so different. These landscapes are now for people, people who live locally but also all those people who come out here from Sheffield and Manchester, and from further afield, at the weekends and in the holidays.

The main point of these upland landscapes is now to serve the public. Some of the old landowners have sold up to organisations like the National Trust, but also the Forest and Wildlife Service of the government is a big landowner in national parks. This has ensured that the taxpayer really does get good value from the hills. Gone are the days when the taxes from some poorly paid care-worker or teacher were going to a duke so he could use them to subsidise his grouse shooting. These days the uplands are open access and are used by the population. Some areas are closed each year, during the nesting season, for birds and other wildlife to thrive, and some access roads have been closed completely, so that you can go anywhere but it's more of an effort. But the really nice thing is that this has reconnected the town and the country-side to an amazing extent. House prices have increased and there are now what used to be called yuppies buying homes in terraces in Glossop and Penistone! Who'd have thought that? The locals don't complain, except about the funny southern accents, because the communities are more vibrant than they ever were – they are richer both socially and financially.

Take my daughter, who's in her forties now. When she was growing up, the places around here were really run down, and although she loved the hills she had to go down south to find a half-decent job. But she came back when things picked up here, with her southern husband, and they've both done really well, and had a variety of jobs that are based on the 'Ecology for All' ethos of the Peak District National Park. And the community in which my two grandchildren are growing up is so much more modern, forward-thinking and diverse than when I was a lad or my daughter was growing up. It's good to see.

The land prices for open moorland swung about like crazy for a couple of decades. There were fortunes to be made and lost if you moved in the right direction at the right time. As shooting came under pressure some saw what would happen and sold out at the top of the market. Some of them, I think, squeezed the moors dry for big grouse bags and then sold up just before grouse shooting went into its terminal decline. Then those shooting types who were stuck with grouse moors where you couldn't shoot grouse were looking at big losses. Some sold to wildlife NGOs, though it pained them to do so, and that's when the National Trust bought land here in a big way. Some speculators bought in, too, thinking that payments for ecosystem services might come in in the end. And they were right. Land values have now increased again. You can see why, too – you need little investment in order to get the payments – they are paying you for letting nature take hold so you just sit back and count the carbon income rolling in.

The Red Grouse is still a well-known bird in these parts, there are still plenty of pubs and hotels, and also some quite fancy wine bars, called the Red Grouse. There's still that one on the Glossop to Hayfield road. I remember supping in there once after a day's beating one September. We'd driven the side of Kinder Scout and been richly tipped for the day's shooting, and spent some of the cash in the pub. But these days the place is really buzzing with walkers and people who've come here for their holidays. Some call the Peak District the 'Scotland of the South' because of the scenery and the wildlife – although you'd have to say the beer's a lot better down here.

It's quite a change. Who misses driven grouse shooting? No one round here. Is there a campaign to bring back grouse shooting? Don't be daft!

*

What I would like you to take away from this chapter:

- There are many possible futures, and they don't have to include driven grouse shooting. Some of those futures could be much better than the present and we shouldn't be afraid to imagine what they might be like – and then act to bring them about.

CHAPTER SEVEN

End game

> If you want a happy ending, that depends, of course, on where you
> stop your story.
>
> Orson Welles

The scenario described in the last chapter is entirely feasible, although of course it is entirely speculative. It would be quite a good place to end up, and there are many other alternative future scenarios that would also be attractive endpoints. But I am sure about one thing: driven grouse shooting's days are numbered, and numbered in the thousands rather than in the tens of thousands. So I can promise you a happy ending.

This can't happen, though, until driven grouse shooting is ended, because of the biological facts of the situation. Driven grouse shooting depends, for its profitability, on massively unnatural populations of Red Grouse, and the management regime that delivers those populations depends on illegal control of protected wildlife by some in the industry and unsustainable land-use practices. Because you can't square that circle, and the grouse shooters are simply fighting to maintain a discredited status quo, then there is no happy ending as long as driven grouse shooting persists.

We could be in for a pleasant surprise – it could all happen very quickly – but it is more likely it will take some time, because the grouse shooters own much of the land, are politically well-connected, are rich and are quite clever at getting their own way. But it's unusual for the few to get their way over the many, and the more publicity that is given to driven grouse shooting the more the ranks of the protesters will swell, and the louder their voices will become in politicians' ears.

The message of this book is that driven grouse shooting is an unsporting 'sport' carried out for the pleasure and the profit of the few, at the expense, socially, financially and environmentally, of the many. If it hadn't been invented in Victorian times we would never invent it now. All we have to do is to imagine the range of better futures that await our economy, our people and our wildlife if we cease driven grouse shooting, and then act to bring them about. And then we will get a happy ending. I promise you a happy ending.

But how about you promise me, and yourself, something too? If you have been persuaded by this book, and by the reading that awaits anyone who wishes to delve more deeply into the details, then why not join in? The happy ending will come sooner if you ask for it than if you close the pages of this book and hope that somebody else does all the work.

The timing of the cessation of driven grouse shooting is up to you and me. If we do nothing but sit on our hands then it will take longer than if we put ourselves about a bit. Here is a list of actions that you can take to hasten the demise of driven grouse shooting:

- **Attend Hen Harrier Day events**: At around the time this book is published Hen Harrier Day 2015 will take place, but there will certainly be more such rallies in future. Indeed, it is likely that they will grow and we may see Hen Harrier festivals springing up. Go along to an event and see what's happening, and give your support to this threatened bird.
- **Write to your MP**: I'm a great believer in making your MP work for you. Make your MP aware of your views and ask them to help by raising matters in parliament and within their own political party. Encourage them to take an interest in the environment, wildlife conservation and wildlife crime.
- **Write to supermarkets and restaurants**: ask those who sell game meat, particularly grouse, whether they can assure you that they know that it is sustainably produced. Ask for it to be lead-free. Ask how many Hen Harriers nest on the grouse moors from which it comes. Say that you will boycott their business if you don't get satisfactory answers – and then do so and write and remind them that you have. When

you get the answers that you want, remember to support those businesses that are prepared to do the right thing.

- **Write to your water company**: if you live in the north of England (or Scotland, or much of Wales), then some of the water that comes out of your taps fell on a hill, and some of that hill may well be owned by your water supplier. Write and tell United Utilities that you are pleased by their role in protecting Hen Harriers in the Forest of Bowland for many years. Write and ask Yorkshire Water, who part-funded the EMBER project, what they plan to do on their own land, and in their catchments, to discourage heather burning and to encourage raptor protection.

- **Write to newspapers**: whenever the news breaks about a raptor being killed, write to the national and local papers expressing your concern and disgust. When articles and news items appear online, comment on the newspaper's website with your views. Add your voice to the mix.

- **Use social media**: it might not last for ever, but the grouse shooters are outgunned on social media. At the time of writing the Moorland Association has only 291 followers on Twitter, and the GWCT (5,500), BASC (10,500) and the Countryside Alliance (15,600) all have fewer followers than me (19,200), Chris Packham (117,000) and the RSPB (145,000). Every time you retweet or like a message then you are helping to spread the word, and the more the word spreads the more people will become activated to play a part.

- **Support BAWC, the RSPB and other wildlife NGOs**: Birders Against Wildlife Crime is not a membership organisation but you can support them in various ways in their work to reduce wildlife crime of all sorts. Follow them on Twitter (@birdersagainst, 2,300 followers already), keep an eye on their website and see what you think as they grow and develop. The RSPB has been the leading wildlife organisation tackling bird-of-prey crime and has also led on many aspects of improving the management of the uplands. The RSPB has done more for blanket bogs than other wildlife conservation organisations. Give them your support and also let them know that you expect the RSPB to take a tough line on wildlife crime and to seek a better future for all UK uplands. The Wildlife Trusts seem to be considering their options at the moment – if you are a member, then let them know what you think. The National Trust has a good vision for the Peak District. If you are a member, tell them you support their vision and ask for updates now and again.

- And finally, keep an eye on my blog (www.markavery.info/blog/) and my Twitter account (@markavery). Recommending this book to your friends is another way of spreading the word. I'd slightly prefer you bought it for them than lent them this copy (and so would my publisher), but no one gets rich from selling books, particularly books with a campaigning theme. If you would like me to come and talk to your bird club, women's institute, conference or lunch group about these issues then I might be up for that, too (email me at mark@markavery.info).

So that's it. The book ends closer to the end of the story than to its beginning, but the happy ending depends on us all. Over to you …

CHAPTER EIGHT

Another year of progress

This chapter provides a brief update on events in 2015 and early 2016, where more progress was made on moving towards a ban on driven grouse shooting.

Brood-meddling and the Hawk and Owl Trust

Throughout 2014 there had been rumours that the Hawk and Owl Trust was promoting the idea of brood management, or at least that their Chairman, Philip Merricks, had been promoting this option with enthusiasm everywhere he went. In early 2015 these rumours strengthened, and I decided to flush them out in a series of blogs on the subject. That certainly worked, and Philip was eager to tell all and sundry how keen the Hawk and Owl Trust was on brood management – or 'brood-meddling' as we, its opponents, called it – and how it was very important to work with grouse-moor managers so that they could get what they wanted.*

The idea behind brood-meddling is that if an estate has 'too many' nesting Hen Harriers they should be boxed up and taken away to a place of safety, and then reared in captivity for subsequent release into the wild (a long way away from their home moor). Compared with diversionary feeding, it seems a very expensive and elaborate activity. This idea was strongly promoted by those organisations not readily identified as the closest friends of the Hen Harrier, and opposed by the RSPB (unless a long list of strict conditions was met). The recruitment of the Hawk and Owl Trust to the grouse-moor managers' camp on this subject, led by their land-owner chairman, was a

*Phillip Merricks attempted to clarify the position of the Hawk and Owl Trust in an article entitled *'The Hawk and Owl Trust Position in the Hen Harrier Debate'*, by Lin Murray. This was posted on the Trust's website on 20th January 2015.

shock to many of the organisation's supporters, to those heavily involved in raptor conservation and to many birders. Not only was it a surprise, it was an unpleasant one. Two polls run by Rare Bird Alert (one in January, showing 71% against brood-meddling, and a second in August that showed 80% against) both indicated massive majorities against the proposal. Most embarrassingly for the Hawk and Owl Trust, their President and long-time supporter, Chris Packham, resigned over this difference of views over policy.

Birders Against Wildlife Crime

BAWC emerged in 2014, but blossomed in 2015. The first BAWC conference was held in Buxton in March 2015. BAWC went on to organise the Hen Harrier Day event in the Goyt Valley, and helped to coordinate other events. BAWC was also at the Bird Fair, and has become a real presence on Twitter and Facebook.

E-petition number 1

All e-petitions, including mine to ban driven grouse shooting, were closed in late March 2015, ahead of the general election in May. In ten months, my e-petition had achieved 22,399 signatures, way short of the 100,000 needed to trigger a parliamentary debate but more than double the sign-up achieved by the previous e-petitions by Chrissie Harper on vicarious liability (10,908), John Armitage's on licensing (10,429) or indeed the GWCT's Andrew Gilruth's e-petition asking Defra to publish its Hen Harrier plan (10,683). It had also energised thousands of people and raised the issue way above its previous level. Every time grouse shooting was now mentioned someone would say something like 'but aren't some people keen on seeing this banned?', which makes life very uncomfortable for the men in tweed.

The total exceeded my expectations, and fuelled my hopes that a future e-petition might do even better. I would have to wait and see where we were after the general election, but I was thinking of the wording and the timing and the tactics for the next e-petition before the first had ended.

The 2015 general election

Wildlife and nature, and even the environment as a whole, played very little part in the general election campaign.

At an environmental hustings in Euston I was able to ask a panel of political party environment spokespeople whether they would ban driven grouse shooting. Not surprisingly, only the Green Party's Natalie Bennett said yes, although Labour's Barry Gardiner (one of the Sodden 570) said many of the right things, as did Baroness Parminter for the Liberal Democrats, though the Defra minister (who lost his job after the election), Lord Rupert de Mauley, didn't seem to think there was much action needed at all.

The election result was a surprise to everyone – particularly in the scale of Scottish National Party gains, the scale of Liberal Democrat losses and the failure of UKIP to make parliamentary progress. Labour was routed in Scotland and in the English countryside and retreated to the inner cities. The coalition government dominated by Tories became a Tory government, and Defra retained the leadership of Liz Truss and George Eustice but acquired Rory Stewart as Parliamentary Under Secretary of State. Mr Stewart would now have to handle the difficult issues of Hen Harrier persecution, grouse-moor management, lead ammunition, and a host of other tricky issues, as well as whatever natural disasters Mother Earth might throw his way.

With a Conservative government in place until 2020 the pace of reform on the issue of grouse shooting is likely to be slow, but it will not be zero. The need for reform is too great and the number of important issues is too many to be ignored. The period between now and the next general election provides a period in which the opposition parties can be brought to a more active position on the need for change in the hills. Progress is already being made.

Henry the Hen Harrier

The idea of being the 'burley minder' while a variety of folk occupied a six-foot tall Hen Harrier costume on the grouse moors of England and Scotland, at the gates of Sandringham,

Balmoral and Buckingham Palace, outside London's oldest restaurant and right to the front door of Defra at first seemed rather silly. It wasn't my idea, but it was what I found myself doing in the summer of 2015.

The costume was made by a company that specialises in outfits for mascots for football teams and the like. Our Henry the Hen Harrier joins a long list of bird mascots including Gilbert the Gull (Torquay United), Eddie the Eagle (Colchester United) and Ozzie the Owl (Sheffield Wednesday), as well as the problematic Harry the Harrier of Kidderminster Harriers who, despite being the club mascot for many years, has not yet moulted into adult male plumage and is still a brown ringtail.

Henry emerged into the world in adult plumage, fully fledged, at the BAWC conference in Buxton in March. Subsequently he visited many of the sites mentioned in this book including Rules restaurant in London, Dersingham Bog in Norfolk, the Langholm moors, the Forest of Bowland, the Peak District, and the headquarters of the Hawk and Owl Trust, the Game and Wildlife Conservation Trust, and Scottish Land and Estates, and attracted a big friendly crowd at the RSPB's base of The Lodge in Bedfordshire.

As well as dodging around the grouse moors of Britain, Henry attended two large events: the Game Fair at Harewood House in late July, and the annual Bird Fair at Rutland Water. At the Game Fair, where I was speaking in a debate, Henry pursued the President of the CLA off the GWCT stand, with the government minister Rory Stewart legging it too, and through the Countryside Alliance marquee. Henry had come to the major event of the grouse-shooting community and was making his presence felt. At the Bird Fair Henry had a whale of a time and was photographed with many wildlife personalities including Chris Packham (not for the first time), Bill Oddie, David Lindo, Nick Baker, Mark Carwardine, Simon King, Simon Barnes and Martin Hughes-Games.

Photographs of Henry on his travels, with commentary of the places he visited, appeared on my blog, the Birders Against Wildlife Crime site and on the Raptor Persecution Scotland blog. Henry introduced a note of levity and silliness into the debate, which was difficult for grouse-shooting interests to combat without looking as though they had suffered a sense-of-humour bypass. And he put a smile, or sometimes a puzzled look, on people's faces.

I am often asked who Henry is – a question worthy of a philosophy essay. Henry is a costume which can be stuffed into the back of a car as his former occupant speeds away from the possibility of a tricky conversation with a local gamekeeper. Henry has been, at different times, Findlay Wilde, Harley Wilde, Chris Packham, Rosemary Cockerill, a guy from California, Ruth Tingay, Susan Cross, Rebecca Walton, Brian Egan, the guys from both Raptor Persecution UK and Birders Against Wildlife Crime, and a few other folk who wish to remain anonymous. But he is also the grey ghost of all Hen Harriers, and he may be coming to a grouse moor or an event near you soon.

E-petition number 2

The Westminster government e-petition site disappeared in the run up to the general election and said it would be back later. It returned on 23 July, with a much improved site, mapping facilities that allowed one to see which constituencies had given most support to each and every e-petition, a lower word-limit on the petition itself, and the necessity to get a few people to sign up to the e-petition before it would be published. All in all, the site was improved and it looked as if this form of public contact with government was here to stay and was being treated fairly seriously. The major change was that the length of life for any e-petition was now halved to six months rather than a year.

The wording for my new e-petition was:

Ban driven grouse shooting

Grouse shooting for 'sport' depends on intensive habitat management which damages protected wildlife sites, increases water pollution, increases flood risk, increases greenhouse gas emissions and too often leads to the illegal killing of protected wildlife such as Hen Harriers.

RSPB, 7 March 2014. '…burning drainage and other forms of intensive land management in England's iconic peat-covered hills are threatening to create a series of environmental catastrophes'.

Inglorious – conflict in the uplands (a book on why we should ban driven grouse shooting).

Dr Dick Potts, scientist, 1998 '...a full recovery of Hen Harrier breeding numbers is prevented by illegal culling by some gamekeepers.'

Chris Packham addressing Hen Harrier Day rally, August 2014. 'We will win!'

My hope was that in a shorter period (six rather than 10 months) this e-petition would surpass its predecessor – 25,000 would be a good score, I thought. But maybe people would be bored with it? Would the broader scope, with Hen Harriers as a smaller part of the 'ask', be effective or lose support? Standing still would look like failure – only more signatures in the much shorter time could be deemed a success.

After a couple of days I was reassured, with thousands of people signing up rapidly. In just over two weeks, and a week before the opening of the grouse-shooting season, the e-petition passed 10,000 signatures, but we had to wait until mid-September for a wholly inadequate government response.

That response included the phrase *'When carried out in accordance with the law, grouse shooting for sport is a legitimate activity and in addition to its significant economic contribution, providing jobs and investment in some of our most remote areas, it can offer important benefits for wildlife and habitat conservation.'* So, when done legally, grouse shooting is legal – thank heavens we have such a bright government to tell us that! And despite Rory Stewart being sent a copy of this book, it seems that its messages had not permeated Defra's thinking at all. Never mind, these things do take time.

Chris Packham and the Countryside Alliance

Chris Packham's passionate stand against wildlife crime, whether it be in the Mediterranean or here at home, and his impassioned and outspoken public position on a range of issues including fox hunting and badger culls, have made him a hero to many (he was voted the *Birdwatch* readers' Conservation Hero in both 2014 and 2015) and a villain to others.

The chief executive of the Countryside Alliance, Tim Bonner, wrote to the BBC asking them not to employ Chris Packham and describing him as 'a disciple of the animal rights movement' who 'signs up to its creed by voicing his opposition to all the usual activities from badger culling to grouse shooting and, of course, hunting'. Mr Bonner must surely have noticed that you don't have to be an animal rights supporter to be against a misguided and ineffective cull of badgers, and you don't have to be an animal rights activist to oppose driven grouse shooting, and he may even have noticed that fox hunting is illegal these days. He might even have noticed that it is perfectly acceptable in this country to believe that animals have rights and that we shouldn't be nasty to them just for our fun. Mr Bonner's angle was that Chris Packham should not be able to speak out on these issues when he is employed by the BBC (and he doesn't) but nor should he be allowed to voice his opinions in those large gaps between BBC employment either. This all seemed a bit nasty to me.

An e-petition was started supporting the Countryside Alliance position and calling for the BBC to sack Chris, but a few days later an opposing e-petition started. The anti-Packham e-petition amassed less than 3,000 signatures; the pro-Packham e-petition gathered more than 81,000 signatures, which I would take to largely be a vote in favour of free speech and against the bullying tactics of the Countryside Alliance rather than an endorsement of Chris's views. Chris then produced a video 'thank you' message for his supporters, which also asked them to join the RSPB and the League Against Cruel Sports, support BAWC, sign my e-petition on banning driven grouse shooting and buy a copy of *Inglorious* – I know for sure that many people did the latter two things.

LACS report

The League Against Cruel Sports produced a report *'The intensification of grouse moor management in Scotland'*, authored by two experts on land use, land reform and upland wildlife, Andy Wightman and Ruth Tingay.

The report rehearsed many of the issues of this book in a Scottish context and also stressed the issues of new tracks being built to enable easier access to the hills for grouse-shooters and fences being erected that reduce access for everyone else. The thrust of the report is that grouse shooting is under-regulated by the Scottish government and over-subsidised by the rest of us. For example, why aren't upland tracks subject to proper planning regulation as they mar the beauty of Scotland's scenery, one of its greatest tourist assets?

The report is also interesting in showing what a successful capital investment this highly-subsidised, under-regulated sport has been over recent years.

Fighting back – business joins in

LUSH produced Skydancer bath bombs – the profits from which will help fund satellite-tagging of Hen Harriers. I bought several and find that they make good air fresheners for the car as well as being excellent in the bath.

The amazing Findlay Wilde continues to show others how to do it. He persuaded Ecotricity, the green energy company, to fund a Hen Harrier satellite tag for 2016.

Restaurants

Some of the Red Grouse that are shot for fun are also eaten for fun, and some of them arrive in swanky London restaurants such as Rules in Maiden Lane (see p239–40). I wrote to Rules in early 2015 asking them whether they were aware of the lead levels in the game (including grouse) that is their speciality, and what they thought of the health issues surrounding lead levels in meat. Their response was to refer me to the GWCT for a response. When I contacted the GWCT they said, not unreasonably, it was nothing to do with them and so I went back to Rules – but with no success. In the top right hand corner of the Rules restaurant menu is the statement *"Game birds may contain lead shot."* Is this statement a sufficient warning for a restaurant to give its patrons on the health issues surrounding its food?

Marks and Spencer and grouse meat

In 2014, M&S were persuaded not to go ahead with their plans to sell Red Grouse meat in London stores after a mini-campaign, where we asked them how they could be sure of the sustainability of their suppliers (p. 214). In 2015 M&S seemed almost ready to stock grouse but used low grouse stocks due to poor weather as a reason, perhaps an excuse, to prolong the delay in selling grouse. This was a blow to the grouse-shooters, who are understood to have lobbied hard for M&S to sell the birds. This, I imagine, was rather more to do with the public endorsement that it would represent than the financial benefit.

M&S Chief Executive Marc Bolland, said to be a keen shooter, announced in January that he would leave M&S in April 2016; it will be interesting to see what line the new senior management team goes on to take.

Iceland Foods and grouse meat

Where they failed with M&S, the shooters succeeded, of all places, with Iceland Foods. The Chief Executive of Iceland, Malcolm Walker, is also a keen shooter. Iceland announced in July 2015 that they would sell Red Grouse at the knock-down price of £8.95 for two. These were, of course, frozen grouse from previous seasons, and were nestling alongside cheap burgers and 'turkey drummers' in Iceland food cabinets. This interesting commercial venture was given a big mention in the *Daily Mail* (editor Paul Dacre, grouse moor owner), but no other newspaper that I saw. It was, perhaps, another public relations exercise for grouse shooting rather than a serious commercial enterprise.

Hen Harriers in 2015

There were 12 nesting attempts of Hen Harriers in England in 2015 – only six succeeded. At five nests that were being guarded to protect them, the males 'disappeared' during the breeding season, and it seems likely that most or all of these disappearances were due to illegal persecution, though some in the shooting industry claimed that it might be due to disturbance by the people protecting the nests. It seems more likely to me that males from nests guarded by the RSPB were actually targeted for killing so that unflattering headlines could be manufactured (see below).

Twelve nesting attempts is better than average for recent years (even though six failures is not great) but a long way short of the 330 pairs that science says could live in the English uplands. It's hardly a cause for much celebration considering the unexplained losses of so many male birds.

The next UK Hen Harrier survey takes place in 2016. We usually see a slight lessening of persecution in these years, possibly because there are a few more fieldworkers tramping the hills and possibly in order to make the figures look a little less damning than otherwise – we will see.

In Scotland, the body of a Hen Harrier called Annie, who was part of the Langholm study, was discovered shot dead on a grouse moor.

You Forgot the Birds (YFTB)

An organisation called You Forgot the Birds appeared on the scene in autumn 2014, attacking the RSPB. I didn't mention it in the earlier edition of this book as I had hoped it would simply fizzle out, and I also didn't want to treat it as if it were at all serious to the issues raised in this book. YFTB is not a major player in this debate but it is an interesting window into the minds of the British grouse industry for they, we discovered, are the funders of its work.

The Times reported (5 August) that a billionaire businessman and keen shooter, Old Harrovian Crispin Odey, is one of the funders of the YFTB campaign against the RSPB. Odey accused the RSPB of engaging in a 'class war' against his hobby.

YFTB aimed a barrage of criticism at the RSPB over its funding, its nature reserves, its ability to protect Hen Harriers and other aspects of its work. The British grouse industry did not argue its case for grouse shooting; instead, it attacked the RSPB for 'forgetting the birds'. As a journalist said to me, 'It's a bit odd that the RSPB gets attacked so strongly when they are hardly the grouse industry's major problem: it's what you are doing, Mark, that is the biggest threat to grouse shooting'.

YFTB tried to turn the outcome of the Hen Harrier breeding season into an anti-RSPB story, and supplied *The Daily Telegraph* with quotes on the subject, but the published story was so inaccurate that a complaint to the independent Press

Standards Organisation resulted, eventually, in *The Daily Telegraph* apologising and printing a correction.

Hen Harrier Day 2015

On 9 August Hen Harrier Day events were held in England and Scotland. The largest was again in the Peak District, this time in the Goyt Valley, and this time it didn't rain. Other events were held in Scotland in Perthshire and on Mull, and in England at the RSPB nature reserves of Saltholme in the north of England and Arne in the south, as well as two events in the Forest of Bowland. Overall attendance was around 1,000 people – a decent increase on last year.

In addition, there was a Hen Harrier evening organised in Buxton on the Saturday evening which included a variety of speakers and performers including Jeremy Deller, author Mark Cocker (who grew up in Buxton), Chris Packham, Findlay Wilde, the RSPB's Mike Clarke and Amanda Miller, and local performers. The following day, after a morning of Hen Harrier Day speeches at the rally in the Goyt Valley, there were stalls in the Buxton Palace Gardens representing BAWC, the RSPB, LACS and the Derbyshire Wildlife Trust. The thought that Hen Harrier Day might spread across the country and turn into a Hen Harrier festival in Buxton was moving into reality.

The Tingay blogs

Ruth Tingay, occasional Henry occupant and raptor researcher, paid a visit to an upland seminar on Red Grouse organised by the GWCT in November and wrote a series of blogs about them. Her blogs provided a fascinating insight into what the grouse-shooting community say when they think that they are talking amongst themselves (even though it was a public event).

It emerged that GWCT staff were concerned at the number of Red Grouse on some moors – there were too many and disease was becoming more of a problem. There are signs that the worming drugs which have helped so much to boost artificially high populations of Red Grouse for shooting are losing their effectiveness if over-used – a familiar story of resistance developing when drugs are used to excess. They were also concerned that a new disease, 'bulgy eye', was spreading rapidly across grouse moors in much of the north of England and into Scotland. The grit boxes that dispense medicated grit to treat the worms may well be a means of transmission of bulgy eye. These are the problems one would expect from such an unnatural system – natural predators are almost absent from grouse moors and so their role in removing diseased individuals from the population is absent. These changes are just another symptom of the complete artificiality of driven grouse management. Which grouse would you like on your dinner plate – the one that had worms or the one with bulgy eye?

At the seminar, Mark Oddy from Buccleugh Estates where the second Langholm project is taking place, came out in favour of lethal control of raptors, saying '...we have to now grasp the nettle and try and put forward a case, which probably in the first instance under licence, will allow some type of lethal control...'. The grouse-shooting community has not been weaned off its addiction to killing birds of prey in order to preserve the profitability of their pointless hobby.

Floods and greenhouse gases

On either side of Christmas 2015 there was torrential rain in the north of England. The resulting floods affected thousands of homes and businesses. The early floods in the Lake District focused attention on upland land use, particularly sheep farming, as a contributory factor in causing problems downstream. Later floods brought grouse moors into the discussion.

Hebden Bridge and nearby communities were again flooded, and a George Monbiot article in the *Guardian* (29 December 2015) discussed the likelihood of the role of grouse moor management in these floods (referencing both this book and Walshaw Moor).

In a parliamentary debate on flooding, the Labour Shadow Secretary of State for the Environment, Kerry McCarthy MP, mentioned the issue of grouse-moor management, as did the Shadow Climate Change Minister Barry Gardiner MP. The wider issues of grouse-moor management, and the damage to ecosystem services, were now becoming a regular part of the discussion of how to combat flooding, and how to get the best from upland land use and the large amounts of public money invested in it.

Earlier in the year the Committee on Climate Change had also mentioned intensive grouse-moor management in the context of greenhouse gas emissions *'The damaging practice of burning peat to increase grouse yields continues, including on internationally protected sites.'*

As predicted in the pages of this book, the impacts of intensive grouse-moor management, for a pointless sport of shooting birds for fun, on wider environmental issues such as flood risk, water quality and climate change would grow in prominence and importance in the debate over the future of the uplands in general, and of grouse shooting in particular.

The Defra Hen Harrier plan

The long-awaited Defra Hen Harrier plan was not published until January 2016. When it came it was a plan for inaction on the issue that affects the Hen Harrier the most – wildlife crime. The plan lacked the most obvious necessity of a decent plan – an objective that can be used to assess progress, or lack of it. Defra's plan was a non-plan from a government that appeared not to care about Hen Harriers but palpably *did* care about the community of interests that are the source of wildlife crime against Hen Harriers and other protected wildlife.

The plan included a nod towards brood-meddling and a reintroduction project in southern England but no resources for either, and a sanguine reading of the report suggested that it promised no new resources for the existing measures either. Despite this hopelessly weak plan, and a complete absence of any mention of government looking at the possibility of vicarious liability for England or of the licensing of shooting estates, the RSPB welcomed the plan. This was a rather feeble response.

Lead in Iceland's grouse

I visited several Iceland Foods stores and bought some frozen Red Grouse in September. Conversations with the staff indicated that they weren't selling well, which is why they were reduced to the ridiculous price of £2.95 for two birds.

My aim was to get these grouse analysed for lead content. Previous studies, of which Iceland and other supermarkets had been made aware, showed that the average Red Grouse would contain more than ten times the lead level that would be permitted in beef, pork or chicken. Analysis of Iceland's grouse meat showed that it had an average lead level of 100 times what would be legal for other meats (though it is legal for grouse meat). One sample had a lead content of 3,699 times that of what would be legal for non-game meats.

Defra is, as I write, sitting on a report by an expert group on the environmental and human health aspects of lead ammunition use. A ban on lead ammunition is on the cards but is being fought by the shooting community, including grouse shooting interests. We'll have to see how this plays out.

Iceland's position is simply stated on their UK website as, *"Game shot with lead ammunition has not be proven medically to have any adverse health effect."*

E-petition number 2 – the final score

My e-petition went to sleep for about six weeks from mid-November until the end of December, but then roused itself to add around 7,000 signatures in its last three weeks.

The new improved government petition website allows one to see how many people have signed up in each constituency (and is updated every day, so the data are almost real time). This showed that the support for banning driven grouse shooting was not evenly spread through the UK. Support was lower, on average, in Northern Ireland and Wales than in Scotland and England – in other words, in those parts of the UK which are not primarily governed from Westminster and where driven grouse shooting is a rare land use.

Also, taking England as an example, those constituencies with greatest support tended (quite strongly) to be Conservative rural seats and certainly weren't Labour inner cities. This gave the lie to the oft-repeated jibe that the campaign was supported by lefties from the towns who knew nothing of the countryside – most of the support came from countryside constituencies.

In the run up to the closing of the e-petition on 21 January we set up a Facebook page and used a small amount of money (around £2,000) gathered by passing the hat around some friends to promote the e-petition to new audiences. This, the impending deadline and the activities of other supporters produced a surge in signatures, resulting in a final total of 33,647 signatures; more than 50% higher than the previous e-petition, and achieved in only six months rather than ten. The campaign has momentum. Watch this space!

Summary

The year 2015 was a bad one for grouse shooters; not only was the weather poor for producing large grouse bags, but the climate of public opinion was also against them. Grouse shooting was more and more under the public spotlight, and the role of grouse shooting in flooding, wildlife crime, destruction of carbon stores, disease in wild birds and lead levels in game meat was under increasing public discussion.

The way I look at it is this: driven grouse shooting is a pointless hobby that is ecologically damaging. The more people that learn about this damage, whether it be to carbon storage, to protected wildlife, to upland landscapes or to flood alleviation, the greater the number that will rise up and voice their opinions, and the quicker we will have uplands that deliver for us all and not just for the tweed-clad few.

The book you have in your hands is part of my contribution to changing our hills for the better. What will you do to help?

Further reading

This is a list of further reading rather than a full reference list. It is a mixture of books, scientific papers and internet links. Some of the links are to my own blog, where you can look back at events and find more links to more details. The internet is a funny place – you may find that by the time this book is in your hands some of the links no longer work (but I have checked them all as a 'last task' before submitting this manuscript to my publisher).

Chapter 1

Amar, A. 2014. Hen Harriers: going, going ... http://www.bou. org.uk/hen-harriers-going-going.

Amar A. and Redpath S. M. 2005. Habitat use by Hen Harriers *Circus cyaneus* on Orkney: implications of land-use change for this declining population. *Ibis* **147**, 37–47.

Amar A., Redpath S., Thirgood S. 2003. Evidence for food limitation in the declining hen harrier population on the Orkney Islands, Scotland. *Biological Conservation* **111**, 377–384.

Amar, A., Picozzi, N., Meek, E. R., Redpath, S. M. and Lambin, X. 2005. Decline of the Orkney Hen Harrier *Circus cyaneus* population: do changes to demographic parameters and mating system fit a declining food hypothesis? *Bird Study* **52**, 18–24.

Amar, A., Arroyo, B., Meek, E., Redpath, S. M. and Riley, H. 2008. Influence of habitat on breeding performance of Hen Harriers *Circus cyaneus* in Orkney. *Ibis* **150**, 400–404.

Avery, M. and Betton, K. 2015. *Behind the Binoculars*. Pelagic Publishing, Exeter.

Baines, D. and Richardson, M. 2013. Hen Harriers on a Scottish grouse moor: multiple factors predict breeding density and productivity. *Journal of Applied Ecology* **50**, 1397–1405.

Balmer, D. L., Gillings, S., Caffrey, B. J. *et al.* 2013. *Bird Atlas 2007–11: The Breeding and Wintering Birds of Britain and Ireland*. BTO Books, Thetford.

BBC Inside Out. 22 Nov 2013. Hen Harrier facing extinction. https://www.youtube.com/watch?v=-GNUonyaHMY.

BBC Nature. Hen Harrier. http://www.bbc.co.uk/nature/life/Hen_Harrier.

BBC News. 25 May 2001. Keeper fined over rare bird death. http://news.bbc.co.uk/1/hi/uk/1352092.stm.

BBC Springwatch. Hen Harriers. https://www.youtube.com/watch?v=9re7hBXHc7s.

Bibby, C. J. and Etheridge, B. 1993. Status of the Hen Harrier *Circus cyaneus* in Scotland in 1988–89. *Bird Study* **40**, 1–11.

Brown, L. 1976. *British Birds of Prey*. Collins, London.

BTO. Summary of all ringing recoveries for Hen Harrier (*Circus cyaneus*). http://blx1.bto.org/ring/countyrec/resultsall/rec2610all.htm.

Daily Telegraph. 26 May 2001. Gamekeeper fined for shooting rare hen harrier. http://www.telegraph.co.uk/news/uknews/1331675/Gamekeeper-fined-for-shooting-rare-hen-harrier.html.

Durham Bird Club. 2012. *The Birds of Durham*. Durham Bird Club, Durham.

Etheridge, B., Summers, R. W. and Green, R. E. 1997. The effects of illegal killing and destruction of nests by humans on the population dynamics of the Hen Harrier *Circus cyaneus* in Scotland. *Journal of Applied Ecology* **34**, 1081–1105.

Etheridge, B., Riley, H., Wernham, C. *et al.* 2013. *Scottish Raptor Monitoring Scheme Report 2012*. Scottish Raptor Study Groups, Inverness.

Fielding, A., Haworth, P., Whitfield, P., McLeod, D. and Riley, H. 2011. *A Conservation Framework for Hen Harriers in the United Kingdom*. JNCC Report 441. Joint Nature Conservation Committee, Peterborough.

Green, R. E. and Etheridge, B. 1999. Breeding success of the hen harrier *Circus cyaneus* in relation to the distribution of grouse moors and the red fox *Vulpes vulpes*. *Journal of Applied Ecology* **36**, 472–483.

Hayhow, D. B., Eaton, M. A., Bladwell, S. *et al.* 2013.The status of the Hen Harrier, *Circus cyaneus*, in the UK and Isle of Man in 2010. *Bird Study* **60**, 446–458.

MacMillan, R. L. 2014. Hen Harriers on Skye, 2000–2012: nest failures and predation. *Scottish Birds* **34**, 126–135.

Mather, J. R. 1986. *The Birds of Yorkshire*. Croom Helm, London.

Moores, C. Interview with Andrew Gilruth, GWCT. July 2014. Birders Against Wildlife Crime. https://soundcloud.com/bawc.

Newton, I. 1979. *Population Ecology of Raptors*. T. & A. D. Poyser, London.

Potts, G. R. 1998. Global dispersion of nesting Hen Harriers *Circus cyaneus*: implications for grouse moors in the U.K. *Ibis* **140**, 76–88.

Redpath, S. M. and Thirgood, S. J. 1997. *Birds of Prey and Red Grouse*. Stationery Office, London.

Redpath, S., Amar, A., Madders, M., Leckie, F. and Thirgood, S. J. 2002. Hen harrier foraging success in relation to land use in Scotland. *Animal Conservation* **5**, 113–118.

Risely, K., Massimino, D., Newson, S. E. *et al.* 2013. *The Breeding Bird Survey 2012*. BTO Research Report 645. British Trust for Ornithology, Thetford.

Sharrock, J. T. R. 1976. *The Atlas of Breeding Birds in Britain and Ireland*. T. & A. D. Poyser, Berkhamsted.

Sim I. M. W., Gibbons D. W., Bainbridge I. P. and Mattingley W. A. 2001. Status of the Hen Harrier *Circus cyaneus* in the UK and the Isle of Man in 1998. *Bird Study* **48**, 341–353.

Sim, I. M. W., Dillon, I. A., Eaton, M. A. *et al.* 2007. Status of the Hen Harrier *Circus cyaneus* in the UK and Isle of Man in 2004, and a comparison with the 1988/89 and 1998 surveys. *Bird Study* **54**, 256–267.

Stott, M. 1998. Hen harrier breeding success on English grouse moors. *British Birds* **91**,107–108.

Thompson P. S., Amar A., Hoccom D. G., Knott J. and Wilson J. D. 2009. Resolving the conflict between driven-grouse shooting and conservation of hen harriers. *Journal of Applied Ecology* **46**, 950–954.

Watson D. 1977. *The Hen Harrier*. Poyser, London.

Wilson, M. W., O'Donoghue, B., O'Mahony, B. *et al.* 2012. Mismatches between breeding success and habitat preferences in Hen Harriers *Circus cyaneus* breeding in forested landscapes. *Ibis* **154**, 578–589.

Chapter 2

Atherden, M. 1992. *Upland Britain: A Natural History*. Manchester University Press, Manchester.

Avery, M. I. and Leslie, R. 1989. *Birds and Forestry*. T. & A. D. Poyser, Berkhamsted.

Barnes, R. W. 1987. Long term declines of red grouse in Scotland. *Journal of Applied Ecology* **24**,735–741.

Cahill, K. 2012. *Who Owns Britain and Ireland*. Canongate Books, Edinburgh.

Committee of Inquiry on Grouse Disease. 1911. *The Grouse in Health and in Disease, Being the Final Report of the Committee of Inquiry on Grouse Disease*, Volumes I and II; with an introduction by Lord Lovat. Smith & Elder, London.

The Field. 28 January 2008. Grouse shooting at Wemmergill. http://www.thefield.co.uk/shooting/grouse-shooting/grouse-shooting-at-wemmergill-22836.

Hopkins, H. 1985. *The Long Affray: The Poaching Wars in Britain*. Faber & Faber, London.

Hudson, D. 2008. *Grouse Shooting*. Quiller, Shrewsbury.

Hudson, P. J. 1986. *The Red Grouse: the Biology and Management of a Wild Gamebird*. Game Conservancy, Fordingbridge.

Hudson, P. J. 1987. *The Red Grouse: King of Gamebirds*. Game Conservancy Trust, Fordingbridge.

Hudson, P. J. 1992. *Grouse in Space and Time*. Game Conservancy Trust, Fordingbridge.

Hudson, P. J. and Newborn, D. 1995. *A Handbook of Grouse and Moorland Management*. Game Conservancy Trust, Fordingbridge.

Hudson, P. J. and Rands, M. W. R. 1988. *Ecology and Management of Gamebirds*. Blackwell, Oxford.

Lovegrove, R. 2007. *Silent Fields*. Oxford University Press, Oxford.

Martin, B. P. 1990. *The Glorious Grouse: a Natural and Unnatural History*. David & Charles, Newton Abbot.

Percy, J. 2013. *Fields of Dreams*. Sporting Library, Grantham.

Potapov, R. and Sale, R. 2013. *Grouse of the World*. New Holland, London.

Ratcliffe, D. A. 1990. *Bird Life of Mountain and Upland*. Cambridge University Press, Cambridge.

Rutland, D. 2012. *Shooting: a Season of Discovery*. Quiller, Shrewsbury.

Scott, G. 1937. *Grouse Land and the Fringe of the Moor*. H. F. & G. Witherby, London.

Stephens, M. 1939. *Grouse Shooting*. The Sportsman's Library Volume XXVII. A. & C. Black, London.

Waddington, R. 1958. *Grouse: Shooting and Moor Management*. Faber & Faber, London.

Watson, A. and Moss, R. 2008. *Grouse*. New Naturalist 107. Collins, London.

White, S. J., McCarthy, B. and Jones, M. (eds). 2008. *The Birds of Lancashire and North Merseyside*. Hobby Publications.

Wightman, A. 2013. *The Poor Had No Lawyers: Who Owns Scotland (and How They Got It)*. Birlinn, Edinburgh.

Yallop, A. R., Thacker, J. I., Thomas, G. *et al.* 2006. The extent and intensity of management burning in the English uplands. *Journal of Applied Ecology* **43**, 1138–1148.

Chapter 3

Amar, A., Redpath, S. M. and Thirgood, S. J. 2003. Evidence for food limitation in a declining raptor population. *Biological Conservation* **111**, 377–384.

Campbell, S., Smith A., Redpath, S. and Thirgood, S. 2002. Nest site characteristics and nest success in red grouse *Lagopus lagopus scoticus*. *Wildlife Biology* **8**, 169–174.

GCT and RSPB. 2002. Hen Harriers and the Joint Raptor Study: a joint statement by the Game Conservancy Trust and the Royal Society for the Protection of Birds. https://www.gwct.org.uk/media/249268/Hen_harriers_and_the_Joint_Raptor_Study_2005.pdf.

Redpath, S. M. and Thirgood, S. J. 1997. *Birds of Prey and Red Grouse*. Centre for Ecology and Hydrology, London.

Redpath, S. M. and Thirgood, S. J. 1999. Numerical and functional responses of generalist predators: hen harriers and peregrine falcons on Scottish grouse moors. *Journal of Animal Ecology* **68**, 879–892.

Redpath, S. M. and Thirgood, S. J. 2003. The impact of hen harrier predation on red grouse: linking models with field data. In *Raptors in Changing Landscapes*, ed. D. B. A. Thompson, S. M. Redpath, M. Marquiss and A. Fielding. HMSO, Edinburgh.

Redpath, S. M., Clarke, R., Madders, M. and Thirgood, S. J. 2001. Assessing raptor diet: comparing pellets, prey remains and observations at hen harrier nests. *Condor* **103**, 184–188.

Redpath, S. M., Thirgood, S. J. and Leckie, F. M. 2001. Does supplementary feeding reduce predation of red grouse by hen harrier? *Journal of Animal Ecology* **38**, 1157–1168.

Redpath, S., Amar, A., Madders, M., Leckie, F. and Thirgood, S. J. 2002. Hen harriers foraging success in relation to land use in Scotland. *Animal Conservation* **5**, 113–118.

Redpath, S. M., Thirgood, S. J. and Clarke, R. 2002. Field vole abundance and hen harrier diet and breeding in Scotland. *Ibis* **144**, E130–E138.

Smith, A. A., Redpath, S. M., Campbell, S. T. and Thirgood, S. J. 2001. Meadow pipits, red grouse and the habitat of characteristics of managed grouse moors. *Journal of Applied Ecology* **38**, 390–400.

Thirgood, S. J. and Redpath, S. M. 1997. Red grouse and their predators. *Nature* **390**, 547.

Thirgood, S. J. and Redpath, S. M. 1999. Raptors and grouse: a conflict in the uplands? In *Proceedings of the 22nd International Ornithological Congress*, ed. N. J. Adams and R. H. Slotow, pp. 2125–2129. Birdlife South Africa, Johannesburg.

Thirgood, S. J. and Redpath, S. M. 2000. Can raptor predation limit red grouse populations? In *Raptors at Risk*, ed. R. D. Chancellor and B.-U. Meyburg, pp. 527-534. Hancock House, Vancouver.

Thirgood, S. J., Redpath, S. M., Haydon, D. *et al.* 2000. Habitat loss and raptor predation: disentangling long- and short-term causes of red grouse declines. *Proceedings of the Royal Society of London B* **282**, 651–656.

Thirgood, S. J., Redpath, S. M., Newton, I. and Hudson, P. J. 2000. Raptors and red grouse: conservation conflicts and management solutions. *Conservation Biology* **14**, 95–104.

Thirgood, S. J., Redpath, S. M., Rothery, P. and Aebischer, N. J. 2000. Raptor predation and population limitation in red grouse. *Journal of Animal Ecology* **69**, 504–516.

Thirgood, S. J., Redpath, S., Campbell, S. and Smith, A. A. 2002. Do habitat characteristics influence predation on red grouse? *Journal of Applied Ecology* **39**, 217–225.

Thirgood, S. J., Redpath, S. M. and Graham, I. M. 2003. What determines the foraging distribution of raptors on heather moorlands? *Oikos* **100**, 15–24.

Watson, M. and Thirgood, S. 2001. Could translocation aid hen harrier conservation in the UK? *Animal Conservation* **4**, 37–43.

Chapter 4

Amar, A., Court, I. R., Davison, M. *et al.* 2012. Linking nest histories, remotely sensed land use data and wildlife crime records to explore the impact of grouse moor management on peregrine falcon populations. *Biological Conservation* **145**, 86–94.

Anon. 2013. *State of Nature.* http://www.rspb.org.uk/Images/stateofnature_tcm9-345839.pdf.

Avery, M. 2011. My Janus moment – looking forward to farming and back on birds. *The Guardian* 4 May. http://www.theguardian.com/environment/2011/may/04/rspb-25-years.

Avery, M. 2012. *Fighting for Birds.* Pelagic Publishing, Exeter.

Avery, M. and Pain, D. 2009. Letter to Defra and Department of Health on dangers of lead. http://www.leadammunitiongroup.co.uk/rspbletter.html.

Bain, C. G., Bonn, A., Stoneman, R. *et al.* 2011. *IUCN UK Commission of Inquiry on Peatlands.* IUCN UK Peatland Programme, Edinburgh.

Benyon, R. 2010. [Parliamentary business, 22 July 2010.] http://www.publications.parliament.uk/pa/cm201011/cmhansrd/cm100722/text/100722w0002.htm.

Chrissie's Owls. http://www.chrissiesowls.com/index.php.

Countryside Alliance. http://www.countryside-alliance.org.

Countryside Alliance. 2011. The RSPB's vanity project. http://www.countryside-alliance.org/ca/campaigns-shooting/the-rspbs-vanity-project.

Dennis, R. H., Ellis, P. M., Broad, R. A. and Langslow, D. R. 1984. The status of the Golden Eagle in Britain. *British Birds* **77**, 592–607.

Everett, M. J. 1971. The Golden Eagle survey in Scotland in 1964–68. *British Birds* **64**, 49–56.

Fletcher, K., Aebischer, N. J., Baines, D., Foster, R. and Hoodless, A. N. 2010. Changes in breeding success and abundance of ground-nesting moorland birds in relation to the experimental deployment of legal predator control. *Journal of Applied Ecology* **47**, 263–272.

Food Standards Agency. 2012. Advice to frequent eaters of game shot with lead. http://www.food.gov.uk/news-updates/news/2012/5339/lead-shot#.UHLz7K74Jos.

Green, R. E. 1996. The status of the Golden Eagle in Britain in 1992. *Bird Study* **43**, 20–27.

Green, R. E. and Pain, D. J. 2012. Potential health risks to adults and children in the UK from exposure to dietary lead in gamebirds shot with lead ammunition. *Food and Chemical Toxicology* **50**, 4180–4190.

Harper, M. 8 December 2011. A promise is a promise. http://www.rspb.org.uk/community/ourwork/b/martinharper/archive/2011/12/08/a-promise-is-a-promise.aspx

Harper, M. 15 May 2012. Hen harriers on the brink: it's time for action. http://www.rspb.org.uk/community/ourwork/b/martinharper/archive/2012/05/15/hen-harriers-on-the-brink-it-s-time-for-action.aspx.

Hawk and Owl Trust. 2011. Sign e-petition to protect birds of prey. http://hawkandowl.org/sign-e-petition-to-protect-birds-of-prey.

Kinder Trespass website. http://www.kindertrespass.com.

Lane, J. 10 December 2012. Guest blog: Jude Lane on the death of a hen harrier. Martin Harper's blog. http://www.rspb.org.uk/community/ourwork/b/martinharper/archive/2012/12/10/guest-blog-jude-lane-on-the-death-of-a-hen-harrier.aspx.

Langholm Moor Demonstration Project. Diversionary feeding. http://www.langholmproject.com/diversionaryfeeding.html.

Lead Ammunition Group. http://www.leadammunitiongroup.co.uk.

Natural England. 2008. *A Future for the Hen Harrier in England?* Natural England, Sheffield.

Natural England. 2009. *Vital Uplands: a 2060 Vision for England's Upland Environment.* https://www.jmt.org/assets/john%20muir%20award/vital%20uplands%20a%202060%20vision%20for%20england%27s%20upland%20environment.pdf.

Pain, D. J., Cromie, R. L., Newth, J. *et al.* 2010. Potential hazard to human health from exposure to fragments of lead bullets and shot in the tissues of game animals. *PLoS ONE* **5**(4), e10315. doi:10.1371/journal.pone.0010315.

Paterson, O. 20 July 2014. Owen Paterson: I'm proud of standing up to the green lobby. *The Telegraph.* http://www.telegraph.co.uk/news/politics/10978678/Owen-Paterson-Im-proud-of-standing-up-to-the-green-lobby.html.

Redpath, S. and Thirgood, S. 2009. Hen harriers and red grouse: moving towards consensus? *Journal of Applied Ecology,* **46,** 961–963.

RSPB. 2007. *The Uplands: Time to Change?* https://www.rspb. org.uk/Images/uplands_tcm9-166286.pdf.

Tharme, A. P., Green, R. E., Baines, D., Bainbridge, I. P. and O'Brien, M. 2001. The effect of management for red grouse shooting on the population density of breeding birds on heather-dominated moorland. *Journal of Applied Ecology* **38,** 439–457.

Thirgood, S. and Redpath, S. 2008. Hen harriers and red grouse: science, politics and human–wildlife conflict. *Journal of Applied Ecology* **45**, 1550–1554. doi: 10.1111/j.1365-2664.2008.01519.x

Thompson, P. S., Amar, A., Hoccom, D. G., Knott, J. and Wilson, J. D. 2009. Resolving the conflict between driven-grouse shooting and conservation of hen harriers. *Journal of Applied Ecology* **46,** 950–954.

Sotherton, N., Tapper, S. and Smith, A. 2009. Hen harriers and red grouse: economic aspects of red grouse shooting and the implications for moorland conservation. *Journal of Applied Ecology* **46,** 955–960. doi: 10.1111/j.1365-2664.2009.01688.x

UK National Ecosystem Assessment. http://uknea.unep-wcmc. org.

Watson, A., Payne, S. and Rae, R. 1989. Golden Eagle *Aquila chrysaetos* land use and food in north-east Scotland. *Ibis* **131,** 336–348.

Watson, J. 1992. Golden Eagle *Aquila chrysaetos* breeding success and afforestation in Argyll. *Bird Study* **39**, 203–206.

Watson, J. 1997. *The Golden Eagle.* T. & A. D. Poyser, London.

Watson, J. and Dennis, R. H. 1992. Nest-site selection by Golden Eagles in Scotland. *British Birds* **85**, 469–481.

Watson, J. and Whitfield, D. P. 2002. A conservation framework for the Golden Eagle *Aquila chrysaetos* in Scotland. *Journal of Raptor Research* **36**, 41–49.

Watson, J., Rae, S. R. and Stillman, R. 1992. Nesting density and breeding success of Golden Eagles in relation to food supply in Scotland. *Journal of Animal Ecology* **61,** 543–550.

Whitcher, D. A. 2003. *Bradfield Area Badger Survey.* South Yorkshire Badger Group.

Whitfield, D. P., McLeod, D. R. A., Fielding, A. H. *et al.* 2001. The effects of forestry on Golden Eagles on the island of Mull, western Scotland. *Journal of Applied Ecology* **38**, 1208–1220.

Whitfield, D. P., McLeod, D. R. A., Watson, J., Fielding, A. H. and Haworth, P. F. 2003. The association of grouse moor in

Scotland with the illegal use of poisons to control predators. *Biological Conservation* **114**, 157–163.

Whitfield, D. P., Fielding, A. H., McLeod, D. R. A. and Haworth, P. F. 2004. The effects of persecution on age of breeding and territory occupation in Golden Eagles in Scotland. *Biological Conservation* **118**, 249–259.

Whitfield, D. P., Fielding, A. H., McLeod, D. R. A. and Haworth, P. F. 2004. Modelling the effects of persecution on the population dynamics of Golden Eagles in Scotland. *Biological Conservation* **119**, 319–333.

Whitfield, D. P., Fielding, A. H., McLeod, D. R. A. *et al.* 2007. Factors constraining the distribution of Golden Eagles *Aquila chrysaetos* in Scotland. *Bird Study* **54**, 192–211.

Chapter 5

Allen, C. 27 October 2014. Guest blog: There is nothing green about these country 'sports', by Caroline Allen of the Green Party. http://markavery.info/2014/10/27/guest-blog-green-country-sports-caroline-allen-green-party.

Avery, M. 1 January 2014. What will 2014 bring for you? http://markavery.info/2014/01/01/2014-bring.

Avery, M. 25 March 2014. Defra response to John Armitage's e-petition. http://markavery.info/2014/03/25/response-john-armitages-epetition.

Avery, M. 25 June 2014. The curious case of Simon Barnes's departure from *The Times*. http://markavery.info/2014/06/25/curious-case-simon-barness-departure-times.

Avery, M. 26 June 2014. Simon Barnes again. http://markavery.info/2014/06/26/simon-barnes.

Avery, M. 27 June 2014. Be an ethical consumer – turn your back on grouse! http://markavery.info/2014/06/27/ethical-consumer-turn-grouse.

Avery, M. 5 July 2014. A grouse with M&S. http://markavery.info/2014/07/05/grouse-ms.

Avery, M. 8 August 2014. Martyn and Joe in Lush Northampton. http://markavery.info/2014/08/08/martyn-joe-lush-northampton.

Avery, M. 9 August 2014. Lush Peterborough. http://markavery.info/2014/08/09/lush-peterborough.

Avery, M. 11 August 2014. A Peak Day. http://markavery. info/2014/08/11/14037.

Avery, M. 13 August 2014. Hen Harrier Day – some 'thank you's. http://markavery.info/2014/08/13/hen-harrier-day-thank-yous.

Avery, M. 2 September 2014. A response, of a kind, from Defra. http://markavery.info/2014/09/02/response-kind-defra.

Avery, M. 5 September 2014. Government response to e-petition 65627.http://markavery.info/2014/09/05/government-response-epetition-65627.

Avery, M. 24 September 2014. Two of our Hen Harriers are missing. http://markavery.info/2014/09/24/hen-harriers-missing.

Avery, M. 1 October 2014. Important new study on impacts of moorland burning on river catchments. http://markavery. info/2014/10/01/important-study-impacts-moorland-burning-river-catchments.

Avery, M. 1 October 2014. And it's not even worth a bean to the economy. http://markavery.info/2014/10/01/worth-bean-economy.

Avery, M. 10 October 2014. Postcards for the Queen. http:// markavery.info/2014/10/10/postcards-queen.

Avery, M. 24 October 2014. Margate and more. http:// markavery.info/2014/10/24/15111.

Avery, M. 10 December 2014. Yesterday's Rally for Nature. http://markavery.info/2014/12/10/yesterdays-rally-nature.

Avery, M. 11 December 2014. Rallying. http://markavery. info/2014/12/11/rallying.

Avery, M. 14 December 2014. Charles Moore shoots grouse. http://markavery.info/2014/12/14/charles-moore-shoots-grouse.

Barnes, M. A love of grouse. *Fieldsports*. http://www.fields portsmagazine.com/Shooting-Grouse/a-love-of-grouse.html.

Barnes, S. 12 May 2012. Hen Harrier extinction looks bad on the old CV. *The Times*.

Barnes, S. 24 August 2013. That thing kills all my grouse. It's got to go. *The Times*.

Barnes, S. 14 December 2013. Saving the Hen Harrier is a serious business. *The Times*.

Barnes, S. 12 April 2014. We're going to watch gamekeepers like a hawk. *The Times*.

Barnes, S. 19 May 2014. Take your partner for the great sky dance. *The Times*.

Barnes, S. 21 June 2014. Some of our grouses are beginning to be heard. *The Times*.

Birch, T. 9 July 2014. Guest blog: The Hen Harrier Affair, by Tim Birch. http://markavery.info/2014/07/11/guest-blog-harrier-affair-tim-birch.

Davies, A. and Miller, R. 2010. *The Biggest Twitch*. Croom Helm, London.

Edwards, R. 27 September 2014. Outrage over mountain hare 'massacre'. *The Herald*. http://www.heraldscotland.com/news/home-news/outrage-over-mountain-hare-massacre.25442597.

Edwards, R. 10 November 2014. Grouse moor owners driving mountain hares to the brink. *The Sunday Herald*. http://www.heraldscotland.com/news/environment/grouse-moor-owners-driving-mountain-hares-to-the-brink.22648639.

HM Government e-petition website. Ban driven grouse shooting. http://epetitions.direct.gov.uk/petitions/65627.

HM Government e-petition website. Introduction of offence of vicarious liability for raptor persecution in England. http://epetitions.direct.gov.uk/petitions/23089.

HM Government e-petition website. Licensing of upland grouse moors and gamekeepers. http://epetitions.direct.gov.uk/petitions/46473.

HM Government e-petition website. Hen Harrier Joint Recovery Plan: publish it. http://epetitions.direct.gov.uk/petitions/67527.

Moore, C. 13 December 2014. Britain would be big enough for the hen harrier and the grouse if it weren't for politics. *The Telegraph*. http://www.telegraph.co.uk/news/earth/wildlife/11291324/Britain-would-be-big-enough-for-the-hen-harrier-and-the-grouse-if-it-werent-for-politics.html.

Roydon Common National Nature Reserve. http://www.norfolk.gov.uk/view/NCC115525.

Webster, B. 25 July 2014. Game over: M&S takes grouse off shelves after boycott threat. *The Times*. http://www.thetimes.co.uk/tto/environment/article4156994.ece.

Wilde, F. 15 November 2014. Guest blog: Wishing you a Harry Christmas, by Findlay Wilde. http://markavery.info/2014/11/15/guest-blog-wishing-harry-christmas-findlay-wilde.

Copyright acknowledgements

Page 164 – extract from RSPB news article entitled: 'Hen harrier on the brink of 'extinction' in England'. Last modified 9 August 2013. © Royal Society for the Protection of Birds 2013.

Page 175 – RSPB quotation from Martin Harper. Extract from RSPB news article entitled A burning issue for England's upland wildlife. Last modified 7 March 2014. © Royal Society for the Protection of Birds 2014.

Page 191 – quotation from Simon Thorp of The Heath Trust, from article National campaign against moorland bog-burning, 13 August 2012 (as published in *Modern Gamekeeping* magazine). © The Heath Trust 2012.

Page 203 – extract from Peak District National Park Management Plan: ES1, Farming and Land Management. © Peak District National Park Authority 2012.

Page 204 – email from Simon Barnes to author. © Simon Barnes 2014.

Page 205–206 – extract from 'Why it's time to license driven grouse shooting' by Martin Harper. Martin Harper's blog, 26 June 2014. © The Royal Society for the Protection of Birds 2014

Page 207 – extract from 'Turn your back on grouse – A popular campaign against greed and intensification on England's grouse shooting estates'. *Ethical Consumer* magazine. © Ethical Consumer Research Association (ECRA) May 2014

Page 207 – extract from 'The Harrier Affair – A Personal Perspective' by Tim Birch. 15th July 2014. © Derbyshire Wildlife Trust 2014

Page 211 – Andrew Gilruth, Game and Wildlife Conservation Trust e-petition entitled 'Hen Harrier Joint Recovery Plan – publish it'. © GWCT 2012.

Pages 176, 221–223, 230 – response from Defra. © Crown Copyright – contains public sector information licensed under the Open Government Licence v3.0 (except where some other form of wording has been specified).

Page 224 – quotes from RSPB and Chris Packham. © RSPB and Chris Packham 2014

Page 226 – extracts from *Independent* article entitled 'Grouse shooting "is warming planet" as peatlands burned to improve conditions for birds' by Tom Bawden. 1 October 2014. © Independent Digital News and Media Ltd 2014.

Page 226 – extracts from *The Scotsman* article entitled 'Cut heather burning for sake of the environment' by Iona Amos. 1 October 2014. © Johnston Publishing Ltd 2014.

Page 226 – extract from *The Times* article entitled 'Burning of grouse moors linked to global warming' by Ben Webster. 1 October 2014. © Times Newspapers Limited 2014.

Page 237 – extract from *Sunday Herald* article entitled: 'Grouse moor owners driving mountain hares to the brink' by Rob Edwards. 10 November 2013. © Herald & Times Group 2013. All rights reserved.

Page 238 – extract from 'The time to save the hen harrier is now' by Martin Harper. Martin Harper's blog, 16 November 2014. © The Royal Society for the Protection of Birds 2014.

Acknowledgements

Chris Packham is a great guy and I'm very grateful to him for his foreword, but even more for all he has done, continues to do and will do for our wildlife. His stance on controversial issues such as the one covered in this book, but also spring shooting in Malta and Badger culling (to name but two), has helped bring these issues more firmly to the public attention. He has used his celebrity status to further the cause of nature conservation, and simply being nice to other living creatures, in an exemplary way. I'm also incredibly grateful to him for agreeing to attend Hen Harrier Day in the Peak District on 10 August 2014 and promoting the day on his own website. And on the day he was an absolute star. Chris is not just a pretty face (I don't think he's that pretty anyway, though I do know others of a different viewpoint) but his face does bring in the crowds, and nature conservation needs some of that.

Charlie Moores has been a great support to me and has sometimes egged me on when I needed egging. As a moving force behind Birders Against Wildlife Crime he has helped publicise wildlife crime to an enormously helpful extent. The podcasts that he recorded, edited and published in the run-up to Hen Harrier Day were all fantastic, and as I write these words he is engaged in setting up the first BAWC conference in Buxton in March 2015. I am proud to count Charlie as a friend and co-conspirator.

The RSPB has been helpful in cooperating with this book. Martin Harper, the conservation director, made several RSPB staff available to me to talk to, and I'm very grateful. In addition Elizabeth George, the RSPB librarian, was very helpful in making me welcome and cups of tea on my occasional visits to her library. Blanaid Denman, Bob Elliot, Alison Enticknap, Andre Farrar, David Gibbons, Rhys Green, Tim Melling, Guy Shorrock, Mark Thomas, Pat Thompson and Jeremy Wilson have shared their thoughts and experiences of Hen Harriers, gamekeepers and grouse moors with me. Many former friends and colleagues in the RSPB have done as much as they could and sometimes more than they should (so, no names and no pack-drill) to help me in the production of this book and some of the actions that are described in it.

The Wildlife Trusts have helped in a great many ways, particularly in the Peak District around Hen Harrier Day, and I am grateful to them for edging just a little out of their very cautious, super-cautious, over-cautious approach to changing the world.

I am grateful to my editor at Bloomsbury, Jim Martin, for his support during the writing of this book, and to Nigel Redman, also of Bloomsbury, for championing it through the commissioning process.

Dominic Mitchell, the Editor of *Birdwatch* magazine, has helped the campaign on Hen Harriers in many ways, allowing me to rant about conservation issues in my monthly column in his excellent magazine, and helping draft the e-petition to ban driven grouse shooting.

The librarian of the Reform Club, Simon Blundell, helped locate dusty copies of Hansard and tracked down a copy of *Who Owns Britain and Ireland* for me.

Mark Constantine and Lush Cosmetics have been incredibly supportive. Their featuring of Hen Harriers in Lush shops across the UK just before Hen Harrier Day brought the issue of wildlife crime from the uplands to the high street and resulted in 20,000 postcards being delivered to the Queen and a rush of signatures to the e-petition to ban driven grouse shooting.

Brian Egan of Rare Bird Alert has been a constant supporter of anything that will help the Hen Harrier.

Mike Price, Jamie Horner, Nick Brown, Nick Moyes, Susan Cross and Tim Birch helped me appreciate the Peak District better and all were present on Hen Harrier Day in the rain.

The guys who run the Raptor Persecution Scotland website (and who have ticked the box for anonymity) have been a great support.

Ruth Peacey, Jez Toogood, Adam Clarke and Nick Wilcox-Brown did a fantastic job in filming Hen Harrier Day in ghastly conditions and then getting a smart-looking video onto the web in double-quick time. Gerry Granshaw helped coordinate things between me and Chris Packham in the hectic days around Hen Harrier Day and the Inglorious Twelfth, and was always a cheery voice on the phone.

Alan Davies and Ruth Miller showed me Hen Harriers, other birds and a good time in north Wales (and I showed Alan an Otter). We cemented our friendship through 2014 and if I ever have the money to go on an expensive (but very good value) birding holiday then I'll try to make it one of their trips for the friendship as well as the excellent birding skills.

Iolo Williams was happy to chat to me about Hen Harriers in Wales.

John Armitage was supportive and deserves praise for launching his e-petition to licence sporting estates.

Chrissie Harper has the warmest of hearts and the mellowest of voices – and her e-petition to introduce vicarious liability in England deserved greater support from the conservation establishment.

The Wilde family are just lovely and it's always a pleasure to see them all, Nigel, Heather, Findlay and Harley.

Barry Gardiner deserves a mention (as does his partner) for attending Hen Harrier Day. It was great to see a politician, and a senior one who might, by the time you read these words, be a Defra minister (fingers crossed), attending a public event of this sort.

Mark Cocker pointed me in the direction of some useful literature and is a fellow traveller on many of these issues.

Michael McCarthy has been encouraging of this project even though he probably doesn't agree with all of it, and is always a useful sounding board for ideas.

Ian Newton is a hero to many of my generation, and to younger folk, too. He talked to me, sensibly and with great knowledge and understanding, about the issues that dominate this book.

Rob Yorke and Roderick Leslie both wrote guest blogs for me on what the future might be like if driven grouse shooting were to be banned, from the perspective of a fictional ex-gamekeeper. So I used the same name, Terry, for the wholly fictional character in Chapter 7.

Rosemary, Thomas and Jennifer had to put up with me disappearing upstairs and being antisocial for many months, and over Christmas 2014, in order to finish this book on time. My conversation tended to be dominated by phrases such as 'I wrote xxxx words today' (or sometimes 'xxx words today' or even 'xx words today') and 'I think I'm ahead of the word count on the Duckworth–Lewis formula at the moment'. That can't have been much fun.

And last, because his contribution came at the end, Hugh Brazier edited my slightly scrappy manuscript and helped enormously to get it into shape. There were some tense moments – both present and past. All the errors and poorly expressed passages remain my own work, but there would have been more of them without Hugh's expert help.

Index

snaring 111, 252–3
Snipe 19, 57
social media 8, 273
South Pennine Moors
    149, 157
South Yorkshire Badger
    Group 116
Sparrow, Tree 44
Sparrowhawk 147, 178, 216,
    248–9
Special Areas of Conservation
    (SACs) 62
Special Protection Areas
    (SPAs) 31–2, 62
Spelman, Caroline 136
Spencer-Stanhope,
    Sir Walter 58
Sphagnum 61, 264
Spruce, Sitka 15
Squirrel, Red 265
Starling 19
State of Nature 163–4
Steiner, Achim 142
Stoat 73, 74, 75, 88, 197,
    252, 259
Stone, Michael 197
Stonechat 179, 208, 247
Strathmore, Earls of 63
strongylosis 76, 83
Strutt and Parker 186
Sullivan, Robert 186
Sunday Herald 237
Sutherland, Dukes of 65
Swallow 180, 198

T

Taylor, Lord Holbeach 136
Teal 181, 199, 209
Tetrao tetrix 51
    urogallus 50
Thatcher, Margaret 135
The Glorious Grouse 60
Thirgood, Simon 87

Thomas, Mark 122
Thompson, Guy 121–2
ticks 75–6
Tilmouth, Alan 160
Times, The 204–5, 214, 220,
    226, 232
Tit, Blue 19
Toogood, Jez 216, 218
trapping 81, 110–11, 116, 147
Trichostrongylus tenuis 76
Trotter, Stephen 218, 244
Truss, Liz 136, 213
Tumblr 217
Tweedsmuir, Lady 200
Twitter 8, 204, 212, 217, 245,
    260, 273–4
    @birdersagainst 174, 273
    @markavery 274
Tynan, Sarah 233, 234

U

UK National Ecosystem
    Assessment 138–41
UN Environment
    Programme 142
United Utilities 188, 224
University of Leeds 225
uplands 7, 54–6, 81
    Natural England *Vital
        Uplands* 129–30
    Newton Rigg College
        conference 184–8
    RSPB *The Uplands – Time to
        Change?* 124–5
    Uplands Stakeholder Forum
        Hen Harrier Sub-group
        158, 211, 221–2, 231
    where are the grouse
        moors? 60–2

V

vermin control 72–5
Victoria and Albert 58